PAM WEAVER

Bath Times and Nursery Rhymes

AVON

AVON

A division of HarperCollins*Publishers*
77–85 Fulham Palace Road,
London W6 8JB

www.harpercollins.co.uk

A Paperback Original 2013

1

First published in Great Britain by
HarperCollins*Publishers* 2013

Copyright © Pamela Weaver 2013

Pam Weaver asserts the moral right to
be identified as the author of this work.

A catalogue record for this book is
available from the British Library.

ISBN-13: 978-0-00-748844-5

Set in Minion by Palimpsest Book Production Limited,
Falkirk, Stirlingshire

Printed and bound in Great Britain by
Clays Ltd, St Ives plc

MIX
Paper from
responsible sources

FSC
www.fsc.org **FSC™ C007454**

BATH TIMES AND NURSERY RHYMES

Adopted from birth, Pam Weaver trained as a nursery nurse working mainly in children's homes. She was also a private nanny. In the 1980s she and her husband made the deliberate decision that she should be a full-time mum to their two children. Pam wrote for small magazines and specialist publications, finally branching out into the women's magazine market.

Pam has written numerous articles and short stories, many of which have featured in anthologies. Her story, *The Fantastic Bubble,* was broadcast on BBC Radio 4 and BBC World Service. She has written two novels, *There's Always Tomorrow* and *Better Days Will Come,* both published by Avon. *Bath Times and Nursery Rhymes* is her first memoir.

Also by Pam Weaver

There's Always Tomorrow
Better Days Will Come

With the exception of my parents and my husband, the real names of the people in this story have been disguised or changed completely. I have altered the gender of some of the children to protect their identity and all of the names of both children and staff have been changed. I have also refrained from giving the exact location of each nursery, hospital or private home where I worked for the same reason.

The stories are true to the best of my memory.

I should like to thank Ann Webb and Sylvia Dennis (Denny) for jogging my memory and for a fantastic weekend together when we all walked down memory lane. I should also like to thank Wendy Germaney, who took the time to write down some of her memories which have been included in this book.

To all the children who were in my care at some time or other, I thank you for the wonderful times we shared together and I hope and pray that you've had a good life despite some of your difficult circumstances. To those who worked with me, thanks for the memories.

This book is dedicated to Jacob and Sophia Sullivan with lots of love from Granny.

Chapter 1

'After you've had your supper, wake the night nurse, and then come to the main hall. The person on "Lates" does the mending.'

Miss Carter, the small ginger-haired nursery warden, barked her instructions at me and left the room. I was doing my first 'Lates' duty in a children's residential nursery run by Surrey County Council. The year was 1961. Yuri Gagarin had become the first man to go into outer space, The Beatles were at the start of their phenomenal success, you could buy a house for two thousand pounds and I was just sixteen.

I had arrived from my village home in Dorset a week before; my only possession, a small brown suitcase and my one ambition, to get a qualification with letters after my name. Adopted at birth, I had grown up as the daughter of my natural mother's best friend in a small village on the Hampshire-Dorset border. My father had been an American GI, who came to this country for the D-Day landings in France and most likely perished there. He was obviously a person of colour because I have an olive skin and at that time, tight curly hair. I had left school in July and began my working life in Woolworths on the broken biscuit counter. I had no real idea of what I wanted in life but it certainly didn't include broken biscuits or a promotion to the ladies' personal items counter, which was on offer as soon as I'd done three months' probation. Selling 'bunnies' (the name we gave sanitary towels because of the loop at each end which you fastened to the belt) didn't really do it for me. The trouble was, there were few other opportunities in my part of rural Dorset. Max Factor had a large factory near Poole and paid well but that was about it. They laid on a bus to collect their workers from round our way so, because I would have no problem in getting to work, my dad was keen for me to join them. I hated the idea of working in a factory even more than selling bunnies.

'Not good enough for you?' he challenged. Dad and I were always at loggerheads.

'No, it isn't that,' I said confidently. 'I don't want to be stuck indoors all day and besides, I want a training. I want to make something of my life.'

He harrumphed and made it plain that I couldn't manage that so of course I had to prove him wrong. I was determined to find something which would give me a certificate and a qualification at the end of it. The only problem was, what? As soon as I could, I spent my lunch hour with the careers officer in the little market town of Ringwood where I worked, and collected a sheaf of brochures.

I could join the Navy – I quite fancied that. I spent the next few evenings browsing through and drooling over the pictures of all those handsome young sailors . . . but as yet I was far too young (I had to be eighteen) and besides, they said you had parade ground duties and the thought of all that marching put me off a bit. What if I became a secretary? But the thought of hours and hours sitting in a typing pool and not being allowed to talk was a complete no-no. My ambition even reached as far as becoming a barrister but that was only because I loved the idea of wearing a wig and gown and arguing in court (thanks to Dad, I was an expert when it came to arguing). But when I looked into it, I didn't have the right education. There was no chance of going to university because Dad was a bricklayer and my Mum cleaned people's houses for 2s 6d an hour. Whatever I did, I had to pay my own way. I toyed with the thought of nursing but there are certain things in life which have no appeal at all and dealing with brimming bedpans was one of them. I had worked my way through the whole pile of brochures when I came across a leaflet on being a nursery nurse. It fitted the bill beautifully. What's more, Surrey County Council offered to train a girl in exchange for a commitment to work an extra year in a nursery when she had passed the NNEB, the initials given to the certificate issued by the National Nursery Examination Board. I sent off the forms and to my absolute delight, got an interview. Mum and I travelled to Kingston upon Thames together and went to County Hall. By the end of the day, I'd been told I was accepted by the person conducting the interview, Miss Fox-Talbot, who was supervisor for children's residential homes and senior child care officer for the county. A week later I received a letter confirming my appointment. It laid out the terms of my training contract, and my pay. I was to be paid £194 a year, in accordance with the statutory agreement with Whitley Council of the Health Service, less £101 a year for my board and lodging. This equated to £1.79 a week in today's money, however all was not lost. After a year's service my wage would increase, giving me an extra £11 per annum! The letter included a list of clothing I would need to bring with me. Despite having a grammar school education and leaving with three GCEs, I had to report to Guildford and take an entrance exam to ascertain my level of education and I also had to arrange to have a chest X-ray. It was very exciting because once all that was done, I was at last taking the first steps towards my career.

Now that I was actually employed in a nursery, I had to make it work. Because I was a minor, Dad had been asked to sign a contract as my guarantor, which committed him to paying back any expenses the council had incurred, should I give up before the end of my training. Because of that, I was more than anxious to please people. It didn't take me long to work out that if someone in authority said you should do something, you didn't argue, you just did it.

Because I was on 'Lates', I had to have my supper half an hour before the other girls. Alone in the staff room for the first time since I had arrived a week before, I ate my supper – lukewarm tin tomatoes on soggy toast – and gulped down a mug of scalding dark brown tea. I cleared away the dirty crockery and reset my place for someone else. I looked at the clock. It was almost seven p.m. so I went into the hall, where the other members of staff had gathered before going off duty. No one spoke to me. The bell went for supper and once again I was left alone.

The first thing I had to do was check on the children. They were all in bed of course and hopefully already asleep. The dormitory rooms were dimly lit but I checked that they were still covered by their blankets and made sure they had their special toy in the bed with them. One or two were still awake so I tousled a head here and there or gave them a goodnight kiss.

Before I went for my supper, I had been shown a small cloakroom and a box full of dirty shoes. I found the shoe polish and set to work. The shoes were all different colours so I polished all the red shoes first, then the blue ones, the brown and finally, the black ones. After that, I had to find the owner (the inside of the shoes were marked with the child's name) and put the clean shoes on top of their pile of clothes ready for the morning. That done, I returned to the main hall and looked into the mending basket. There was a jacket with a button missing, a skirt with a torn hem, a coat with a ripped pocket and a pair of trousers with a broken zip. The zip looked far too complicated and surely I would need a sewing machine to do that, so all things considered, I reached for the button box and sat down.

It was taking a bit of getting used to but everybody used abbreviated names for our various duty times. 'Lates' meant that a girl (who had already been working since seven in the morning)

4

would come off duty at six-thirty in the evening, eat a quick supper and then go back to work until nine o'clock, when the night nurse arrived. Sometimes, the night nurse would arrange with a friend to do a 'Stand-in'. That meant the friend would come back on duty at nine and the night nurse could have an evening out before going on duty.

As it turned out, that evening Miss Carter was doing a 'Stand-in' for Nurse Adams. I carried on with the mending in between checking the children about every twenty minutes. The nursery was quiet. Everyone was asleep. Miss Carter came to relieve me at nine, assuming that her friend had already gone out with her boyfriend, and I went into the staff room to enjoy some TV.

There were three girls in the sitting room. One was writing a letter at the table, a second was cutting her toenails over a waste-paper basket. Only the third girl looked up when I walked in. Isolde worked in the Toddler room, a tall girl and, at nineteen, older than me, with very short fair hair and mischievous eyes, was more interested in travelling than working with children. A free spirit, she made no secret of the fact that she hated the discipline and routine in the nursery.

'Well?' she said. 'How was your day?'

'Fine,' I lied.

'Good for you,' she murmured. 'Personally, I can't stick this bloody place. I'm jacking it in. Three months of this hell on earth is quite enough for me.'

I stood in the doorway, feeling a bit awkward. What should I say to that? I hated it too and I was homesick as well, which was something I certainly hadn't bargained for. I had thought I might miss Mum and Dad and the dog a bit, but I had this gnawing ache in the pit of my stomach all the time. It made me feel ill and I couldn't eat properly. I couldn't admit defeat but already I was beginning to think anything would have been better than this, even the make-up factory or selling bunnies. The staff

5

were so unfriendly, I was terrified of putting a foot wrong and the work was relentless and hard. I longed to be back in the little two-up, two-down cottage where I had grown up and already, the draughty little sitting room with its meagre coal fire had taken on a romantic, rosy hue. I swallowed hard. I mustn't start crying again – they would all think I was a big baby. Surely things couldn't get any worse?

'Don't just stand there,' said the girl cutting her toenails. 'For goodness sake put the wood in the hole. You're creating a hell of a draught from where I'm sitting.'

I slunk in, closed the door and sat on the edge of the chair. It was Wednesday night and on the TV, the credits for *Wagon Train* were already rolling against a backdrop of the dashing Flint McCullough played by handsome Robert Horton. I sighed. Things had just got a whole lot worse. It was my favourite programme and I'd missed it.

All at once the door burst open and a furious-looking girl burst into the room. The door banged against the table behind it and an HP sauce bottle on the top fell over. The girl's blonde hair was dishevelled and her eyes still red and puffy from sleep.

'Who was on Lates?' she blazed.

I gulped. That was me. Oh Lord, what had I done wrong? Think, I told my panicking brain. What did you forget? I went through everything I'd done in a split second. I'd done the mending (apart from the zip), I'd remembered to check the children every twenty minutes and when Miss Carter took over, everything was fine. I'd polished twenty-two pairs of shoes, hung up the nappies in the laundry, and put out the drinks tray ready for the morning. What else? Whatever it was, it was obvious who was to blame. Everyone else in the sitting room looked up at her in mild surprise. I was the only one who was beetroot red and already feeling utterly suicidal.

'Me,' I squeaked as I tried to make my voice sound as small as I could.

'Why the hell didn't you wake me?' she bellowed.

'Wake you?'

'The person on Lates is supposed to wake the night nurse,' she shouted.

'Er . . . I'm sorry . . .' I tried my best to ignore the fact that she was standing there, screaming at me with only her see-through nightie on. 'Nobody told me.'

Actually, that was a lie. Miss Carter had told me but I had forgotten.

'You stupid little fool!' she ranted. 'I was supposed to be meeting my boyfriend at eight!'

'I'm sorry . . .'

'What am I going to tell him? More importantly *how* am I going to tell him? I don't even have his phone number!' She was beginning to sound hysterical.

'I'm sorry . . .'

'You stupid idiot. You've ruined my whole life . . .'

'I . . . I'm sorry . . .'

'Didn't Miss Carter tell you to wake me?'

I shook my head. 'No.'

That was another lie and now I had a new dread. What if Miss Carter walked in right now and heard me saying she hadn't told me to wake the night nurse? I looked anxiously over Nurse Adams' shoulder.

'I'm sorry . . .'

'And stop saying you're sorry, you silly cow!'

'I . . . I'm . . .'

I froze. She was so angry I felt sure she was going to hit me. She glared for a few seconds and then swept out of the room and slammed the door. This time the glass in the window frame shook.

'Ha, ha, ha!' Isolde rolled herself backwards on the sofa and kicked her feet in the air. 'That was terrific. What a laugh!'

'Actually,' I confessed, 'I think Miss Carter might have mentioned waking the night nurse.'

'Who cares,' Isolde laughed.

'Serves her right,' said the girl cutting her toenails. Her voice was toneless. 'She always was a stuck-up old cow!'

'Miss Carter?'

'No, you goon! Audrey Adams.'

I was too upset to comment. 'I think I'll go to bed,' I said, slinking out of the room.

Oh Lord, what had I done? I had signed myself up to a year in this place, then two years training in another nursery and finally a further year somewhere else when I'd finished my training. Alone in my room, I undressed and lay my head on my pillow. I wept silent tears as I wondered just how much of the money my dad would have to pay the council if I turned up on the doorstep tomorrow. Should I go and see Matron in the morning and tell her I wanted to go home? But even as the thought entered my head, I knew I wouldn't do it. Somehow, I had to stick this out.

The person in charge, Matron Thomas, lived in a flat within the building. Matron was a highly-strung woman, who constantly complained about 'having a dreadful head'. We didn't see a lot of her except perhaps when there was a new admission, or the parents came to visit. We would hear her coming, her blue nylon overall with its pleated skirt rustling as she walked into the nursery, usually to complain that the children were too noisy or somebody had left something where it shouldn't be. She was a little aloof but came down on us like a ton of bricks if she saw something she disapproved of.

Life in those nurseries was hard. A lot has been written about the injustice done to the children, and quite rightly so. It's heartbreaking to hear about children being beaten and abused, especially in a place which is supposed to be a place of care, but I have to say that in the nurseries where I worked, everybody did their best to give the children a happy experience. Sometimes the girls, myself included, took a child out on their days off. We would buy an extra toy out of our own money for the children who were upset and we were always there for a quick cuddle when it was needed. The rigid routine was hard for the free-spirits like Isolde but equally difficult for people like me. I didn't mind being told what to do, but sometimes it felt as if I was owned body and soul by those in charge of the nursery and it was hard to please everybody.

At sixteen I was only a few years older than the oldest child, and we nursery assistants were all treated like dogs. We worked a twelve-hour stretch, with two hours off during the day. Off duty was either 9.30–11.30, 2–4 or best of all 5–7, because tea was at 4.30, so it meant you had an extra half hour and a lovely long evening to yourself. Having that afternoon break was a definite advantage in the summer, but the evening was great if you were going out. We were only allowed to stay out until ten p.m., or if you had a 'Late Pass', you could stay out until 10.45 p.m. It made having a social life hard because by the time you'd come off duty at seven and got ready, you were lucky to have two hours away from the Home. Matron Thomas didn't seem to understand that dances went on until 11 p.m. and had hardly warmed up by the time you had to leave and catch the bus. It was tough if you were going to the pictures as well. You didn't always get to see the end of the film because you had to make the bus stop in time for the last bus up the hill. I saw most of the films of the day in two halves. You could walk into the pictures any old time so I would get there in time to see the end of one showing and then stay for the beginning. *Whistle Down the Wind, A Taste of Honey, Carry on Regardless* . . . I saw them all, back to front. And when you got back to the nursery, if you rang the doorbell to get in after 10.45 p.m. you would forfeit some of your precious off duty another time.

Anyone out after 10.45 p.m. was, according to Matron Thomas, 'up to one thing and one thing only.' She was probably right.

We *would* be up to one thing and one thing only – running like mad up the hill because we'd missed the bus and we wanted to get to the door before 10.45 p.m!

We did 'Lates' two evenings a week and everybody had to take turns to do ten nights of night duty, which lasted from 9 p.m. until 8 a.m. After the ten nights on duty, the bonus was that you got two days off together. Normally we had one day off a week but you could never guarantee when it would be. You might get Monday off one week and then Saturday the following week, which meant you'd work eleven days on the trot. Because of the uncertainty, it was hard to commit to anything outside the nursery or to join a club.

Not only did we work long hours but we also had very low pay. My first salary was nine pounds, four shillings (nine pounds, twenty pence), which in today's money worked out at two pounds, thirty pence a week! That was for six weeks' work because we always worked 'two weeks in lieu', as they called it. That meant when you left a post, you would get the extra two weeks pay in your final wage packet. And when I started my training a year later, my salary actually went down because the council took back some money to offset the cost of training me. As a result, for two years, from 1962–64, I had an average of six pounds, fourteen shillings a month. At that time, a shop girl would be on three pounds, five shillings a week – i.e. thirteen pounds a month, but of course she would have to pay her living expenses out of that. Our wage was what they called 'all found', which meant all living expenses had already been taken out.

Life in the nursery was also very insular. With so little time off duty, the rest of the world passed us by. Of course we saw the news on TV, but the milestones of history meant little to us at the time. But perhaps that's always the case – you only realise the importance of an event with the passing of the years. Hence, the inauguration of President Kennedy in January 1961 was only worthy of note because he was relatively young at the time. By comparison Harold Macmillan, our own Prime Minister, seemed like a dinosaur. Personally, I found listening to The Shirelles singing what I considered the best song ever written, 'Will You Still Love Me Tomorrow' on my Dansette radio far more exciting.

Back in my room after upsetting Nurse Adams, I lay on my back, staring at the ceiling as I chewed over the events of the day. The room itself was a mishmash of conflicting colours. The walls had two completely different wallpapers, both floral, but neither of them complemented the other. One was a very busy flowery pattern in predominantly yellows and browns while the other three walls had pink flowers on a bright blue background. The candlewick counterpanes were both purple but not matching and the furniture – two bedside lockers, two chests of drawers, one with its own built-in mirror – were a heavy dark brown. There was a kitchen chair painted white in one corner and an easy chair with wooden arms and mustard yellow fabric covering the seat in the other. The curtains were yet another floral pattern. Above the door was a plain glass window, which let in the light from the corridor.

When I had arrived at the nursery the week before, I was told I would be sharing my room with another girl but as yet, I hadn't met her. She'd been on holiday when I arrived but the others had done their best to fill me in.

'Her dad's a vicar,' said Margaret.

'And she's very religious,' Isolde informed me. 'She sings hymns all night. And of course,' she went on, 'she's an awful lot older than you.'

I could just picture her. She was bound to be an ancient po-faced religious bigot, who would spend all her time trying to force me to join in with her holy activities. Oh boy, I could hardly wait to meet her! I switched off the light and sometime later, she crept in, but after my brush with Nurse Adams I didn't feel much like singing hymns, so I rolled over and pretended to be asleep.

When the night nurse brought us our early morning cup of tea at six, Hilary and I peered gingerly at each other over our bedclothes. Her appearance was quite a shock. She was older than me, but only by a couple of years, and she was slim and attractive with dark curly hair and an engaging smile. It turned out that her dad was indeed a vicar, but she never let that deter her from doing exactly what she wanted.

When we got to know each other we discovered that the others had good-naturedly done their best to wind both of us up. Apparently I was from the deepest part of Africa and my father had been a missionary-eating cannibal! They had been so convincing, she was really nervous about sleeping in the same room as me.

Hers was the first really friendly face I'd seen at the nursery. She was working with the toddlers and I was in the baby room, but the house wasn't that big. We'd wave to each other, or meet at meal times and have a chat and she promised that if we could both wangle the same day off, she would arrange to take me to her house. From the moment I met her I began to feel a whole lot better. She was lively and fun to be with, but she also had a dare-devil streak. Hilary wasn't afraid to try new things and with someone to lead the way, I wasn't either! I began to feel that perhaps being a nursery assistant wasn't so bad after all.

The home had about thirty children altogether. They were in care for many different reasons. Homelessness was the main one but some had a sick parent who had no one to look after them while they were in hospital; some had been ill-treated or were living with parents who couldn't cope with small children; some parents were alcoholics or had no job and no income; others were in the process of being adopted. Some stayed for only a few days while others were in the home for long periods of time, perhaps years. Apart from the times when we all met in the garden, the children were totally segregated by their ages. The rooms were divided into Babies, Tweenies and Toddlers. The

Baby room took the little ones until they were a year old, the Tweenies were aged one to two years old and the Toddlers room was for the three to fives.

As a direct result of this policy, it would churn me up to see brothers and sisters clinging desperately to each other when they met. No one had, as yet, realised the devastating effect this kind of separation had on the children. The poor kids must have felt punished for something they didn't understand and at times the feelings of loneliness must have been unbearable. Cut off from a mother and sometimes a father too, your brother or sister might be somewhere in the building but you'd only catch a glimpse of them once in a while. You would be put in a room full of strangers behind a closed door and it must have been very hard to adjust. We were all taught to obey the routine at all costs, which was hard enough when you're sixteen and you've made your own choice, but when you were only three, how bewildering life must have seemed. The whole routine in Tweenies seemed to revolve around potty training. The basic philosophy appeared to be pot them every half an hour and they will be trained! As a consequence we gave them breakfast and went to the toilet. The children played for half an hour, either in the Tweenie room or in the garden, and then went to the toilet. We took them for a walk and then they went to the toilet, etc. etc. all through the day.

For all its faults, routine brought stability into the children's lives and we never ill-treated anybody. It may have seemed a little cold at times because very close attachments were frowned upon. The staff would probably move on in life, whereas the child would have to remain; the thinking was that the child had to be protected from another sense of loss and bereavement when you left. The trouble is, we all crave relationships and this edict left a lot of children feeling unloved and unwanted. Yes, the system was misguided but for all that, I remember lots of laughter and plenty of cuddles.

I began my career in the Baby room. It was a light airy room with six little babies in six little cots. It was considered a great privilege for a nursery assistant like me to be allowed to even touch a baby and in those first few days I certainly wasn't permitted to hold one. First, I had to prove my worth. This meant endless floor polishing, bin changing and nappy washing. The floors were like mirrors, and as my mother would say, 'you could eat your dinner off them.' Every day it was part of the routine to sweep, wash and polish them. The sweeping and washing was done by hand and on your knees, as was the application of the polish. The nursery had an electric polisher to get a decent shine, but it was a real skill learning how to use it. Press the control on the handle a little too hard and you'd be flying around the room and banging into everything. Press too lightly and you couldn't get a decent shine off the linoleum floor. The whole exercise was a back-breaking and thankless task.

Before I was allowed to handle the babies, my other job was nappy washing. Funnily enough, bearing in mind my squeamishness about bedpans, I didn't mind doing it and besides, they taught us how to make an art form out of it. All the nappies were sluiced in the nursery, and then rinsed in cold water in the laundry. The laundry itself was outside the main building and cold, freezing cold in winter. It was also dark and damp. After the nappies had been boiled for what seemed like forever in huge boilers like vats, they were pulled, scalding hot, over to the sinks with wooden tongs. (I wonder what today's Health and Safety regulations would make of that!) Then we rinsed them twice by hand and spun them in an industrial spin-dryer. When I arrived at the nursery, the industrial spin-dryer wasn't working so we had a domestic one. There was a loose connection on the lid so you had to sit on it in order to make it work. It really shook your bottom but one girl reckoned she'd lost pounds by sitting on it, so nobody minded too much. Soap powder was strictly rationed and Matron Thomas watched us like a hawk. We were constantly suspected of using the washing powder for our own clothes but poor as we were, none of us wanted to wash our clothes in those stinking soapsuds. They smelled like Jeyes Fluid (a very pungent disinfectant with a distinctive smell of its own) and stale lavender all rolled into one.

The hand-knitted baby cardigans and other delicates were washed in soap flakes but they were the industrial type and the devil to get to melt in the water.

If the weather was too damp or wet to dry the clothes outside we used to hang them in industrial driers, which were lit by gas. It was little wonder that the laundry had its own unique smell but the one blessing of laundry duty was that it gave a homesick sixteen-year-old a few moments to cry alone without being castigated or ridiculed. I was embarrassed to be seen to be upset and felt I should be grown up enough not to want my mother, but it was a struggle.

The person directly in charge of the Baby room, Sister Weymouth, had a staff nursery nurse and a nursery assistant to help her look after six babies. Sister Weymouth was an older woman, perhaps in her fifties. She was a skinny woman with a stooped back and spindly arms. Although a little distant, she was fair. She wore a navy coloured sister's uniform but without the cap and cuffs. With such a high level of staffing it's easy to understand how we managed to keep the place looking so spick and span and the reason why the type of children's home I was working in became a thing of the past. That number of employees would cripple today's councils with their ever-tightening budgets.

Working in the milk kitchen was like being in a pure white space capsule. We wore masks and gowns. We were taught to wash our hands between each feed preparation and the whole milk kitchen was washed from floor to ceiling every day. Incidentally, all the babies were fed on National Dried Milk, a government issue basic milk powder. I had been in the nursery for three months before I was allowed in the milk kitchen and even then I was strictly supervised. Sister Weymouth peered at me over the top of her facemask. 'Level each scoop exactly,' she said. 'Too much and the baby will overdose on his vitamins and may become very ill. If you don't fill the scoop right to the edge, the poor baby will starve.'

I was still so scared of putting a foot wrong, it never occurred to me she might be exaggerating. Three grains of National Dried Milk powder too many and I'd blow the kid up. Three grains too few and I could be accused of running a concentration camp . . . oh Lord, what a responsibility!

The system of child care by today's standard was very old fashioned. For instance, meal times were rigidly adhered to for even the tiniest baby. If a baby had to be fed at six o'clock, that's exactly what happened. I was once made to sit with a crying baby on my lap, willing the stubborn hands of the clock to move from 5.50 to 6 p.m., but not daring to put the teat in his mouth until the appointed time. If I had been caught feeding the baby before 6 p.m. it would be back to the nappy bins and floors for me. Of course it was totally ridiculous for the baby. If he had been crying for twenty minutes, he was often too exhausted to take his bottle anyway, but the rules were the rules.

My turn for being on 'Lates' came around again and Nurse Adams was still on night duty.

'Don't forget to wake the night nurse this time,' smiled Isolde and I went to get my early supper.

She had to be kidding. After the fiasco of the week before, that was the last thing I would do. My supper was steamed cod roe on toast. It looked horribly grey and was swimming in milk, which had made the toast all soggy again. I had never experienced such 'delights' before but first of all I had a job to do. I took a cup of tea to Nurse Adams, making absolutely sure it was just the way she liked it, milky with no sugar. My hands were trembling slightly as I walked up the back stairs to the pokey little room in the attic where the night nurse slept. At the top of the stairs, I steadied my nerves, tipped the small spill in the saucer back into the cup, knocked lightly on the door and walked in.

'Good evening, Nurse Adams,' I said.

At exactly the same moment as I walked in the door, her alarm clock went off. She stirred slightly, reached out and switched it off but she said nothing. I stood still, waiting for her to sit up and take the cup but she didn't.

There was a small locker on the opposite side of the bed. The room itself was so small I would have to squeeze my way past her clothes at the end of the bed to get round there so I decided to lean over her to put the cup on the table. It seemed to be the path of least resistance. And after all, she was still half asleep.

But wouldn't you know it? At the precise moment the tea was halfway across the bed, she flung her arms up to stretch and yawn. There was a loud clatter as the cup and saucer parted company and the lukewarm tea fell onto the bed. 'Oh! I'm sorry . . .'

'You!' she shrieked, opening one bloodshot eye. 'Get out, get out!' A soggy pillow followed me out of the door and I had gained the reputation of being the village idiot.

Chapter 2

Mr Swinnerton was a man with deep-set eyes and a serious expression. He'd married late in life but to his great joy his Hungarian wife had presented him with a baby girl. They called her Geraldine and she was the light of his life. Mona, his wife, loved her daughter but since the birth of the baby, she had changed. She found it stressful, particularly when Geraldine cried at night. Mr Swinnerton did his best to help, but he had a full day's work ahead of him and needed his sleep. The baby was what they called 'colicky'. They tried home remedies and Mona took her to the health clinic for advice, but she still struggled with the complexities of English.

The Swinnertons lived in a small flat surrounded by lots of neighbours. At first, they welcomed the little baby but their joy soon turned sour. She disturbed their afternoons and their evenings with her continual crying. Mona became more and more depressed. They had no family that could help them. Mr Swinnerton's mother had died some years ago. Mona's family still lived in Hungary, or at least they had done until the Hungarian Revolution of 1956. Mona had escaped the troubles but her family stayed behind. She had never heard from them since and she supposed they were among the two hundred thousand people who perished when the Soviets crushed the rebellion. Then one evening Mr Swinnerton came home to find that his beloved wife had killed herself. Nowadays we understand a lot more about post-natal depression but back then, a mother would be told, 'you've got a beautiful baby girl and a loving husband, what more do you want? Pull yourself together and get on with it.' Geraldine was taken into care and came to live in the nursery where I worked. Her father had to pay a percentage of her childcare costs but she got over her colic and began to thrive. Visiting hours were only on a Sunday, but Matron Thomas felt sorry for the quiet man. He used to cycle to the nursery after work to see his little daughter, who grew into a serious-faced toddler and the spitting image of him. Eventually Geraldine moved from the Baby room to Tweenies (the rooms where the children between the ages of one and two were looked after) and still he kept coming, riding up the hill on his battered old bicycle. Social workers tried to persuade him to let her be adopted, but he just couldn't do it: he loved her too much to let her go.

I was on duty when Geraldine was admitted. All the children's clothing came from a central store and so the same jumper often popped up in various sizes throughout the building. However, the one redeeming factor was that everything was labelled, so no child actually wore somebody else's outfit. We scratched the child's name onto white tape with a rusty old pen dipped into indelible ink and sewed it inside each garment. It was a long and tedious job, doing every single item of clothing.

At first, Mr Swinnerton found the 'no personal things' rule a little hard to take. The children had no private space of their own but they had their own individual combs and hairbrushes, etc. Geraldine was allowed one personal toy, which was usually kept on the bed. He didn't make waves, but he would give you this 'injured' look which made me realise the pain he was going through.

At the time Geraldine came to the nursery the children's personal pegs were identified by a picture of a teddy or a spinning top or something similar. It seemed like a good idea at the time, but the practice was stopped after some visiting dignitary knelt in front of a child and asked a child, 'and who are you?'

'I'm the golliwog,' came the reply.

Once she'd settled down, Geraldine was a contented little girl, although she never lost that serious expression. When I left the nursery, she was still there and her father still cycled up to see her. I'd like to think that he eventually found another wife and made a home for his little girl but maybe that is only a pipe-dream. Back then, bringing up a child as a single parent was even more difficult for a man because the woman was always considered the primary carer.

On Sundays some of the parents came to visit. This was a mixed blessing; the children who had nobody to visit them must have envied those who did. It was wonderful for the visitors who came to be together as a family but then everyone had the grief of parting again. They would linger as long as they could to have a protracted farewell but we had to persuade them to say goodbye and leave at once. Everybody would be upset but it only made it a lot worse if we allowed the child to become hysterical and cling to the parent so hard that we had to drag them off. The parents had no privacy when they came to visit either. Sometimes that was deliberate. If they were suspected of being cruel to their children, nobody wanted to leave them alone to repeat the offence. Others felt embarrassed by their own tears when they saw their children, or self-conscious with all of us hanging around the room. Most of the parents had their children taken into care because of homelessness or maybe an illness had incapacitated them for a while. These people loved their children and they were grief-stricken to be separated. For that reason, I hated ringing the four o'clock bell, which signalled the time to say goodbye.

The house was set in quite large grounds. There was plenty of space for the children to run around, but they had few toys. Miss

Carter, the nursery warden (a kind of nursery teacher), kept the better things under lock and key. Some of them only put in an appearance on special occasions, usually when someone important came to visit the home. Appearances were all-important, and money was tight. I remember one time when we had had a delivery of something in three large boxes. We put the boxes in the playroom and the children had a wonderful time playing in them. It all came to an abrupt halt when Cassie fell over and sliced the top of her finger off on the edge of the box. Of course Matron Thomas went bananas, not only because the poor child had been injured but also because the powers that be would be onto her like a ton of bricks. Cassie was rushed to hospital for treatment (she was fine and amazingly, her fingertip grew back) but the boxes were removed and banned.

The nursery backed onto a park and we often took the children for walks there. We never simply 'fancied a stroll' – each walk had to have an objective in view. It might be to pick flowers, or to spot how many different kinds of car we could find, or to look for wildlife in the park. The idea was to teach the children how to be observant and to help them foster a keen interest in what was going on around them. Of course in talking to them we were also giving them a good command of language and understanding. Sometimes a child's comment would raise a bit of a smile. Mark was nearly two years old. Back in the nursery, we were showing the children pictures of the things we had seen on our walk. 'Look,' I said, 'a tree.'

Mark studied the picture and beamed. 'One, two, tree,' he said.

Because they were so young, we couldn't do much with the babies. We sometimes took them for 'walks' but of course they slept a lot. When they were awake, I was taught to speak to them even if they didn't understand and I began to see that it was a wonderful way of creating a bond between child and carer. The big prams meant that the baby always faced the person pushing it so it was easy to keep up a conversation with the baby. The modern buggies have the child facing away from the person pushing it and although it means the child can see what's coming rather than what has passed, something is lost in the relationship he can have with his nurse. I didn't stay in the Baby room all the time. We were constantly being moved around so that we could have a well-balanced understanding of the needs of the children in our care. When I was with the toddlers, the girl in charge of the room even wanted them to listen for and recognise bird song when we went out for walks. I had lived in the country all my life so I could easily recognise the birds we heard in the park – blackbird, pigeon and the occasional robin, but those who had been city dwellers all their lives struggled a bit. The nursery warden never liked us to use slang words either. For instance we had to teach the children that it wasn't a 'conker' tree but a horse chestnut tree and it was never a 'doggie' but a dog.

Being observant wasn't exclusively for the park setting. We had to use the same values when we walked about in the built-up areas or down the town. Thus the children knew all about zebra crossings, pillar boxes and the blue and white police box (made famous in later years by *Dr Who*), where members of the public could dial 999 were all part of our outdoor classroom.

When we went out we were expected to walk in such a way that the children felt happy to talk to us. Of course if the staff went out in convoy or just two prams, with toddlers walking beside it, we would talk to each other but the children took priority and we would answer any question as fully as we could.

Whenever we crossed the road we took time to teach the children Kerb Drill. The mantra was 'Halt! Look. Quick March!' The Royal Society for the Prevention of Accidents issued a booklet about the adventures of Tufty Fluffytail, a red squirrel, in 1953. Tufty was the invention of Elsie Mills MBE and proved to be so popular that in 1961 they formed The Tufty Club for under five-year-olds, which in its heyday had two million

members. Kerb Dri...
The Green Cross C...
cross carefully'.

I enjoyed the walks in...
the children through the ...
them in the air. Sometime...
a deer walking in the distan...
day-trippers and families hav...
the older children to run whe...
burn up their excess energy an...
Often the home conditions they'd ... ...far
they hadn't had a very healthy upb... ... not have
had a healthy diet before they were ... ...o care and that
could have affected their mobility and ...ing skills. Some had
been stuck in high-rise flats with no play areas or in one room
with several other siblings and a sick parent. Being in the park
always brought fun times and laughter. One day we found some
blackberries. It was late in the season so they weren't all that
wonderful and some had maggots but we managed to eat a
couple straight from the bush. I was also taught never to laugh
at a child, so when Alice got back to the nursery and she told
one of the other girls all about it, I suppressed a grin.

'Did you bring some back for me?' asked Hilary.

'Oh no,' said Alice gravely. 'They were full of magnets!'

It was important to make sure we allowed enough time for
the walk home. If we had been running about in the park, the
children might be feeling tired. If we had a pushchair all well
and good, but for the children walking beside the pushchair we
had to make sure we didn't overtax them.

When we were out for walks it was a good opportunity to
talk about stranger danger and that the man in the policeman's
uniform is our friend. Back in the nursery, we would sometimes
create a street in the playground and give the children the opportunity to practise crossing the road in front of a child in a pedal

such a way that it was a fun
attitudes and understanding which
they got older.

wanted to be a nursery nurse, I had always regarded
something children did to while away the time. It had never
occurred to me that play was important to a child's development.
I began to understand that play was not simply a way of letting off
high spirits and excess energy but it was also an outlet for emotions
and helped children to prepare for life. We often learned a lot about
a child's history by the way he or she played. When Sarah was in
the Wendy house, she handed a dolly by the foot to Ian, saying,
'Here, you can have the little bugger – he's driving me bloody mad!'
It didn't take much imagination to work out what might have been
going on in her home before she was taken into care.

The staff in the nursery helped me to notice how children
played. I began to see that play helped them develop social skills
as well. Up until a child is about two years old, they mostly play
on their own. From two years onward, they are aware of another
child and play in a parallel way. In the Wendy house, for example,
they'd still play their own game, but they were now conscious
of the other children with them. It's only as they get older that
children learn the concept of sharing, taking turns and finally
creating a world of their own together.

I began to see how concentration developed. It might start with
building a short tower of bricks or making a simple puzzle, but it
would gradually move to more complex games. By the time a child
had progressed into Toddlers, it was possible to play simple board
games like Lotto, where you match animal cards, with an adult. Play
not only helped the children develop intellectually but it also helped
with their physical progress. Their large muscles were strengthened
by climbing, jumping, running, pushing and pulling, while their
smaller muscles developed by picking up and placing things or
painting, modelling with clay or playing with the water tray. Even

in the Baby room I saw them changing. At first a baby would use the third finger and palm to pick something up and then that progressed to the thumb and forefinger as hand and eye coordination got better. Even throwing toys out of the pram meant the baby was using his arm or learning how to release his fingers.

Perhaps the most intimate form of interaction between the staff and the children came through storytelling. I have always loved storytelling myself, which is why whenever a child asked for a story I was keen to do it. The book corner was well stocked with good books. The children had their own little chairs and we always tried to make it homely so there was an adult chair where we could sit with a child on our lap, if required. Books which talked down to children were frowned upon, which is why we didn't have a single Enid Blyton book in any of the council nurseries. It didn't matter that children adored her books. I had been one of them. I'd read all the *Famous Five* books and the *Secret Seven* but in the early 1960s, probably because she had dominated the children's book market for so long, the professionals were quick to voice their disapproval. Later, when I moved on and became a nursery student my college lecturer, Mrs Davies, quoted from Enid Blyton. Apparently she once told a reporter, 'I sit at the typewriter and it just drips from my fingers.'

I'm sure if she did say such a thing, Enid Blyton meant it in an entirely different way but Mrs Davies wrinkled her nose in scorn and said, 'Well, that sums up her writing skill perfectly.'

The sort of stories which met with approval were books like *The Happy Lion* by Louise Fatio, *Millions of Cats* by Wanda Gag and anything by Beatrix Potter. Magic was considered taboo for the under-fives (I don't know why), as were very 'wordy' stories.

One thing always puzzled me. When I had gone to the council offices for my interview for the job, like all those before and after me, I'd met the nursery supervisor for the council, Miss Fox-Talbot. A formidable woman, she was short and stocky in build but famed for her fabulous hats and her racy red mini car. She told my mother and me that my uniform would be 'an attractive pink gingham dress'. It turned out to be a shapeless, round-necked garment with a matching covered belt and a Peter Pan collar. It had three rubber buttons down the front, so that they could be boiled, and apparently size twenty fitted everybody. The skirt was just below the knee and considering the rest of the world was waking up to the sack dress and later on, the mini skirt, we all hated it. Most girls hoiked up the skirt and took in the sides in an effort to look a little more twentieth century than eighteenth century.

The thing that puzzled me was this. In the letter Miss Fox-Talbot had sent me was a list of things I'd need to take with me to the nursery. At the bottom of the page, alongside a tooth-brush and comb, it said two pairs of 'garden knickers'. My mother and I scratched our heads. What on earth were garden knickers?

I was all for leaving it, but much to my acute embarrassment, Mum dragged me round all the major stores in Bournemouth but in every single department we were met by blank stares. Mum even insisted we go to a corset department where some old fossil, who had probably been working in the shop since Mrs Noah left the ark, suggested they might be powder blue silk drawers with an elasticated waist and long legs, which stretched as far as the knee. As soon as I saw them, I recognised them as the type of garment my old granny used to wear. I rarely, if ever, defied my mother but I put my foot down right there and then.

'There is no way I'm going to wear them!' I said in front of the shocked assistant. 'I'll work in the garden with no knickers at all if necessary, but I won't wear them!'

I worked for the council for four years. Nursery assistants like me came and went. We discussed the subject of garden knickers ad infinitum but I don't think any one of us ever discovered what they looked like and although I never carried out my threat to go bare bottom in the garden, I certainly never wore my granny's silk drawers.

Chapter 3

One early morning we got a call. It was an emergency admission. A mum had been rushed to hospital with internal bleeding. It was possibly a miscarriage so there was no telling how long or short her stay would be. If Mum had already lost her baby, it would only be for a few days. If the baby had survived, it may mean months of complete bed rest until it was born. Whatever happened, someone had to look after her other child, a little boy. The problem was that Mum and Dad were Polish and only spoke Polish.

We had never had a Polish child before, and the prospect of such a child coming to the nursery threw everyone into a complete flap. It was nothing to do with prejudice – after all, we had children whose parents had come from the four corners of the world. They might be West Indian, African, mixed race, English, Irish or Welsh but they were dealing with the same problems as everyone else. Homelessness, illness and unemployment can come to anybody. The problem here was that nobody spoke Polish. How were we going to communicate with the poor child? Our sympathies were aroused. To be torn from the arms of your mother would be bad enough, but to be thrust into a situation where you were unable to communicate or make yourself understood would be horrendous.

We wanted to make the usual preparations but even that wasn't possible. Usually by the time a child arrived in the nursery a pile of clothes would be waiting, and once we were sure of the size, each item marked with the child's name. The child's personal clothes would be put into a box and kept until he or she was ready to leave the nursery for good. No one had told us the name of the child or whether we were to expect a boy or a girl.

About half an hour later, a police car drew up outside and a WPC climbed out of the back seat with the child in her arms. To everyone's surprise Robin Kowalski turned out to be eight months old and his mother was English so there was no need for an interpreter after all! He was a delightful baby. As bald as a coot, he was quite content even though his mother wasn't with him. Robin only stayed a while. Sadly his mother had a complete miscarriage and she would nurse her pain and loss for years to come. Robin accepted his lot and smiled his toothless grin as a few days later we waved him goodbye and good luck.

I had only been in the nursery a couple of months when I began to feel increasingly ill. I was born with narrow Eustachian tubes in my ears and so a cold quite often resulted in me going deaf. Usually after a few days, my hearing would return and I'd be back on top but in the winter of 1961–62 my cold simply got worse and worse, and I remained completely deaf for more than a week.

I desperately wanted to go to the doctor but I was under the impression that I needed Matron's permission to do so. She exploited that belief and kept me working. In fact, rather than address the problem, she put me on night duty. It was not a good move. She had removed the problem of everyone having to shout at me and the irritation people feel when they can't make a deaf person understand what they want, but how could I possibly look after the children properly if I couldn't hear them? At least in the daytime there were other people about to cover my back and make sure the children were well cared for.

One night, as I was preparing the children's morning orange juice, Miss Carter appeared in the kitchen. It was the wee small hours of the morning and she was in her night clothes and dressing gown. Using hand signals, she made me go into the night nursery. When I switched on the light, every child was sitting up in bed and screaming. I have no idea who or what started them off, probably one child waking up after having a bad dream, but I hadn't heard a thing. Even when I was standing in the room, I still couldn't hear them.

By the time I came to the end of my ten nights, I was feeling a tad better. I went home to West Moors and a couple of days of Mum's cooking and pampering had me feeling a lot better. However, as soon as I got back into the nursery, I was ill again and before long, I had two lumps in my neck. The pain was becoming unbearable but still Matron turned a blind eye. I should have just gone to the doctor myself but by then I had learned that the way you spelled the word Matron was G-O-D. She cleverly avoided my pleas to have time off to go and see him.

One day, I had two hours off duty in the afternoon and I was feeling so lousy I went to bed. I was supposed to be back on duty at 4.30 but when someone came to find me, I refused to get up. 'I'm too ill to get up,' I whined. 'I need a doctor.'

The girl went away and about half an hour later, one of the more senior staff came to summon me to Matron's office. To say that Matron Thomas was unsympathetic would be an understatement. She gave me a right rollicking, threatening to write to my mother to say I was not fit to be a nursery nurse and to ask her to take me home. I was devastated. To get a qualification was the only thing I really wanted. I couldn't bear the thought of failure. How could I go back to the village with my tail between my legs? I'd endured months of homesickness, which still hadn't fully gone away, and the slave-like conditions and now she was threatening to stop me from going for my training. She finished off by telling me to go back on duty at once.

'But I need a doctor,' I whimpered.

'Then go,' she said. 'And when he sees you, he'll tell you you're making it up. He'll tell you there's nothing wrong with you.'

I crawled away in tears. The doctor was a bus ride away. My head was banging, I felt dizzy and sick but if I was to get that sick note, I had to get there somehow. I had to make my own way and I was unfamiliar with the roads. Being completely deaf didn't help either. If I asked directions, I couldn't hear them and it will surprise you how often people turn their heads away from you as they give directions. Without seeing the person's mouth, with perhaps the small hope that I could lip read, it was useless. The night itself was foggy and dark. The Clean Air Act had been in force since 1956, so the fog wasn't as bad as the infamous London pea soupers but it certainly added to the stress of the journey.

Sitting in the waiting room, waiting for my turn, I only knew I'd been called when several other patients gesticulated towards the doctor's office. He examined me and told me off for coming out with a temperature of 102°F, but he signed me off sick. I was so relieved.

Next I had to find a chemist to get the prescription made up. I dared not turn up without my medication. Matron Thomas would have left it until the next day before sending anyone out for it and I was desperate to be well again.

With my medicine safely in my pocket I set off for the nursery again but in my misery, I got on the wrong bus and added a half-hour walk to my destination. Matron was furious when I got back and gave her the sick note. She snatched it from me and the look on her face said it all; she obviously hadn't expected the doctor to sign me off. Her pet worry was that the nursery would be short-staffed and so girls worked all the time when they were unfit and should have been in bed. Back in my room, I crawled under the covers. My roommate was away for a few days, so I was alone. No one came to see me all the next day and frankly, I was too ill to care. Luckily I was right next to the bathroom so I managed to get to the toilet and I drank water from a tooth-mug on the window ledge. It was a miserable time.

Things get a bit hazy after that. I had a pot under the bed and because I felt too ill to go into the bathroom, I used it. No one came to see me or to ask if I wanted food or drink and when the pot was full, I was forced to stagger to the loo with it myself. My salvation came in the form of the doctor. He must have been slightly concerned about me because he turned up a couple of days later, unannounced. That was the first time Matron Thomas came to my room, and she stayed while he examined me. There was a heated discussion at the foot of my bed and they both left. A few minutes later, Matron came back up again, this time with a bowl of water, a flannel, a towel and one of her own nightdresses. She washed me and changed my bedclothes and an hour later, I was in an ambulance and on my way to hospital.

It turned out that I had an abscess on each eardrum and at last Matron understood that I wasn't making it up, nor imagining it. I was put onto four-hourly penicillin injections and given heat treatment on my neck. Both abscesses were so large, I had already discovered that when I lay on my side, I rested on the lump and not my neck. The only way I could sleep was to lie on my back. Matron Thomas' uncaring attitude was extended to my parents. No one informed them that I was in hospital, or ill for that matter and it was only after I'd been in hospital two days that they discovered I was there. A working-class home with a telephone was virtually unheard of back then. My mother had asked the local farmer, Mr Wellman, if she could use his phone in a case of emergency. When the hospital decided to operate, because I was still a minor, they needed my father's permission, so they rang him.

When the call came, Mr Wellman set off from Woolslope Farm to find my mother. She was at work but she left immediately and used the public telephone to call my dad's boss. My dad was a builder and Mrs Hayward ran two miles across open fields to reach the bungalow Dad was working on at Ashley Heath, near Ringwood. There was panic all round but Dad gave the hospital verbal permission and the next day he and Mum came all the way from Dorset by train. Ward sister allowed them in, even though it wasn't visiting hours until the afternoon, and I was overjoyed to see them.

By now, the penicillin was taking effect and I was making a slow improvement. Matron had invited Mum and Dad to go to the nursery for tea and Mum told me afterwards, she put on the performance of her life. She appeared distraught, wringing her handkerchief and saying, 'If only Pamela had told us she was ill. We had no inkling she was unwell.'

Mum bit her tongue. She knew I was terrified Matron would stop me doing my training, so much against her better judgement, she said nothing. Years later she told me just how hard that had been. 'I was furious with that Matron,' she said. 'Everything in me wanted to confront her and tell her I knew she was lying, but you had asked me not to say anything.'

Once I started getting better, I made some friends in the ward. It was very large and if I close my eyes I can still smell the floor polish and disinfectant. The girl in the bed next to me had had an illegal back-street abortion and almost died. I think she was about twenty. She seemed so sophisticated, so grown up, and she wore her make-up in the most amazing way. Her mascara was halfway down her cheeks like a spider's web, making her eyes look enormous. She had the palest pink lipstick, giving her an almost ghostly look, and her bouffant was parted down the middle and framed her face. It was a look which was soon to become very fashionable.

As my health improved, I was able to join in the fun and laughter patients share on a ward. We were all made to rest after lunch and I woke up one afternoon to the sight of a female patient, aware that men might be around, backing out of her bed to go to the toilet. She told us afterwards she did it that way because she didn't want to swing her legs over the bed because she had no panties on. The only trouble was, she was wearing a hospital gown which opened down the back and only one of the tapes, the one at her neck, was tied!

Then there was Nurse Driver on the ward. She was an SEN (State Enrolled Nurse, a title given to girls who had completed the three-year training course but had failed their exam. They were limited to general duties and were not allowed to do the medicine trolley). One day, the morning drinks had just been served when she turned up at my bedside.

'Have you got a headache?'

'No.'

A little later, after the ward round, she was back.

'Do you need something from the medicine trolley? Shall I tell Sister?'

'No, thank you. I'm feeling a lot better today.'

Just before lunch time I saw her coming back again.

'Are you feeling all right?'

'Yes, I'm fine, thank you.'

In the end, she was driving me potty so in the vain hope that she would go away, the next time she made a beeline for my bed I said, 'Actually, I have got a bit of a headache.' I lay down, thinking she would leave me alone to sleep.

Five minutes later she was back with two enormous pills and a cup of water.

I didn't want them, or need them so I refused as politely as I could. 'And in any case,' I smiled, 'I couldn't manage to swallow anything as big as that.'

She hurried off only to reappear with the pills crushed in a dessertspoonful of blackcurrant jam. As I forced the disgusting mixture down she gave me a loud lecture about not suffering in silence.

It was Nurse Driver who had an accident with her stocking

suspender. She was busy on the ward when it broke. I think the whole thing had come away from her girdle because usually if only the button at the end came off you could put a sixpenny piece in its place to keep your stocking up. Nurse Driver had tied a bandage around the top of her stocking to keep it up. During her shift, it gradually came undone and we had to bite our cheeks so as not to laugh as she dashed up and down the ward with a long trail of dirty bandage trailing behind her uniform.

And then there was the window. Someone said they felt hot. It was probably because she had a fever, but never one to rest on her laurels, Nurse Driver tried to open one of the windows. Being an old-fashioned building, they were of the long sash cord variety. Short, but undaunted, she found a step ladder and yanked the window down. Now we had half a gale blowing through the ward and of course, the window was jammed and so no one could shut it. It stayed like that for about an hour until two men came from the workshop to fix it.

After a week or so in hospital, I was allowed to go back home to Dorset. I can't remember who took me home but I'm sure I wouldn't have been expected to travel by train or coach. My recovery was hampered by a bout of glandular fever and it was three months before I returned to the nursery. I was keen to go back but once I began to feel better, I did enjoy my time at home. As usual, Dad went to the pub every night, so Mum and I watched *The Avengers*, *Juke Box Jury* and of course the handsome Clint Eastwood as Rowdy Yates in *Rawhide*. I spent some days over at St Leonards with my Aunt Betty, just 'chilling out' as they say now. I met friends and we went to Bournemouth to the pictures or shopping. I went to a Tramp's Ball at the West Moors youth club, which turned out to be the last time the kids I grew up with got together. By now, we were all out in the world of work and beginning to make new friends. I remember the time fondly for so many reasons, not least because one of the lads tried to get on the bus to get to the youth club but his tramp's outfit was so convincing the conductor chucked him off! We had a great time.

The following Monday, I went back to my GP and was signed off. The silly thing is, if Matron had let me go to the doctor right at the start, I would probably have needed only a couple of days off sick but because of the delay in getting treatment, she had been without a member of staff for three months. There was also an assumption that we would do anything to 'skive' off work. What a shame she didn't trust us more. If she had, she would have seen that we were loyal, both to the nursery and the children, and would only have taken time off if it were really necessary.

Chapter 4

Not everyone who lived in the home looked after the children. Some were unmarried mothers, who worked as cleaners or in the kitchens. Back then, having an illegitimate child still carried an awful stigma, but the first faint rays of change were coming into the care services. Most mothers were forced to give up their children for adoption. I have been told some very harrowing stories by my contemporaries in life, who were badgered and browbeaten into signing their babies away. A popular mantra was, 'You want the best for your baby, don't you? What could be better than to give him a Mummy and a Daddy who will love him and give him the best in life?' Under duress they signed their babies away and some girls were actually locked in a room at the mother and baby home when their child was taken, in case they made a scene. These women may be in their sixties and seventies now but recent programmes on TV show only too well that they are still traumatised by events that happened when they were young. It hurts them all over again when they finally meet their offspring and they don't really believe their mother put up enough of a fight for them. For those who wanted to keep their child, there was little or no public money to support children staying with them. Today's society has little or no concept of how difficult it was, especially if the family were too ashamed to help. I have heard young people saying, 'There's no way I'd have given up my child.

Nothing would have got in my way.' But one wonders how they would have managed with no family support, no day nurseries, virtually no social security, and back in the sixties even the most caring of employers were reluctant to offer work to women with children, especially young children.

The mothers living in the nursery may have been only offered very meagre wages in exchange for their services but the system meant that they could at least keep their babies with some dignity. The children stayed in the nursery itself, and were well cared for by trained staff. Best of all, the mothers had them to themselves in their off-duty hours.

We may have all been far more subservient to authority than today's society, but that didn't mean we were passive doormats. Everyone developed ways of getting their own back on the powers that be and one of the best ways to do so was to shock. One of the mothers we had in the house was a fourteen-year-old school-girl. Social services spent a lot of time with her, pressurising her into naming the father of the baby. In the end, she retorted, 'Look, if you'd eaten baked beans on toast and you got indiges-tion, would you know which bean gave it to you?' Matron Thomas nearly fainted and the child care officer (which was what they called the social worker back then) almost fell off her chair.

That story was repeated in every nursery I worked in until it became legend. We all admired anyone with real spunk. The best of it is, the girl may have still been at school, but she'd only had one boyfriend and, as young as they were, they loved their baby and planned to marry as soon as she was sixteen. I often wonder if they did.

The unmarried mothers weren't always young. Mary wasn't the sharpest knife in the drawer but she had a good heart. She had led a sheltered life, first in an orphanage and then in a hospital. She was the sort of girl hardly anyone notices. When she was discharged from the home where she grew up she was placed in the local hospital, where she worked doing routine chores and errands as a ward orderly. She enjoyed her work and people liked her. Her corny jokes were legendary. 'I've got a frog in me throat and it won't jump up,' was one of her favourites, and if you said, 'Are you all right?' she would reply, 'No, I'm half left,' and think it hugely funny.

Mary met the love of her life towards the end of the Fifties. He paid her a lot of attention and she fell hopelessly in love. Though her teenage years were by now far behind her, Mary was an innocent; he was more worldly wise. Their love affair was brief but intense and before long she began to notice the changes in her body. A visit to the doctor's confirmed her worst fears: Mary was pregnant.

At first, although she was upset, she wasn't unduly worried. After all, her man had declared his undying love every time he had climbed the back stairs to her room. She was confident he would 'do the right thing,' but her whole world was shattered when she found out what the rest of the world knew, that he was already married. For the first time in her life, Mary's gentle spirit was crushed. She was ill for some time but thankfully, the world was moving towards more enlightened times. Twenty-five years before, in the 1930s, girls like Mary were still declared insane and shut up in mental homes, sometimes for the rest of their lives, but the doctor dealing with Mary was a lot more understanding.

As part of this fairly new initiative, as soon as Jennifer was born, Mary was moved to our nursery. She worked in the kitchen while her daughter was looked after in the nursery. It was an ideal arrangement. The council had a 'permanent' member of staff (where else could Mary go with her baby?) and Jennifer was with her mother.

Mary was a loving and devoted mother. Nearly all her hard-earned cash was spent on her daughter and she also spent every spare minute of her off-duty time with Jennifer. They made a contented pair and the light had returned to Mary's eyes. Because

Mary had what we now call 'learning difficulties', she needed the guidance of others to help her with her child's upbringing. She was also a bit scatty. One evening she called me into her bedroom. She had knocked a water glass off her bedroom table and absent-mindedly stepped straight onto a small shard of broken glass, which was embedded in the sole of her foot. One of the other girls called Matron, who wasn't best pleased, because she worried constantly about staffing levels. Mary went by ambulance to the local hospital and once X-rayed, the doctor gently pulled the glass out and there was no lasting damage. When Mary came back, complete with bandaged foot, she dined out on that tale for weeks to come.

For women working in the nursery with their children, it could only ever be a temporary arrangement. The nursery only catered for children until they were five. Once they were ready for school, they either moved to another children's' home or into foster care. I left the nursery in 1962, when Jennifer was just over a year old. Mary may have been offered a similar situation in another children's home when Jennifer was five. I hope so – they belonged together.

I wish now that I had written down some of the things the children said. We would repeat them at staff meal times and perhaps to a friend outside the nursery but so many of their quirky remarks are long since forgotten. Of course we never ridiculed them but some of the things they did were so sweet. The children all had their own individual combs and although they were marked with their names, they were supposed to keep them in their own pocket, which was hung over the radiator guard in the bathroom. I can still see Paul, standing with his legs akimbo and his hand on his hip in exactly the same way Matron Thomas did. He'd even captured her cross face as he boomed out across the playroom, 'Julie, let me tell you somesing. You have left your comb on the top of the raid-it-ator card!'

Or Gary, who was dragging his feet when we were out for a walk. Knowing that Matron would complain if he scuffed his shoes, I said languidly, 'Gary, pick up your feet.' He stopped walking and looked behind him. Turning back to me, he said with a quizzical expression, 'But I haven't dropped them.'

Then there was Kelvin, who ate only the middle of his sandwich.

'Kelvin,' said Hilary, 'Cook cut you some lovely sandwiches but you always leave the crusts.'

'I know,' he sighed. 'She just doesn't get it.'

I managed to get a day off on my seventeenth birthday in April. No one else was off so I had to spend the day alone. I went up to London and did some window shopping. At some point I walked past a cinema. It was showing *High Society*, starring Bing Crosby, Grace Kelly and Frank Sinatra. It was by no means a new film, as it had been released in 1956, but I had never seen it. When I walked into the cinema, it was like walking into another world. The usherettes wore black uniforms with a frilly apron like a maid and in the interval, they actually served tea on a tray, with a teapot and china cups. I had no idea you could order it alongside your ticket, so I made do with the usual Lyons Maid ice cream! The *Pathé News* was full of stories about East Germans escaping the Berlin Wall. It had been built to prevent the massive defections of East Germans to West Germany. It was an horrific time but somehow it appealed to my sense of romance, with brave young men risking their lives and all that.

Being an institution, we were legally obliged to have regular fire drills. When the fire bell went off, the person in charge of the room had to make sure every child was taken to the assembly point. Matron or Sister would have a clipboard with everyone's name on it and they had to be checked off. In this way, every person in the home was accounted for and safe. The nursery nurses and assistants helped with the children and Mary was given the job of making the 999 call. She took her responsibility very seriously.

'When I was in the 'ospital,' she used to say, 'they told me that if I saw a fire, I was to grab one of the 'oses, and 'ang out the winder and 'oller for 'elp.'

I held my hand to my face to surpass a giggle.

'Well, there's no need to do all that,' said Matron sniffily. 'Just make sure you're in the cupboard under the stairs (where the telephone was housed) to ring for the fire brigade.'

One day we had a surprise fire drill. All the staff and children gathered at the assembly point and in due course we were checked off.

'Are you in the cubby hole, Mary?'

'I am Matron,' came the reply.

Matron was pleased with the plan and we all started going back to work. But then we heard the sirens and the next minute two fire engines hurtled down the drive. In her enthusiasm to get it right, Mary had actually made the call.

When I got back from my long illness, nothing much had changed. Matron Thomas was still totally neurotic. She was always complaining of a 'headache' – at least it seemed that way whenever she appeared on one of her brief sorties to the nursery. In fact, she really didn't need to put in much of an appearance because the day-to-day running of the place was such a well-oiled machine. Nobody questioned or altered anything. The mantra of the day was, 'We do it this way because we've always done it this way.'

Hilary, my roommate, developed a huge sty on her eye. As soon as Matron saw it, she said all in the same breath, 'Oh, Hilary, it's huge! It's as big as a shilling (about the same size as a five pence piece) but you can't go off sick because we don't have enough staff.' Hilary soldiered on in great pain but

41

was forced to go off sick a few days later when she not only had to contend with the enormous sty but had also developed yellow jaundice!

With Hilary off sick, I made a new friend. Evie Perryer, a pretty, bubbly girl, arrived. We hit it off straight away. She had a real joie de vivre and we were always laughing. Evie was the kind of girl all the boys fell over to be with. In fact, she was never without a boyfriend and the two of us started going to the International Friendship League meeting.

I think someone my mother worked for must have told us about the International Friendship League (IFL). The Sixties saw a big rise in the numbers of foreign students coming to Britain, especially from the African continent and India. The IFL had branches all over the country and was run along the lines of a church youth club. They promoted clean, healthy interaction between young people and the one we attended was held in a church hall. The meetings usually began with a 'talk' by someone who was an expert in his/her field and then, after a cup of tea, the rest of the evening was given over to a dance. The only talk I can remember was one given by an ex-policeman, who shared a story of how a murderer was caught by a spider's web on the victim's trouser leg. Using this, the police pin-pointed the spot where the murder had taken place and even found the exact spider who had made the web. Fascinating.

The dances gave everyone the opportunity to meet boys from just about every country in the world. There were no English boys there and the people we met were polite and knew how to make a girl feel like a princess. One was an Italian boy, immaculately dressed in a suit with its own waistcoat and a camel coloured coat. He was good-looking and a brilliant dancer. The only trouble was, he was much, much less than five foot. I watched him going around the hall, asking the girls to dance and every one of them refused him. He finally got to me and I couldn't bear to disappoint him. I said 'yes' and from that moment he kept coming back. Finally, he wanted to walk me home and tried to persuade me to come out on a date but that was a step too far for me. Nice as he was, I didn't want to date him. Later, I met Chaw, a boy of Asian extraction who came from North Africa, Joe (I think he was called Joe because no one could pronounce his name) from the Yemen and Nafis from Pakistan. Evie met Coover. I don't know where he was from but he was breathtakingly handsome and made me go weak at the knees. I fancied him like mad. No one had any money. Although their parents had sent them to England for an education, most of them had sacrificed everything they had to be there. Their meagre money covered the cost of their digs and the tuition fees so a date might be an evening at the pictures, or a walk in the park.

I was luckier than most. When Chaw asked me out, he had a Vespa scooter. It terrified me – it backfired all the way up the hill and it was a wonder it got us back to the nursery. When it came to knowing the facts of life, I was rather naive. At school we had studied the reproduction system of the frog. I could tell anybody about what frogs do but it wasn't much help when it came to men. I understood that you had to be married before you could have a baby, but after the wedding night quite what the man did, I hadn't a clue!

I enjoyed being kissed so when we arrived at the gate, Chaw politely asked if he could kiss me goodnight. I eagerly agreed but as he kissed me, he pushed himself against me. I can't say I felt the earth move but something did and I fled. Chaw was my first-ever date, and so all the girls had waited up to hear about it. When I saw them, I was so upset I couldn't speak. I raced to my room, threw myself across the bed and wept.

After a few minutes, Hilary came in and sat beside me. 'Whatever's wrong?'

'He's done it,' I wept. 'I didn't want him to but he's done it.'

She asked me to be more specific and so I told her everything. Hilary may have been a vicar's daughter but everyone agreed she knew just about everything there was to know. She was a bit concerned but she said she felt sure I would be all right. Putting her arms around me she said quite seriously, 'I know you can do it with your clothes on, but I don't think you can do it with your coat on, especially when it's still buttoned up.'

I was so relieved to have the benefit of her experience and she certainly reassured me that it would be all right but I was more than relieved when my period began a couple of days later. As for the coat that saved me, it was thick brown mohair with three coaster-size buttons down the front. Boy, was I glad I was wearing it!

Joe who came from the Middle East fell in love with me. A big man with dark skin and a ready smile, he was a student and although his parents were wealthy, he never seemed to have much money either. He was kind and loving and I have always regretted that I didn't stop the relationship sooner. I'm afraid that I unwittingly hurt him deeply. He came home and met my parents, which of course must have given him hope that our relationship would go further but he was a Muslim and I wasn't prepared to change my culture or beliefs, something which would have been required of me. Joe's father was a well-respected newspaper publisher, regularly commuting to New York and the UN, where he represented his country.

At the beginning of our relationship, Joe complained of the cold English winter, so I told him I would knit him a sweater. We chose some bright red wool and big needles and I began. When I decided that I wanted to break up the relationship I still had to knit the wretched jumper and because I knew it had cost him a lot of money, I felt honour bound to complete it. He was a big man and it took forever but eventually I'd finished. He was so proud of it, but then I dumped him. I was trying to do the right thing, but looking back I obviously sent out some very confusing messages.

Another boy I met was called Nafis, who came from Pakistan.

One time when Nafis and I had a date, he was looking very sad. He kept shaking his head and saying, 'I wish I hadn't done it.'

'Hadn't done what?'

'Last night Marilyn Monroe telephoned me from Hollywood,' he said. 'She begged me for a date but I said I was busy. I told her I was taking you to the pictures and now look what's happened.'

It was a bit of a sick joke but I laughed from politeness. It was August 1962 and Marilyn Monroe, reputedly the sexiest girl in the world, had just been found dead. Nafis didn't last very long as a boyfriend either. Not because of his bad taste jokes or the fact that his mouth tasted like an ashtray; the problem was that he was tiny. I thought I was overweight, although looking at photographs at the time, I wasn't really. But I hated being made to feel big and Nafis made me feel like an elephant. He never knew why I dumped him.

Then there was Coover. He used to send Evie red roses. How I envied her, with all those lovely roses *and* Coover.

When she got back to nursery, Hilary decided Evie was too prudish for her own good and so when she was in the bath, Hilary rattled the bathroom door until the bolt slid back. She and I marched in while poor Evie struggled to cover her ample bosom with the smallest of flannels. We were being heartless really and I don't think for one minute we thought we were going to change how Evie felt but the event was typical of the tactics Hilary enjoyed.

I became something of a dressmaker. One time Evie didn't have a thing to wear and she was going on a date. I had a day off so I said I would make her something. In her morning off duty, she hurried into town and bought something which looked an awful lot like curtain material. I spent the afternoon making her a sack dress. It had three large sunflowers down the front, a scoop neckline and no sleeves. I finished it just as she came off duty and she wore it that night.

Now that I had a little money in my pocket, clothes became increasingly important. 1962 saw the rise of Carnaby Street in London. It was near Oxford Street in Soho and was full of fashion boutiques. Hilary and I were still stuck in the 'everything to match' era of the late 1950s but that didn't stop me drooling over dresses which I couldn't afford. My best outfit of the day was a patterned orange and brown blouse, worn with a brown pencil skirt and a big orange cardigan. Hilary looked very smart in her pink swagger coat over a navy dress. She had navy stilettos, matching handbag and long navy gloves. Contrast that with Mary Quant's mini skirts and the sack dress and you can see how radically different the fashions were becoming. The bright bold colours were amazing.

There wasn't a great opportunity to help the children develop a taste in dress and appearance although just like every other child, the children in care showed some interest in clothes. They liked nothing better than to see us in our 'going-out clothes' as they called them. Often a girl would promise the older children to come back into the nursery and show them her 'party' dress if she was going somewhere special. I remember going into the night nursery to show the children my new dress when I was on my way out. I did a couple of twirls in the middle of the room when Rosie climbed to the end of her bed. 'What are those?' she asked, as she patted my chest.

'They're my boobs,' I said.

'My daddy's got some of those,' she said gravely.

The only real way to foster a personal interest in what you wear is when you are given a choice. The children in the nursery had little of that. I do remember the odd occasion when a child hated a certain dress or pair of trousers and in that case we would change it for another item from central stores but that isn't really choice. Even so, sometimes getting dressed could be fun. Cory was supposed to be getting dressed but instead he was fooling around. 'Cory,' I said, 'would you like to put your socks on?' 'No thank you,' came the reply. 'I think I'll wear my feet today!'

The one time when children did have choice about what to put on was when we got out the dressing-up box. It was interesting to note that sometimes the shy child seemed to come out of his or her shell when they had something different on. Our dressing-up boxes were really good. Sometimes when the children had chosen their outfits we would put on a record or switch on the radio and have music and movement as well. There were always a few items of dressing-up clothes in the Wendy house and an apron or a hat could transform any game into something much more exciting.

For me, the discovery of boys was a welcome distraction but we still worked incredibly hard. Matron would move us around, especially if she thought we were making what she called 'an attachment'. Every day began at 6.30 a.m. when the 'duty girl' came round with a cup of tea. Everyone had to be on duty at 7 a.m. so the scramble for the bathroom was pretty hectic and you had to be quick. No time for a bath of course, as there was a queue of girls behind you, all rushing to be on duty at the same time. We all took it in turns to be the 'duty girl'. The night nurse would bring a large teapot to your room and leave it. Then the duty girl had to pour the tea and make sure everyone else in the house was awake.

The decorators were in and Hilary's and my room was top of the list. While it was being done, we both had to move. I think I got the better deal because Hilary's bed was squashed into a room with two other girls while I was asked to share with Christine.

Christine's room was on the ground floor in the 'cottage'. The room had once been part of the stables of the big house. I was duty girl for the morning, so the night before I had laid out the cups and saucers on a tray and put them on the floor in between our beds. That night we had a fierce summer storm, which was highly atmospheric. During a brief lull, we heard the distinct rattle of cups.

'What was that?' I said into the darkness.

'I don't know.' Christine's voice was little more than a strained whisper.

The sound of rattling cups echoed through the room.

By now my heart was bumping with fear. Neither of us had a bedside light. The only light was from the light switch by the door. 'Get out and put on the light.'

'I'm not getting out of bed,' said Christine. 'I'm too scared. *You* get out.'

I couldn't do it either, so the pair of us lay in bed utterly terrified and unable to sleep. Who or what was in our room we hadn't a clue, but we were both thoroughly spooked up. I imagined it to be a snake or a rat or a ghost. Daylight was painfully slow to come and it was first light before we finally dropped off. But when the night nurse switched on the light as she brought in the teapot, we couldn't believe our eyes. Rolled in a neat little ball in the middle of the tray, spilled cups of milk all around him, lay a very sleepy hedgehog!

Hilary and I moved back into our newly painted room. It was much better although not quite as wonderful as we had been led to believe. The wallpaper was the same all around the room, which was a blessing, but it was large turquoise blue poppies. We had new curtains in turquoise, although not the same shade of colour and we still had the same mismatched purple counterpanes. As we still hadn't reached the psychedelic atmosphere of the 1970s, it seemed rather odd.

There were a few girls who never did make it to do their training. Isolde, the girl who laughed in the sitting when Nurse Adams missed her date, left a couple of weeks after the event. Another girl was Laura Duncan. She was older than me, about nineteen, and had lived a very sheltered life. She became the butt of comment and jokes and for a time, I joined in, but then I could see that she was really struggling. I remembered my own struggles with homesickness and the sheer relentless hard work and I began to feel ashamed. As a result, when we worked together I tried to help her whenever I could. She was a plain-Jane who looked a lot like Joyce Grenfell, with big teeth and a long face. She was gawky and awkward in her movements and although obviously well educated, she was totally impractical. One morning we were assigned to sweep up one of the playrooms and Laura almost fell over the long-handled brush. I actually had to show her how to use it!

Because I was kind to her, she stuck to me like a limpet. I liked her but we had little in common. Her parents were very over-protective and would come to the nursery to spend her off-duty with her. They never gave the poor girl a chance to be her own person. Sometimes they would take her into town for a coffee and a look around the shops but if it was raining, they would simply sit in the car together on the driveway. It wasn't her fault but it was little wonder that people laughed at her. A couple of times, when we shared the same off duty, she would come with me into town or to the pictures. That's why her mother invited me to their house. Laura was on holiday and I had a day off so I caught the Green Line bus to Dorking, where she lived. I had asked for the name of her road and the driver called it out as we arrived. To my dismay, Laura wasn't there waiting for me as she had promised. I didn't realise but the road was in the shape of a large horseshoe; I had got off at one end and she was waiting at the other.

Still, I had the name of the house and the number so I set off to find it for myself. The houses in her street were very large with huge gardens. It was clearly the sort of place where bankers and pop stars lived. Laura's house was a tad smaller than the others in the road but it was detached and in its own grounds. As soon as her mother opened the door, she almost had an apoplectic fit. She put her hand to her head and leaned dramatically in the doorway.

Slightly confused, I introduced myself. 'Hello, I'm Pam, Laura's friend.'

Putting both hands on her head she cried out a tirade of words, 'Oh Pamela, poor Laura! She's waiting for you at the bus stop. She went that way and you've come up from the other side. She'll be devastated that you haven't come. Oh, I can't bear it! You must go and find her. You must go to her, Pamela. Go. Go now!'

Bewildered and a little shocked by the amateur dramatics, I turned tail and ran down the road. I met Laura coming back. 'Your mother was terrified that you'd think I hadn't come,' I smiled awkwardly.

Laura seemed unperturbed. 'I guessed what had happened,' she said.

When we got back, her mother fussed over us like an old hen. She offered us coffee and went to the kitchen to prepare it. When she came back, she set up a folding stand and put a big brass table on the top of it.

'We live very humbly here, Pamela,' she assured me. 'People think because of the area, we are rich but as you will see, that is not the case.'

Well, she certainly looked well off to me, not that I cared one jot.

Laura and I had quite a nice day but her mother was totally overbearing. She gave us coffee in the sitting room, insisted we sat in the garden until lunchtime, and after the meal, sent us up to Laura's bedroom until it was time for the brass table and a pot of afternoon tea.

It was shortly after that that Laura left the nursery. We simply got the message that she wasn't coming back. I really hope it was nothing to do with me, but I can't help wondering. Perhaps after our day together, her mother decided that she didn't want her well-bred daughter mixing with the likes of me. I felt sorry for Laura and even more sorry that I never got to say goodbye.

Things were about to change. It was the end of August 1962 and I had completed my year as a nursery assistant. Latterly, I had enjoyed my time there and I think I had gained a little more confidence. I had finally overcome my homesickness, made new friends and I had taken on board some of the more important aspects of childcare. Now I was moving to the nursery, where I was to begin my two-year nursery nurse training. I was keen to get on with the job and a little nearer that all-important qualification. If I'd thought I'd had it hard as a nursery assistant, life had been a picnic compared to what I faced now.

Chapter 5

My new nursery was a large bleak building surrounded by rolling lawns. The rest of the grounds that had surrounded it when it was a private house dwelling had been sold off. Some had been developed and given over to council housing and shops. The whole estate was entered by a long sweeping driveway, ending in a cul-de-sac and the house.

The home was run by a Matron who was very large. She always wore a navy nylon overall and because of her great weight, she lumbered along. She had short dark brown hair, a round face and looked a lot like the Queen Mother before she grew very old; she also had a rather high-pitched whiney voice. The day I arrived, she called us new girls into the office, one by one. There were four of us who began as students together. Hilary had come with me to the same nursery but Evie had gone to another one, somewhere else in the county.

When it was my turn to meet her, Matron Dickenson (we called her 'Dickie' behind her back) gave me a limp lettuce handshake and puffed up her ample bosom. 'We are all happy in this nursery,' she barked. 'And you *will* be happy.' It was more of a command than an invitation.

Hilary and I were faced with more or less the same kind of routine so it didn't take us very long to settle in. The hall landing and stairs were very dark and even in bright sunlight we had to have the light on upstairs. There was a lot of dark wood panelling; dark parquet floors and the mahogany doors were heavy. Once again the children were divided into three groups, Babies, Tweenies and Toddlers, and we spent most of the day cleaning.

We may have been slaves to the routine in the new nursery but there was still a lot of fun to be had. The day began at 7 a.m. when we arrived in the nursery to begin dressing the children. Every child had a wash in the morning. The babies and tweenies were 'topped and tailed' and the older children went to the bathroom to make a valiant attempt to wash themselves. We had to get everyone dressed by 8 a.m. when it was time for breakfast. The children ate in their own groups. Babies were bottle-fed in the baby room, while the tweenies and the toddlers were together in the children's dining room. The meals were enormous. For breakfast they would have either cereal or porridge, then a cooked breakfast, which might be bacon, egg and half a slice of fried bread, or maybe scrambled egg on toast. The night nurse had made marmalade sandwiches for everyone. Tweenies had half a slice of bread made into a sandwich each, and the toddlers a whole slice of bread (two sandwiches). They drank milk or milky tea. After breakfast, everybody went to the toilet. At 9 a.m. the girls who had had their breakfast at 8.30 a.m. came back to relieve those who had stayed to look after the children. There was free play in the playrooms until 9.30 a.m. In the tweenie room, the children, after another visit to the toilet, then went into their prams outside. Sometimes we took them for a walk, but mostly in the morning, they slept in the pram shed or out in the garden while we cleaned the nurseries. The toddlers had the better toys under the supervision of the nursery warden. We also had water, sand and painting for them to do. They were divided into two groups and half the morning was spent with the messy stuff, and the other half in the playroom. If it was fine, everybody was outside in the garden. Lunch was around twelve noon and they would have two courses. After lunch, it was time for a rest. The toddlers slept on stretchers in the playroom, while the babies and tweenies were in their cots.

Many years ago, I met one of the children I'd looked after as a little one. He was in his twenties and he enjoyed reminiscing about his stay in the nursery. One thing puzzled him.

'You used to make us sleep on the table,' he told me.

I couldn't believe what I was hearing and then realised he'd obviously thought the stretchers were tables!

After lunch it was back to the playroom, going out for a walk, or having a spell playing in the garden. Tea was at 4 p.m. and they had bread and butter, maybe a boiled egg, and cakes. After tea we told them stories until it was time to get ready for bed.

Two of us did the bathing from 5 p.m. Another girl collected the children from wherever they were (in the playroom or the garden) and brought them upstairs for us. As soon as they were undressed, we gave them a short time of free play in the bath. I loved bath time. The children had toys to play with and sometimes we'd splash and make a mess. Bearing in mind some of the awful conditions these children had come from, there was nothing nicer than putting a warm, happy child, smelling deliciously of talcum powder, into a clean bed. The children themselves were usually keen to come up for their baths. I remember the time when Mark came upstairs from the garden, where he'd been running about in the evening sunshine. He looked hot and sticky. I went to help him undress but he told us he was a big boy and could get undressed himself. As he whipped off his trousers he looked down at himself and said, 'Awww, look. My willy has gone to sleep!'

Everybody had a milky drink and they would have a bedtime story in the nursery before we kissed them goodnight. After that, we sorted their clothes ready for the morning and then it was time to go for our supper at 7 p.m.

My two new roommates were Marilyn, a bubbly girl with short dark curly hair, who loved sailing, and Paula, a rather austere-looking girl. The old feeling of homesickness came back but this time I was better able to cope with it. Off duty was more or less the same as it had been in my nursery assistant days, with the same long hours and one day off a week. The big difference was that now I was going to college as well. That meant I would work two weeks in the nursery and then have one week in college. To get there, I would leave early in the morning to travel to Guildford by train, returning to the nursery at about 4 p.m. We had to work until 7 p.m when we got back to the nursery but the best bit was that we'd have Saturday off as our day for that week and Sunday off for the next week. A whole weekend every three weeks, what bliss! It meant I could catch the Royal Blue coach from Guildford High Street to Ringwood in Hampshire and then the bus to West Moors and be back with Mum and Dad at around 9.30 on Friday night. I'd be back on the bus to Ringwood at three on Sunday afternoon and I'd arrive in the town at around eight. It was a tidy walk to the nursery, but it didn't matter, not even when it was dark and lonely. Back then it didn't bother anyone being out alone at night.

We trained at Guildford Polytechnic, doing childcare and child education. I had hoped Evie Perryer might be there, but she went on a different week so I met and made friends with whole new set of girls. They were a friendly lot; one, Elspeth, was very elegant and had expensive clothes and Arlene was the class swot. Another girl ended up being called 'Brown Susan'. Her name was Susan Brown and as top of the list on the register, whenever our lecturer called her name, she always got it round the wrong way and it stuck. Our lecturers were Mrs Davies, who taught us child education, and Miss Mountford, who was an ex-district nurse and taught us child development.

Miss Mountford was very forthright and she loved to shock. The first time we ever met her she swept into the room and said, 'Dear, dear, somebody in here smells! Which one of you didn't wash her knickers last night?'

We all froze to the spot, dreading that she might point to one of us with a much more personal remark. She was perfectly capable of doing that. She once drew me aside and advised me to buy a new underarm deodorant. I was so mortified, as soon as I got back to the nursery, I threw the handknitted jumper I was wearing into the bin.

Almost as soon as I settled in, I realised I had a problem. Marilyn was alright, but Paula and I didn't get on. She was volatile and I always managed to rub her up the wrong way. She would make snide remarks and I rose to the bait every time. What began as a prickly relationship quickly deteriorated into not speaking and vindictiveness. The thought of spending two years in the same room together was pretty daunting for both of us. I don't remember exactly how it happened, but in the end we made an agreement not to antagonise each other. It was quite incredible because we stuck to the arrangement and although I can't say we were ever best friends, there was a kind of mutual respect between us and we learned to rub along together.

As time went on, Paula found herself a policeman boyfriend and he got her pregnant. Back in the early Sixties, people still 'had to' get married, but we students had signed an agreement with the council. Our parents had promised to pay back whatever expenses the council had incurred for our training, if we left before our two-year contract was up. This left Paula in a tricky position. She not only faced being an unmarried mother and homeless but she would also be landed with an enormous debt. In the twenty-first century, homelessness is considered a misfortune, nobody cares about being an unmarried mother anymore and debts are an inconvenience. Back then, all three carried a huge stigma of shame. Paula was at her wits' end.

Surprisingly, she confided in me. She burst into tears and wept on my shoulder. As I comforted her, we worked out that if she could continue to work until her due date and then take the couple of weeks' holiday she was owed, that meant that she would be able to complete her contract. That was one problem solved. Next I encouraged her to tell her boyfriend what had happened. She was terrified at the thought but when she told him, he was keen to marry her anyway and as a policeman he could get help with housing. Another problem solved. In fact, the council waived the contract, having decided that a heavily pregnant girl on the premises would be a bad influence on the rest of us! Paula left to get married in her seventh month of pregnancy.

Once again, it was time for me to work in the baby room, this time with a Nurse Astley, who was lovely. The routine was as rigid as it had previously been but now I was allowed to handle the babies straight away. I would come on duty, wash the babies and dress them in their day clothes. Then they would have their feed or breakfast. I would then go to the staff dining room for my breakfast. After breakfast, the babies would go out in their prams and then it was time to clean. The baby bathroom, milk kitchen and playroom all had to be spotless. The washing had to be taken downstairs to the laundry room for whoever was on laundry duty. Then it was time to make up the feeds in the milk kitchen. Lunch time was another round of feeding, and then time for my lunch. In the afternoon, after the babies had had a rest, we might take them for a 'walk' or park them in their prams in the garden. At 4 p.m. it was tea time and then we would bath the babies and give them their night feed before settling them down. In between times, I might be the girl on laundry duty, or perhaps I'd be cleaning prams. Life was still hard work but I was doing what I wanted at last, training to be a nursery nurse.

We had to keep a file on a child in our care. It was to be a kind of diary, charting the child's progress day by day. My first child study case was a five-month-old boy called Peter Chippers. I had to keep a record of when he fed well, any illnesses he had, the day he first crawled and sat up on his own, when we began his weaning and keep a check on his weight. I was allowed to take photographs of him and I made an attractive album out of a scrapbook. The object of the exercises was to make me observant. Sadly the scrapbook was destroyed once I had finished my training and I often think how sad it was that nobody kept it for him. His mother, who through no fault of her own had put him in care, wasn't offered the opportunity to have that diary, nor did she know it existed. It should have been easy enough for the powers that be to keep that record with Peter's personal papers and he would at the very least have had some record of his childhood. He was a sweet child and made good progress. I watched him roll over for the first time and eventually begin to crawl as I encouraged him by putting a toy just out of reach. He had a warm chuckle and he loved eating the homemade rusks they made in the kitchen. Cook would soak bread fingers in milk and then put them on a baking tray in a very slow oven. The children loved them and they were a lot cheaper than the shop-bought varieties.

When I began my case study book, Peter was only four months old. I thought it would be hard to find something interesting to write but I soon discovered the value of the exercise I had been given. As it turned out, I didn't have to look for interesting things, Peter *was* interesting. He enjoyed his bottle, giving little grunts of pleasure as he drank it, and sometimes he patted the bottle or stroked it as well. His eyes were beginning to focus and if I talked to him, he managed a lopsided smile. When I offered him a toy he could distinguish between us. He would study the toy and then look to me for guidance. Of course, I would be smiling so he would know the toy was something good. By six months he was beginning to pick things up or manipulate toys within his reach. He loved to be bounced on my knee as I sang nursery rhymes. He especially loved 'This is the Way the Ladies Ride' and he would chuckle uproariously as I jigged my knees faster and faster with each verse.

We were moved around the nursery during the two years I was there. This was to ensure we had an all-round education. The next child I had as a case study was Keith Devlin. He had a sister in the Tweenie room called Jane and they were very close. Keith was in Toddlers and he had a more active life. He loved painting and what might have looked like a blob on the paper had real meaning for him.

'What's that, Keith?' I would say.

'A man on a bike,' he'd say proudly. Or 'Our Jane eating a biscuit.'

Keith and Jane were in care because of homelessness. Their parents were East Enders who had fallen on hard times. Slum landlords were charging extortionate rents and unscrupulous landlords such as Peter Rachman (who didn't achieve notoriety until a year later during the Profumo Affair) built up their property empires on the backs of people like Mr and Mrs Devlin. If they couldn't pay the rent, they were intimidated or evicted. The council was duty bound to take in a homeless child while the parents had to fend for themselves. Mr and Mrs Devlin were probably on the council house waiting list but with Britain only just coming out of the austerity years after the Second World War, they might have a long wait.

Keith could count up to ten and he was learning the concept of size. 'Mine is bigger than yours', he'd say. He enjoyed reading books and could do just about every puzzle in the toy cupboard but he hated playing with clay. I can't say I blame him – I've never liked the feeling of clay under my fingernails either.

Gradually, I settled into the routine but it was during one of my weekends at home that Dickie began a reign of absolute misery in the nursery. During her final rounds of the day, she found a small window open in the sluice room and demanded to know who was responsible for leaving it open. Nobody owned up so with everybody gathered in the staff dining room for supper, she marched in and announced that she had stopped everybody's off duty. Everyone was upset about it. It was the weekend and some of the girls had planned to meet friends. We weren't allowed to have telephone calls at all and they were forbidden from going down the village to use the public call box.

Hilary led a rebellion of the disgruntled girls. Everybody was upset about having to work a twelve-hour day with no break. It seemed unfair and besides, she was sure it was illegal.

'If I go into the office and tell her it's illegal, will you all stand by me?'

'Of course we will,' they said.

Psyched up by their encouragement, Hilary strode to the office and knocked on the door. Dickie listened to her complaint and told her to go back to work. Then shrewdly, she called the other girls into her office, one by one. When faced by Matron on her own, every girl denied knowing anything about it; Hilary was left out on a limb.

When I came back from home after my weekend in West Moors, the whole nursery was tingling with suppressed resentment and anger. The girls had worked the whole weekend without any off-duty periods and they were all exhausted. Dickie had spent most of Saturday and Sunday in her office and the whole atmosphere in the place was awful.

On Monday, Miss Fox-Talbot, the nursery supervisor, turned up in her red Mini and Hilary was summoned to the office. We all waited anxiously, wondering what her punishment might be. I was convinced she'd be asked to give up her weekend after college but in the event, they told her she might not be allowed to continue her training. She was sobbing with fear when she came out of the office but we all felt that this was merely a threat to pull her into line.

'If they were really going to do it,' I assured her, 'they'd have done it straight away. They wouldn't leave you wondering about it.'

Hilary decided she would spend the week buttering up Miss Hill, the nursery warden – a middle-aged, bony woman with a passion for tea.

'If I can get her on my side,' she said, 'I reckon it'll be all right.'

Sadly we were both wrong. Miss Fox-Talbot came back on the Thursday and Hilary was once again summoned into the office and told she was sacked.

It's still never very pleasant to be sacked but in 1962, it could ruin a career. Angry as she was, when given the choice of leaving immediately or working her month's notice, Hilary realised that it would be far more difficult for Dickie if she stayed, so she elected to work the month's notice.

I was still in the Baby room. She came to me in floods of tears and I just couldn't believe it. I had mixed feelings as well. She was my friend. If I had been there that weekend, I would have gone in the office with her and that would have meant I would have been sacked as well.

From that moment on the whole atmosphere of the nursery changed. Dickie must have sensed a great deal of hostility. Hilary's decision to work her notice only served to increase the tension. She left at Christmas, her career blighted forever. She had managed to get a job as a mother's help but because her employer was 'taking a risk' her wage was reduced to three pounds a week (which was very low, even for a mother's help) and for that she was expected to do just about everything. It was imperative that she got a good reference from her new job, because the one she got from the nursery was so damning. Dickie had certainly vented her spleen when she wrote it. Poor Hilary had a very hard time but give credit where credit is due, she stuck it out for a couple of years. We stayed friends and met up quite often on our days off, and she was still fun to be with and daring in what she did.

Matron and the nursery supervisor had tried to break her spirit but they never succeeded.

I have already mentioned having the dressing-up box out when we put on a record or had music on the radio but there were other ways of stimulating the children's interest in music. Of course we had a lot of singing of nursery rhymes but we would also get out the percussion instruments and the children would bang a drum or shake a set of bells to the music. The nursery had a piano but nobody could play it.

We also improvised with instruments. A cigar box with a series of strings tightly drawn over it made a good sound. We would put a little dry rice in a tin or a few pebbles and then glue down the lid so that nobody could eat them or stick them up their noses. Then we would paint them bright colours. The children loved to shake them in time to the music. A string of buttons or beads and even some Formica samples on a chain from the kitchen shop made great shakers. Somebody stuck some glass paper onto two blocks of wood. When rubbed together, they made a great rasping sound although I'm not sure today's Health and Safety police would approve of that one. We had a music corner in the playroom. It had pictures of musical instruments on the walls and the nursery warden had three recorders, which she produced every now and then for the children to play. The all-time favourite was 'The Grand Old Duke of York' and when we sang it, we would all march around the playroom with the instruments. It worked for the children and it worked for us too. For a few minutes we could forget our aching backs and our tired feet. We didn't care about our hands rubbed raw by washing nappies – with everything banging and blaring out loud, we could stamp our feet and march up the hill and back down again with the rest of them.

Despite the way Matron had separated us over Hilary, for the most part, whatever we were doing, we had a feeling of us 'all being in this together'. We supported each other whenever we were in trouble or covered up to prevent someone getting told off. Whenever a girl needed a shoulder to cry on, she didn't have to look very far. We enjoyed beating the system whenever we could, although our acts of rebellion may seem a little tame by today's standards. Watching the end of a TV programme that finished at 10.15 p.m. when we were supposed to be in our bedrooms by 10 p.m. or skimping on the cleaning if we were behind time, or even letting someone go off duty a bit early so that she could catch the early bus, they were all on our list of achievements. I was there to learn about the care of children but I also learned about loyalty and camaraderie, compassion and friendship, lessons which would hold me in good stead for the rest of my life.

Chapter 6

Having a baby should be a joyful occasion but Mrs Field knew the minute her baby was born that there was something wrong. The nurse whisked her away without showing her to her mother. As they waited for the placenta to come, Mrs Field's stomach was in knots.

'Can I see my baby?' she asked over and over again.

'In a minute . . . nurse is just seeing to her . . .'

She still hadn't seen her child when the midwife had cleaned her up. As she finished, she leaned over and whispered, 'Before you see your baby, Mrs Field, the doctor wants a word.'

'I'm so sorry my dear . . .' was all she heard. His mouth was working but she had already shut the words out.

After he'd talked to Mrs Field, they brought the baby, washed and wrapped in a snowy-white towel. She regarded her mother with an unfocussed stare but Mrs Field turned away and faced the wall.

Barbara Field had been born with no ears. She had a dip on one side of her head where her ear should have been and a sealed hole on the other side. Her birth defects were caused by her mother taking Thalidomide, a sedative which was introduced in the late 1950s and used to treat morning sickness. It was prescribed by doctors from 1957 until 1961, and at the time scientists didn't think any drug taken by a pregnant woman could pass across the placental barrier and harm the developing foetus.

Sadly it proved to be the cause of many horrific birth defects. As many as ten thousand children from forty-six countries were affected, many of them dying at birth. Barbara was one of the four hundred and sixty-six survivors born in the United Kingdom.

Barbara was Dickie's favourite. She would take her into her office-cum-sitting room and give her special toys to play with. She was an adorable kid, cheeky and with a mischievous streak.

One day, while we were bathing the children, Barbara grabbed a bottle of shampoo and drank some. My roommate Marilyn managed to snatch it away before she'd taken too much but it gave her the hiccups. Barbara was quite literally blowing bubbles.

'Blimey,' said Marilyn. 'Now what shall I do?'

There was no way of getting the shampoo back so I said, 'Give her something else to drink. She probably grabbed it because she was thirsty anyway.'

Marilyn gave Barbara some of her bedtime cocoa. Now she was hiccupping chocolate bubbles.

'Is she going to be alright?' Marilyn asked anxiously.

We kept a close eye on her and happily she was fine.

Things took a definite turn for the better for Barbara when she was three. During a play time, one of the girls blew a toy whistle behind her head. Barbara immediately turned around and grabbed the toy for herself. We were so excited. Barbara could hear after all. The whole thing was repeated several times, with exactly the same result. It was time to call Matron. Staff nurse blew the whistle behind Barbara's head and she duly turned around. Dickie was thrilled. She immediately called the doctor and an appointment was made to see an ear specialist. Surprisingly, apart from her babyhood examinations when Barbara had been declared profoundly deaf, no other follow-up examination had been set up. Barbara was to stay in care all her life anyway. Her mother blamed herself so much for her daughter's defects that she'd had a complete breakdown.

Barbara would be sent to a home for the deaf as soon as she was five.

We waited in quiet anticipation for the appointment with the specialist and at last it was only a week away. One afternoon, I used the same toy whistle to play the game with Barbara. As she turned towards the sound, she put her hand up to her neck and a horrible realisation began to dawn. Barbara probably couldn't hear the whistle at all, but she could feel the rush of cold air from the toy as it was blown. Marilyn and I looked at each other in shocked surprise.

'We'd better tell staff nurse,' said Marilyn.

So we did.

'We'd better tell Matron,' said Staff nurse, looking straight at me.

'You tell her,' I said. I didn't want to be the one to tell her we'd all made a mistake – I knew what she was like. She'd do her nut and take it out on me for weeks. The others didn't argue. They were just as cowardly as me.

A week later, Barbara went for her appointment. It was just as well that we hadn't told Dickie and had her cancel it because they did find a small degree of hearing in Barbara's ear and she came back with a hearing aid. They couldn't fix it in the normal way because with no ears, there was nothing to latch on to. Barbara was given what looked like a radio announcer's head phones, which were attached to a battery on her chest by a specially made harness. For the first few days, she walked around with a slightly bemused expression on her face, sometimes stopping to listen to a sound she clearly had never heard before. A whole new world was opening up for Barbara and she began to change. However, she never lost her personality. If she was upset or angry with us, she would pull the plugs out of the battery, effectively 'switching us off'.

Christmas 1962 will go down as the most miserable I ever spent. The atmosphere was somewhat subdued after Hilary's departure but we were all making an effort to get back to some kind of normality. Dickie spent Christmas afternoon alone in her office. We caught the odd glimpse of her walking through the hall and she seemed to be in a bad mood. We didn't see her properly until we all assembled for Christmas dinner at six and she swept into the staff dining room. We had a splendid meal – turkey, sausage, stuffing, Brussels sprouts and peas, roast potatoes, followed by flaming Christmas pudding and custard – but the atmosphere was so bad, the whole meal was eaten in utter silence. I felt as if everyone could hear every mouthful going down. We couldn't look at each other and the meal seemed tasteless and instead of being a long fun-filled chatty time, the whole thing was over in fifteen minutes. Even with such tiny wages, we had all clubbed together to buy Matron and Sister a Christmas present. One of the staff nurses had spent ages in the town looking for something nice and we were pleased with her efforts, but Dickie didn't even bother to open it. As soon as she'd finished her pudding, she stood up and we all stood up as well.

'Thank you, girls,' she said grudgingly. 'I'm sure it's very nice.'

As she and Sister left the room, the door slammed and some of the girls burst into tears.

'What's the matter with her?' Bridget wept.

I put my arm around her shoulder and shrugged.

'Sister Hemmingway took her photograph when she was giving one of the children their Christmas present,' said Marilyn and suddenly we all knew why she was in such a foul mood. Dickie was very conscious of her weight and hated having her picture taken. 'As soon as the flash went off,' Marilyn went on, 'she glared at Sister and stormed out of the room.'

'She didn't even look at her present,' said Staff Nurse. 'I spent the whole day looking for that.'

'This has to have been the worst Christmas ever,' said Bridget.

I couldn't disagree with that.

The council had generously allocated extra monies for their

nurseries at Christmas. Some was for the children's presents, which came from proper toy shops, and the rest was for the staff. It paid for a meal (which we had just eaten) and a present for each girl living in the nursery. When we opened our presents, every girl, senior staff and student alike, had exactly the same thing: a bar of Palmolive soap with a promotional 'pearl' necklace attached. It must have cost all of a shilling (five pence). When we saw it, everyone tried to laugh it off but the truth was, we were all very hurt and close to tears, if not already crying.

The next day, Boxing Day, Dickie's mood was even worse. Sister must have said something about her behaviour because before long we heard the most almighty row coming from the office. I was in the Baby room, which was directly above it. I couldn't make out what was being said, but I could certainly hear the angry voices and the protracted row. After that, Dickie wandered through the nursery, finding fault with everything and everyone.

Throughout the day, girls would appear at the door and asked if I would like them to feed a baby. In reality, they were hiding from Dickie to lick their wounds. Just about every girl who fed a baby that day did so red-eyed and with a wobbly chin. Things got so bad, one of the staff nurses walked out during the afternoon and spent the rest of Boxing Day with her sister, who lived locally. Bridget left altogether without even bothering to pack a case. She sent her sister to collect her things a couple of days later and we never saw her again. When she came back later in the evening, the staff nurse gave in her notice and Dickie's reaction was to put another present outside her bedroom door. I happened to be walking past when she picked it up. It was beautifully wrapped, with pretty paper and a ribbon, but when she opened it, she found a wooden spoon with a luggage label tied to it. The message on the label read, 'To stir it up'. Staff Nurse threw it across the room and burst into tears.

The atmosphere for the staff was unbearable and to be frank, by the end of the day, I wondered if I could stick this out.

Late that Boxing Day afternoon, the children had suddenly become very excited. They all rushed to the window and began shouting and waving. We went to look and couldn't believe our eyes. There in the grounds was a man with a sled. He was dressed as Father Christmas and he waved to the children. His sled had an empty sack on it, so the children were convinced he was the one who had left their toys. We never found out who that man was. I wish he could have known that he was the one nice thing that happened that day. Bless him, whoever he was. He gave some of us the courage to go on and for me in particular, the belief that not everyone was a miserable old cow who took pleasure in spoiling other people's Christmases.

For me, the greatest miracle of all that Christmas was not so much the celebration of the birth of Jesus Christ but the fact that the children didn't seem to notice what was going on around them. They had the best time opening their presents and playing with their new toys. There were extra sweeties and Christmas crackers. They wore their Christmas shirts and dresses and enjoyed their day, and we, unhappy as we may have been, put aside our feelings and joined in their excitement. Our heartbreak may have been self-centred but it gave us a small insight into the difficulties the parents faced when they smiled and pretended all was well when they visited their children in the nursery.

The system of childcare has altered quite a lot since the Sixties when a radical re-think of the care of children unable to be looked after by their parents began to evolve. Social services didn't exist then – that came into being in the Seventies – and up until then the various council and government departments were fragmented. Child care officers were not formally trained. They had been boarding-out officers, who cut their teeth as war-time evacuation officers and welfare workers. It wasn't until 1971 that all social work and children's departments came under one umbrella, the Department of Education, and also included services for young offenders, disabled children and approved schools. Today, children under eighteen who are in residential or foster care are called 'looked after' children and according to the government website in 2012, seventy-three per cent were in foster care, seventeen per cent were in residential schools or placed with their parents under supervision and only ten per cent were in children's homes.[1] Back in the early Sixties, the percentage of children in homes was much higher.

In the Sixties, Parliament set up the children's branch of the Home Office General Supervision Department and gave it the responsibility to see that the Children's Act of 1948 was being implemented. That Act made it the duty of the local authority to look after children who had come from a broken home, or who were abandoned or neglected, orphaned or illegitimate. One such abandoned child who came into the nursery had been found outside a block of flats. He was about a month old and well wrapped up, which was just as well because it was close to Christmas. The staff of the hospital who checked him over called him Noel and because he was found outside Shelby Court, he was given the name Noel Shelby. Poor little boy! We never did find out who his mother was but happily, a few months later, he went for adoption.

We also looked after children referred to us from the courts who might have been ill-treated or any child whose parent was incapable of caring for them. Whenever they could, parents were expected to contribute towards their child's care, as was the case with Mr Swinnerton, who had to pay a fee to the council for the care of his daughter Geraldine.

The way children's homes and nurseries were staffed also

1 Department for Education website 'Looked after' statistics 2011. www.education.gov.uk

varied. A council-run children's home was headed up by a Matron who was an SRN. The second in command would be a Sister who would most likely be an SRN as well. The individual rooms (Babies, Tweenies and Toddlers) were overseen by staff nurses who were NNEBs. Then came the student nursery nurse and finally, the nursery assistant. Each nursery would have a nursery warden who was a trained teacher. The residential nurseries were inspected by both the Ministry of Health and the Department of Education.

As I continued with my training, they taught me to recognise the various ways a child would react to being placed in care. Some, especially older children, would be very upset. We might have to be put up with the child screaming or desperately trying to get away by biting or kicking. This usually only lasted a while because no child had the physical strength to keep it up for long. We would talk quietly and soothingly and try to build bridges but it was always distressing. We also had to be aware that a quiet child may be hurting just as much as the one who acted aggressively. That child might even behave as if he or she had accepted the situation. The same child could carry on for days, weeks or even months, playing with toys and complying with the routine of the nursery, but never having given up the hope that their mother might walk through the door at any moment. When the penny finally dropped that Mother wasn't going to come and take him home, the child probably wouldn't react in the same aggressive way as the first child might have done. He'd be more likely to sob from within. It was important to be loving and understanding and to make sure that each child had room to grieve. We had to be there when they needed us and even though we had a lot of work to do in the nursery, we would rather risk being in trouble than rush anyone who needed us. The welfare of the child was of paramount importance. Whereas the defiant child might be destructive, resort to bullying, refuse to conform or spitting, the more submissive child might resort to head banging, rocking or masturbation. Some children who had been fully toilet trained when they came into the nursery might have a lapse and we learned the importance of being patient and understanding.

Mark Cooper hadn't been neglected nor had he been ill-treated in the usual way but he had almost been killed with kindness. He was born a healthy seven-pound baby (3.18 kg) but Mark had been left in his cot for long periods and every time he opened his mouth, someone stuffed a bottle in it. As a result, when he came into care at six months old, he weighed a staggering twenty-three pounds (10.4 kg). His bottom was very sore, so sore that as the staff nurse removed his nappy, his skin came away as well. For all that, Mark was a happy little soul. His mother simply couldn't cope and because he had remained in the cot for long hours, he had been unable to explore a wider surrounding. His huge weight hindered him but eventually he managed to move further afield. Once he was put on a diet, or perhaps I should say more precisely, a normal diet, his weight began to stabilise. I never remember Mark's mother coming to see him – I think it may have been because she was relieved that somebody was looking after him and she didn't want to be persuaded to take him back. The people from children's committee (the governing body which actually sent out the child care officers) only shared what was absolutely necessary for us to know, and although Matron would have had all the facts, she took the same view. This probably sounds odd nowadays, but I think it was a kind of respect for someone's privacy. No matter what they had done or how spectacularly they had failed, unless it was deliberate cruelty, their dirty washing was never aired in public. We didn't ask and they never said.

Every nursery had its share of pets. At my previous nursery it had been a rabbit. The children would take it for walks around the garden on its harness. It was a fairly large animal and difficult to handle but if the child was sitting down, it was quite happy to be put on a lap for a while. We had to take it to the vet regularly to make sure its claws were clipped in case anyone got scratched. The rabbit was kept in a large hutch in the garden and the girls working in the Toddler room had the responsibility of feeding it and cleaning it out. Although the children were never allowed to help with cleaning the hutch, they did take it in turns to change the water or put in the rabbit pellets. The kitchens kept it well fed with lettuce and other vegetables.

In the nursery where I trained the children had a guinea pig. The purpose of keeping pets was to teach the children respect for animals and we were always careful to make sure who was in charge of them. We had heard a horror story about a nursery where the pet canary had died of thirst because the girl who normally looked after it was on holiday. Nobody wanted a repeat of anything like that in our nursery. The older children felt very 'grown-up' when they were given the opportunity to take it in turns to feed the animals. I can't help thinking that for some of them, that sense of responsibility would have gone some way to compensate for the feeling of helplessness they may have felt: they couldn't change their own situation but they could make sure another living creature was loved and cared for.

The choice of pet was always down to the Matron. My friends in college worked in places where they had hamsters, mice or fish. Hamsters were okay but mice usually attract wild mice and because they have weak bladders they urinate as they move. Fish cannot be handled, only be watched, and whereas they may be attractive, I would find it difficult to get excited by a fish. That being the case, I was glad my nurseries had a more child-friendly pet. Guinea pigs can be interesting. Ours was a tough little creature and didn't seem to mind clumsy handling, although we took care to make sure no one was too rough. The children enjoyed scouring the garden for dandelions to feed it and the kitchen kept it well supplied with free vegetables.

To sum up life in care, the authorities were doing their best to give the children everything they needed in a physical way to survive and it was our job to try and lessen the scars they would inevitably gain from the trauma of being separated from their parents. The council acted *in loco parentis* and we were the softer part of that touch. It was far from ideal of course, but it was the best we could do.

Chapter 7

The winter of 1962/63 was one of the hardest winters on record. It began on Boxing Day and snowed continually until March, the bitingly cold winds bringing blizzard conditions and huge snow drifts. By the middle of February, every news bulletin on the radio was gloomier than the last. Water froze in firemen's hoses, and the plumbers were doing a roaring trade fixing burst pipes. The Thames froze right over and they recorded 36°F of frost at Heathrow. Along the south coast, the sea froze as well. We heard about milkmen doing their deliveries on skis, old people, particularly those living alone, dying of hypothermia in their own homes and livestock being been found frozen to death in the fields. The nursery had plenty of coke and was well stocked with food, which was just as well as prices rocketed with eggs doubling in price to four shillings sixpence a dozen (twenty pence) and potatoes reached a record seven pence a pound (two pence). Hospitals were bulging at the seams with patients with broken legs and broken hips all with complications, caused by people falling in the icy conditions.

Surprisingly, although it was extremely difficult to get around, the country didn't come to a total standstill, but at one point the nursery was completely cut off. Four of us were sent down into the town to get some milk. We wrapped up well and set off with two crates of empty bottles. It was okay going because we took it in turns to carry the crates and they didn't weigh very much, but the snow was so thick, walking was hard work. In some places, it had obliterated the road signs. You might place one foot but as you put weight on it, you'd go knee deep before you could lift the other. It was hard to find the path and in some places, the drifting snow had buried vehicles up to the car roof.

Coming back home was even harder. By now we were very tired and the crate of milk was too heavy for one person to carry. We made little progress trying to carry it between us because we kept falling over but then we had the brilliant idea of threading our belts through the crate and making a rope to pull it. I got slower and slower and when I turned around, I found that I'd ended up dragging an ever-increasing snow drift behind me! That twenty-minute walk took us two hours. We consoled ourselves that when we got back, at least we'd have the evening to ourselves, but not a bit of it. As soon as she saw us, Dickie told us to have a cup of tea and go back to work!

The South of England was bad but not as bad as the North. I still managed to get to college every three weeks and better still, home to West Moors on the Royal Blue coach and then the local bus. Only one journey was disrupted. I caught the bus from my parents' village to Ringwood and usually had about twenty minutes to wait until the Royal Blue coach came. There were about eight people waiting at the coach stop with me. We had been there about an hour when someone came from the bus station to tell us the coach had been cancelled due to the adverse weather conditions. There was no alternative but to go back home. The only trouble was, I had just watched my bus leave and I would have to wait another hour before I could get another one. On top of that, there was no guarantee that it would come. Those same adverse weather conditions might mean all buses were stopped but thankfully, I was in luck. The bus came and I headed home. When I got indoors I nearly collapsed. I had never been so cold in the whole of my life. It felt as if the very core of my body was frozen and my mother was really worried that

I had hypothermia. Dad got out the brandy bottle and I was plied with hot laced tea and given a hot water bottle then sent to bed to get warm. The next day, Mum rang the home from the local call box to tell Matron that I had been stranded and that I would come back as soon as I could. I caught another coach halfway through the day. Thankfully, although I had walked from town, I arrived at the nursery in the early evening and guess what? My day off had been changed. Instead of having the following Friday off, I'd just had my next day off travelling back to the nursery in the coach!

Going back a bit, when Mum and I got back home the day we'd been into Bournemouth looking for garden knickers, the back-yard of our two-up, two-down cottage was littered with old doors, wooden window frames and chicken wire.

'What the . . .?' Mum began.

A head peered round the shed and Dad, all covered in sawdust and enthusiasm, beamed. He lifted his hand in protest as soon as he saw Mum's look of disapproval.

'Now before you say anything,' he began, 'hear me out. This idea will work – I know it will. Just give me a year and we'll all be rich.'

Mum and I glanced at each other and I gave her a half smile. She pursed her lips and shook her head. Just give me a year and we'll all be rich . . . How often had we heard that line?

My dad spent his whole life looking for the big thing that was going to make him rich. He'd always lived in the village, apart from a spell in the army during the Second World War. He was sometimes laid off from the building work because of his bad back and although Mum was content with her lot, Dad wasn't and there were times when his entrepreneurial ambitions knew no bounds. The problem was, they never seemed to work but ever the optimist, Dad was always convinced his latest project would change our lives.

Mum drew herself up to her full indomitable five-foot nothing and took in her breath noisily. 'So,' she said coldly, 'what's it to be this time?'

'Rabbits,' said Dad.

Mum and I looked at each other and chorused, 'Rabbits?'

'What do you think people want these days?' The question was rhetorical. He didn't wait for the answer. 'They're half-starved. They've got no money. What they need is something to look forward to.'

I couldn't argue with that.

'That's why I've decided to breed rabbits. Just what the doctor ordered . . . rabbits. Easiest thing in the world to breed rabbits. I've got it all worked out. First I'll make the cages, then I'll get a buck and a doe and, they'll . . . they'll . . . breed like rabbits!'

Mum was having none of it. She harrumphed and stalked off indoors.

I don't know why. Of all his zany ideas this one sounded quite a good one to me. I liked rabbits. But Mum had every reason to be upset: Dad didn't have much of a track record when it came to his entrepreneurial skills. Take, for instance, his money-saving envelopes. He spent the whole of one Sunday afternoon cutting out a metal template. The next time we went into Bournemouth, he bought three rolls of drawer lining paper and some strong glue from Woolworth's. The Sunday after that found him folding the paper, then I watched him trace around the metal shape with a pencil. I was eight years old at the time and my thirst for knowledge knew no bounds.

'What are you doing, Dad?'

'Making envelopes.'

He began to cut the paper with a Stanley knife. 'After this, it's simply a question of fold and stick. Easy peasy.'

But it wasn't quite as easy as he thought to get the bits that had to match together. His rejects mounted up and up, but the thing about Dad was that he wasn't daunted. By the time his first envelopes came rolling . . . well, limping, off the production line, he could already see himself as a tycoon, and Mum and me in flouncy pink dresses.

'Envelopes today,' he said proudly. 'Brown paper bags and cardboard boxes tomorrow. The sky is the limit.'

The Stanley knife probably wouldn't have cut butter and Dad didn't have a very straight eye. Actually, he was blind in one eye, so maybe he had the wrong one shut. He had paper everywhere and the dog thought it was a great game. I was virtually up to my knees in offcuts by the time my bedtime came but he had eight perfect envelopes and one with a kink in it.

'Ernie!' said Mum in acid tones. 'For goodness sake, just look at this mess.'

Dad glanced up at the clock. 'Good Lord, is that the time? I'll do the rest next Sunday – I'm off to the pub.' Needless to say, he didn't make any more envelopes but at a time of an acute paper shortage, I had a lovely lot of drawing paper.

You can't keep a good man down. After the envelopes came the knitting phase. Actually Dad didn't knit himself. He was a man of his time, a product of the Thirties and Forties when men didn't do 'women's work', as they called it. This time he fancied himself as supervisor of a cottage industry and Mum was press-ganged into being his first outworker.

'It'll be a doddle,' he told her. 'You love knitting, don't you? All they want is a size ten, short-sleeved jumper in double knitting wool in twenty-one days. You do it and I'll pay you ten bob. I can't say fairer than that now, can I?'

Somehow, Mum managed to do it in between all the housework (we didn't have labour-saving devices like a Hoover back then) and cleaning the local doctor's surgery, and fetching me from school, and weeding the garden and a few other little jobs she had. The jumper was finished and Dad sent it off. The firm was delighted. Two weeks later, Mum got ten bob. She was well chuffed. Dad was quite pleased too although I'm not sure if she knew that he had a ten bob note as well. Mum's next assignment was a twinset in four-ply wool. I got a bit fed up with it – she was always knitting. When she met me from school, sometimes she used to take me over to the swings. She didn't any more.

'I haven't got time for all that!' she snapped. 'I've got to get that knitting done.'

She was grumpy too. Trying to listen to *Educating Archie* with Mum click-clacking away was almost impossible. If I looked her way, she'd glare back at me. 'And you can shut up about it too!'

'What?' I protested indignantly. 'I didn't say anything!'

'Any more nonsense out of you,' she snapped, 'and you can go to bed!'

No one was more delighted than me when two weeks later she had another ten bob and the knitting stopped.

'The next order has come through,' said Dad, opening a letter one morning.

Mum didn't look too thrilled. 'What, already?'

'You're a great little knitter,' said Dad. 'They love your work.'

Mum's cheeks flushed with modest pride.

Dad read aloud. 'They want you to do a man's forty-two inch sweater in three-ply wool to be done in ten days.'

Mum swiped Dad with her apron. 'For just ten bob!' she snapped. 'Bloody sod it!' and Dad's cottage industry died there and then.

Well, now it was rabbits.

It took an awful lot of Sundays before Dad had created enough hutches for his new outworkers. I was living and working in the nursery by the time he was ready for his first buck and doe. The rabbits came from the market in Ringwood, five miles away. Mum wasn't too happy about it. She wrote and told me that Dad had carried them home in her best shopping bag and it was ruined by pellets and pee in the bottom.

When I was at home recovering from my spell in hospital, helping with the rabbits was very therapeutic. I loved to watch them but when the first of the babies came I wasn't allowed near in case the doe ate them.

It wasn't long before Mum and Dad had rabbits everywhere and Dad had to build more hutches. As I recovered from glandular fever, I helped clean them out, gave them water and food and sometimes held one of them.

There were pet rabbits in my first nursery but the nursery warden guarded them jealously. The children got to stroke them or walk them around the garden on a lead but so far I hadn't been allowed to be part of that.

Mum began to get orders. 'So far,' she said, 'I've got eleven and the butcher wants another four.'

'At five bob a time,' Dad said, his eyes sparkling, 'that's almost four quid.'

'Remember to keep one for our Sunday lunch,' Mum beamed.

I was used to eating hand-reared livestock. We had kept chickens for years and once Dad won a pig at skittles. The chickens supplied eggs and as broilers, Mum cooked them slowly. The pig went to market but I think Dad lost out on that one. He didn't have a car and by the time he'd given his mate petrol money and a pint, he was out of pocket.

The next day, Dad – dressed in an apron and wearing rubber gloves – took all the rabbits into the shed and closed the door. He was gone all morning.

At lunch time, he came indoors looking pale and shaken.

'A well-deserved four quid,' said Mum, giving him a peck on the cheek. 'Where are they?'

'Outside,' said Dad. 'I'm off to the pub.'

'Good old Sunday lunch,' said Mum, putting on her coat to go and get one.

Dad caught her arm. 'None of us will be getting rabbit for Sunday lunch this week,' he said. 'I couldn't bloody kill 'em, could I?'

It took him several days to pluck up the courage to do the

awful deed, but finally he made it. When I went for training, he would donate a couple to the nursery every now and then. I would travel on the Royal Blue coach with my suitcase and a brown paper parcel with two dead rabbits. When I got back to the nursery, Sister and I would skin them and prepare them ready for the cook next day. Matron was pleased to have them, but sadly it never did make me her blue-eyed girl.

As part of the daily routine in the nursery, the younger children were always taken outside for some fresh air. If the weather was bad or it was raining, they would spend the morning in their prams in the pram shed. It was a dingy place but the prams were lined up side by side, the children put into a blanket bag and strapped in. We made the blanket bags ourselves – we used old worn blankets and stitched up the sides. Then we put tapes at the top. The babies and tweenies were put into the blanket tube and the tapes tied on the shoulder. They may have kicked off their covers but inside the bag, they never got cold. We gave them a few toys to play with, which usually ended up on the floor, and most of them fell asleep for a while although I suspect it was more from boredom than tiredness.

The prams had all been donated to the home and were in fairly good condition. They were all coach-built, or made of fibreglass. (The Marriet was coach-built and the Pedigree was fibre glass.) We preferred the coach-built pram because it kept the baby warm in winter and cool in summer. They were large prams and had 'C' springs to ensure a smooth ride for the baby. The back wheel was larger than the front wheel to make it easier to push up and down the kerb. The tyres were rubber and the handle firmly bolted to the body. It had a rubber grip, which made it easier for pushing, and the pram had a good foot brake, which meant that the adult could keep both hands firmly on the handle at all times. The lining was padded to make sure the baby didn't get knocked and all prams had a hood and storm apron in case of bad weather. In the summer, there was a sun canopy which could be fixed under the screws holding the hood. This would go right over the baby and protect him from the bright sunlight.

We also had a quad pram. This was a coach-built pram in which four tweenies could sit up and enjoy going for a walk. Even though there were four children inside, it was easy to push and we would often use it to take the children out. Once I was pushing the quad pram. I had a child with blonde hair, a child with flaming red hair, a black child and a child with an oriental look about him in it. As I was pushing the pram around the shops, a woman came up to me. 'Oh,' she cried. 'Aren't they sweet? Are they all yours?'

I shook my head and smiled politely but as I walked away, I couldn't help wondering if she'd thought I had a rainbow-coloured husband!

Being a nursery nurse makes you very observant. We may not have known an awful lot about sick babies but we did know a healthy one and that often became the yardstick that would make it obvious if a child was unwell. At a month old, a baby lies more or less helplessly on his back, usually with his head to one side and the arm on that side extended. He has a good sucking reflex and it can easily be elicited by touching his mouth. His eyes move but are as yet unfocussed although he will respond to loud noises. Sarah was only a few weeks old when she was admitted but I knew something was wrong. When she cried, she would push her head back so far it almost touched her spine. I pointed it out to the nurse in charge and she was seen by the doctor. She was taken to hospital with cerebral irritation, perhaps a birth injury but more likely because she had come into the nursery because of neglect. Nothing was ever proven and we all hoped it was caused by a birth injury rather than ill-treatment. Sarah didn't come back to the nursery.

At four months old a baby spends more time awake and moves

his arms and head freely. He can now focus his eyes and he will smile when you talk to him. In every other way, Andrew was a healthy and happy little boy but held his head in a rather odd way. Up until he came to the nursery, he had been placed in exactly the same position every time he'd been put in his cot. We always changed the side we laid babies down so that this sort of thing didn't happen. As time went on, Andrew's balance became better, but he always held his head at a slight angle the whole time he was in the nursery. He came into the nursery because his mother was unwell. The family had several other children who were being looked after by relatives but there was no one to look after the baby. Happily, Andrew's mother recovered and after a few weeks, he went home. The child care officer would have advised Andrew's mother about varying the sleeping position of her baby.

By nine months old, the baby has a few teeth. He has a preference for sitting up and he can raise himself up or roll over. Some babies can stand if they have something to hold onto. He can drink from a cup and is able to pick up small particles of food with his fingers, usually using the thumb and second finger. Christopher chewed everything and the day I put his small chair a bit too close to the artificial Christmas tree, in his enthusiasm to get one of the baubles, he wrecked it. Luckily for me he didn't manage to put one in his mouth!

At a year old, baby is awake for half the day. He is an agile crawler and ready to walk but his balance is insecure. Usually he can say a few words and he's beginning to show his emotions a lot more clearly. Pleasure, fear, annoyance, anger and how to attract attention are all skills he has learned. He can feed himself and will cooperate in his dressing and undressing. Lisa came to life when she was in her bath. She would slash and kick her legs and although we gave her extra time in it, she was always upset to come out of the water. As soon as we undressed her, she would say the one word in her vocabulary, 'Bubbles!' I often wonder if she became a swimmer. She was adopted so the chances of her being able to do something she enjoyed would have been markedly enhanced. Her parents waited a long time to have her and were desperate for a little girl.

By eighteen months, baby would have anything up to twelve teeth. Walking well, he can sit easily and climb into a chair. He would enjoy going bump-bump down the stairs on his bottom and he could pull a wheeled toy. He likes to 'help' in the nursery and can respond to simple commands. His curiosity is being developed, as well as his powers of observation. Peter was so excited when he went out for a walk. 'Bus,' he cried as a red double decker sped past. Back in the nursery he got a book from the book corner. 'Bus,' he said, pointing to the picture. 'Clever boy,' I said. Peter 'read' that book until it almost fell apart. I can't actually remember what happened to Peter but isn't it strange how some children are frozen in the memory? Peter looking at his bus book is one of those indelible memories for me.

By the time a child has reached three years old, he has all his first twenty teeth. He can walk and run freely and with confidence. Balance and coordination has reached a level where he can ride a tricycle and walk up and down stairs on his own. He understands rewards for good behaviour and he is dry at night; he also enjoys drawing and has favourite toys. Delroy was concentrating on getting dressed. No, he didn't want help. When he'd finished, he had his underpants on back to front, his shirt buttoned all wrong and he'd forgotten to put his vest on but never mind, he was very proud that he had got dressed, 'all by my own.'

The child in the nursery was moved on at the age of five. By this time, he had confidence and independence. He could play imaginative games, dress and undress and brush his hair. He could draw fairly well and had a vocabulary of about two thousand words. He was talkative and enjoyed having a conversation.

We all sat at the dinner table with our eyes closed and our hands together.

'Thank you, dear God, for our food,' I said. 'Amen.'

All the children responded with a loud 'Amen'.

Calum frowned and looked at the boy next to him. 'Old men?' he queried.

For all her meanness of spirit, Matron Dickenson could sometimes do something very nice. We were a little bit nervous when she did, wondering where the catch was, but she wasn't all bad. A popular ITV programme at that time was *Sunday Night at the London Palladium*. It pulled in an eye-watering twenty-eight million viewers and starred some of the world's greatest entertainers. To our amazement, Matron got tickets for the students to go. They were free but because the show was so popular, they weren't easy to get hold of. She arranged for a skeleton staff to cover our absence and we set off for London. Everybody was hoping that The Beatles might be the star turn, or perhaps the Rolling Stones. The night we went, there was a brand new group called The Seekers on stage. We'd never heard of them before but they became mega-stars from 1965 onwards. They sang a beautiful song and the lead singer, Judith Durham, had the kind of voice that made your skin tingle when you heard it. I think they sang, 'I'll Never Find Another You', the song which catapulted them to fame shortly after. The host of the show, Norman Vaughan (we'd missed the very popular Bruce Forsyth), was quite good and we all enjoyed *Beat the Clock. Beat the Clock* involved married couples, picked from the theatre audience, playing silly games in which they had to complete within a set time period with a chance of winning a £1,800 jackpot – a lot of money in those days. We clapped a lot. Every time a man appeared at the corner of the stage, he held up a card which said 'clap' and we did so until our hands hurt. The main star of the night was Buddy Ebsen. We'd never heard of him but later in the Sixties he was to become famous as Jed Clampett in the TV sitcom *The Beverly Hillbillies*. Sadly that night we weren't very impressed, mainly because he seemed to be so old!

The professionals made us laugh, but the children did it better. Like the time when Nurse Christine had a birthday. In the Toddler room, we all sang 'Happy Birthday To You' and then Kelvin said, 'How old are you?'

'You shouldn't ask a grown up how old they are,' Miss Hill the nursery warden said.

'That's okay,' smiled Christine. 'I'm nineteen.'

Kelvin regarded her with a look of deeply-held respect. 'You're *very* old aren't you?' he said.

'That's nothing,' Carole, aged four and three quarters, piped up. 'My granddad is sixty-six and he isn't even dead yet.'

And then there was the time when Alan made us laugh in the garden. He had been running about for ages, boasting that he 'could run very, very fast.'

As he came back to me, I said, 'You're all out of breath.'

'Don't worry,' he smiled. 'I've got some more.'

And finally, several children were playing doctors and nurses in the Wendy house together. I looked over the top of the wall to see Johnny lying across the table with his pants down. Sarah, resplendent in her nurse's outfit, was hovering over him with a construction straw in her hand. Horrified, I gasped, 'What are you doing?'

'Just taking his temperature,' came the serious reply as I quickly removed the straw.

Whenever things like this happened, I knew just why I had chosen to become a nursery nurse. I loved the things the kids said and their innocent seriousness made it even more enjoyable. Some were natural comedians and others more like accidental ones, but whenever they made us laugh, we could never resist giving them an extra hug. Studying their progress was enjoyable too. If I hadn't known what to look for, years later I might have missed those milestones when I had children of my own.

Chapter 8

When I look at my childcare notes for that era, it's startling to realise that we were still being taught how to look after children with diseases we never hear about today. I have a whole section on recognising the symptoms and the care of a child with polio-myelitis. Thank God, vaccination has all but eradicated that terrible disease from this country but even in the Sixties, children were still getting it. I remember in the Fifties a girl in my class at school had to wear a calliper on her leg as a result of contracting polio. Diphtheria was another one. If someone was complaining of headaches, shivering, rapid pulse rate and had a throat with a greyish-white appearance, we were exhorted to get that child to hospital because the complications could be catastrophic. The nursery nurse is unlikely to come across these diseases today unless he or she works in third world countries.

Another disease, which is totally treatable in this day and age, was caused by an under-active thyroid gland. Lily was a cretin. Until I met her, I had always thought of the word only in terms of a particularly nasty form of insult. I had no idea it was a real condition. Cretinism is a term that is now frowned upon but it happens when there is a severe lack of thyroid hormone. This condition is usually detected within a week or so of birth because all babies are screened on day six by a blood sample taken by a pick on their heel.

Back in the Sixties I'm not sure that that screening or

treatment was available. Certainly Lily wasn't on any medication in the nursery and she was typical of children with the condition. She had dry wrinkled skin and her tongue was a tad too large for her mouth. Her fingers were broad, and she had a small hernia near her belly button. The whole of her body was covered in thick downy hair and her wild auburn hair was very thick and tufty. If untreated, the condition results in mild to severe impairment of both physical and mental growth and development, and I recognised that Lily fitted into that category perfectly.

She did, however, have a good level of understanding. One day a fly was buzzing around the Baby room and Lily became very excited. Pointing at it, she kept repeating the word 'fly' in her deep, manly voice and in the end all of us were in stitches, including Lily herself. Today, a child with Lily's condition would be treated with Thyroxin, given in tablet form, crushed and mixed with expressed breast milk, formula milk or water.

The one thing Lily hated was carrots but Dickie had a policy that the children had to eat everything put in front of them. If anything went back to the kitchen, she would accuse the staff of being too lazy to give it to the children. Mostly we covered up their dislikes by eating it ourselves, or stuffing what we could into our pockets. We sent our uniforms to the laundry each week and when her clean clothes came back, one of the students – Norah, a rather studious girl with thick pebble glasses – found a brown paper bag in her laundry box. Someone had written on the bag, 'returned in case you feel peckish'. Inside was what had once been a marmalade sandwich, which some child had refused to eat at breakfast time. Norah couldn't face it either, so she'd stuffed it in her pocket and forgotten all about it. Now rock solid and a delicate shade of grey, it gave us all a good laugh as I'm sure it did the laundry workers who found it.

When we gave Lily her dinner, we dreaded the days when it was carrots. Dickie didn't believe a child under five could have a hatred of something. She regarded resistance as naughtiness so she would make a child eat whatever was on their plate. We all hated to see her doing it but we couldn't help poor Lily. Today's nursery nurse has far more clout. The fact that anyone can be a whistle blower or refuse to do something they believe is wrong is a right which had to be hard-fought for and won by the people of my generation. We take it for granted now and quite rightly so, that Lily, young as she was, should have been allowed to state her preference. Back in 1962, she had no choice but a year later, when Sister Hemmingway came on the scene, she made it quite clear right from the start that no child in her care would be made to eat something they didn't want. She stood up to Dickie and once the battle lines were drawn, although things were very unpleasant for a while, Sister got her way.

The child care officers were always keen for unmarried mothers to name the child's father. Lily's mother was put under that pressure and she came up with a unique definition of her pregnancy. Those who knew the family situation were convinced that she had had an incestuous relationship and that Lily's grandfather was also her father. He was a loud, self-opinionated and domineering parent, so it was hardly surprising that Lily's mother stoutly refused to talk.

'I ain't been with nobody,' she told them, rolling her eyes innocently. Then looking a little more thoughtful she added, 'Ooh . . . I sat in me brother's bath water after he'd finished. Could that have been when it 'appened?'

Lily was still in the nursery when I left. I guess she would have stayed there until she was five and then been moved to another children's home. No child care officer worth his salt would have sent her back to her mother's home while the father/grandfather was still alive. Her mother of course had no such protection. Being an adult, she would have been deemed to know she could leave at any time.

In 1963 I had been on night duty over the weekend while the night nurse was on holiday so I had a sleeping day on Monday and a day off on Tuesday. It was Wimbledon week. I had been junior tennis champion at school for two years so I jumped at the chance to go and see the stars. Special outings were a rarity. For a start there was little money to spare and because the off duty was only done the week before, there was little opportunity to plan ahead. Sometimes a girl would swap her day off, with you and you could request a certain day off, but there was no guarantee that you would get it. I had managed to save a couple of quid so after sleeping for part of the morning, I caught the train to Wimbledon and walked to the All England Lawn Tennis & Croquet Club. I sauntered through the gate and wandered around, looking for the best place to watch. First, I went to one of the outer courts and watched the British hope, Mike, Sangster, go out in the first round. Then I went onto the centre court and enjoyed a match there. I had to stand as there were no seats available but it was worth it. Tired but happy, I went back to the nursery.

'It's amazing,' I told everybody at the supper table that evening. 'I had no idea it was free.'

I decided to go back again the next day but this time, I went for the whole day. The queue was horrendous (there had been none the day before) and when I got to the gate, an official asked to see my ticket. I didn't have a ticket so he pointed me in the right direction to get one. There was another horrendous queue but that didn't put me off. It was the ticket price. At twenty-two shillings it was more than a sixth of my monthly wage! How I had managed to wander around the whole of the day before without being stopped I never knew. Perhaps it was because I looked so confident! Whatever the reason, it was my first and only excursion to that hallowed ground.

Perhaps the starkest reminder of how different the children in a residential nursery were came to me after a visit to a nursery school in Bermondsey, Southeast London. I went as part of a group from college in 1964.

Nursery schools were under the Ministry of Education. They were staffed by a head mistress, teachers and assistants in class 1 and class 2. Open from 9 a.m. until 4 p.m., they took school holidays. Parents paid five shillings (twenty-five pence) a week for meals, plus a fee. The children were from two and a half to five years. Some schools had a nursery class attached to the school itself. It was staffed and run in the same way as the nursery school although in that case, the Head of the school was also the Head of the nursery class. The children who went to nursery school and nursery class were usually in a settled home environment. They might find it difficult to adjust to a new environment but it was nowhere near as traumatic as being taken into care.

The children took no notice at all of visitors whereas the children in the residential nursery would crowd around a stranger and try to get their attention. There was a long corridor which linked the rooms but each room was run independently from the others. There were sixty children who were full time in two of the rooms and the other room cared for those who were part-timers. We only had twenty-five to thirty children on our books whereas the nursery school had one hundred and twenty!

My first impressions were of a vibrant, noisy and fast-moving place, where the language was a bit ripe at times. One child pushed another away from the car he was playing with and issued a resounding, 'Fuck off!'

The layout of the rooms was similar to the ones in the residential nursery except that they remained static. We spent a large part of the day putting one lot of things away and getting something else out. Here, each room had a Wendy corner, book corner and music corner, as well as table toys and dressing up things on a clothes horse. The children moved freely among them. The Wendy corner had a real telephone in it, and the book corner had a table for the children to sit at, with more books on it and it also had an old car seat for comfort. In the centre of the room, there were groups of tables with playdough, puzzles and cutting-out things. The scissors were tied to the leg of the table with string. There were also floor toys, such as bricks and floor puzzles. A sand tray was available and an adult was supervising some painters, each working at their own easel. In just the same way as the residential nursery was decorated, the walls were covered in paintings. The children in the nursery school had a pet goldfish and a budgerigar.

Outside in the paved area, a water trolley was available for any passing child who wanted to play and there was even a wooden work bench complete with hammers and nails and, of course, wood. One of the teachers was grating carrots with the children and some were washing toy boxes. We had the same sort of equipment but it was rotated so that the children wouldn't get bored with it all. That meant it would be the sand tray on Monday, the water trolley on Tuesday, the painting easels on Wednesday, etc. Here, everything was available all the time.

The children moved from toy to toy with the bicycles and cars freely available and they also had a life-size United Dairies milk float someone had donated to the school. There was also a small car (real) in a far-off corner. The doors had been removed to prevent any squashed fingers and the engine was gone as well. The boys in particular loved 'driving like Daddy'.

The thing that struck me most was how independent the children were. They enjoyed helping each other to wash and often refused any help from an adult. Our children were far less sure of themselves. They waited to be told what to do and seldom had the confidence to boss another child around. For the first time in my experience I became starkly aware that the residential child was damaged by the experience. They were well looked after and apparently happy in their environment, but meeting the Bermondsey children showed me how rudderless the residential nursery children were. It aroused a deeper under-standing and a greater sense of loving concern for them.

The three big sandpits outside in the play area were movable and at one point the children decided to push one of them out of the sun. Some boys in another part of the play area had a large flag and a box. The game appeared to be to run in and out of the box and avoid being touched by the flag. It lasted a long time, maybe as long as twenty minutes, and I realised then that the degree of imagination was way beyond the boys of a similar age in the residential nursery.

At lunch time, the children helped to lay the tables and we were all struck by the fact that they had glass wine glasses and a glass water jug. We were so safety conscious in the nursery that would never have happened. Everything in the residential nursery was plastic or Bakelite. It had never occurred to me before how limited their experience was. The meal itself was beef, Yorkshire pudding, cabbage, carrots and gravy . . . the same sort of meal our children would have had but the nursery teacher made no attempt to encourage table manners, something which would have been anathema to my Matron. The meal time was noisy and full of conversation. That was lacking in the residential nursery situation too. Our children were allowed to talk at meal times but there wasn't so much excited chatter around the table. The children had a rest on stretchers after dinner, in much the same way as our children did, but once again they helped the teachers and classroom assistants to put the stretchers up. Our children would be in the toilet while the nursery student put up the stretchers for them. After their rest, the children played again. One girl had some home-made stilts made out of tin cans and string. I have no idea if she had brought them from home, but I resolved to try and make some with the children in the nursery when I got back.

The whole visit made a lasting impression on me. Now I could see what our lecturers meant when they talked about the residential child being a deprived child. Our children lacked confidence and initiative. They had been damaged by their experiences and it was going to take a long time to help them back into 'normal' life. We all came back from Bermondsey with a renewed determination to try and make a difference for the children in our care. It wasn't easy because Matron resisted change but I do remember making some stilts out of some empty Robinson's jam tins and the children had great fun with them.

Outings for the children were something of a rarity but they did have them. I went with Sister and six children to Brighton for the day. The children were very excited as we waited in the car park of a local pub for the coach to come.

'Is it coming soon?' asked Gary, his face glowing with excitement.

'Soon,' I said.

Two minutes later he asked again. 'Is it here yet?'

'Keep looking that way,' I said, pointing in the direction from which it would come. 'You'll see it coming along the road.'

Sure enough the coach was on its way but Gary was still looking. As it pulled into the car park I said, 'Here's the coach.'

Gary looked a little disappointed. 'But there's no horses.'

It must have been obvious that we came from a home because when we got out of the coach along Brighton seafront, the driver had started a collection. He handed us a hat full of coins and we were able to buy everybody a second ice cream! The biggest disappointment was that Brighton is a pebble beach. Coming from Bournemouth, I was used to miles of golden sand but luckily the children enjoyed themselves with what little sand they had and at least we didn't get it in our sandwiches.

We could also take the children out on our days off. I took four-year-old Freda and her younger sister Angela to Chessington Zoo for the day. They had a great time. At one point, I bought two bars of identical chocolate and handing them out, I said to Freda, 'Which one would you like?'

'Angela's.' came the reply. Now that was a tricky situation.

My roommate Marilyn had a tricky experience on the Greenline bus as she brought a child back to the nursery after a day out. While she was at home, she had had a bath. The child had seen her getting dressed but at the time made no comment at all. Coming home on the bus, they were sitting on the long seat right at the back. Her small charge waited until the bus had stopped at a bus stop to let on new passengers. Conversation had died and the only sound was that of the engine ticking over until a small megaphone voice piped up, 'Auntie Marilyn, why have you got hairs between your legs?' And then every head in the bus turned towards the girl with the scarlet face on the back seat.

Matron Dickenson never really changed but she did mellow a bit. We were never allowed telephone calls but one day I was called into the office. Hilary was on the phone and asking to speak to me.

'I just wanted to tell you we can't pick you up until seven,' she told me.

We had arranged that I should stay the night at her house and go out together the next day. 'Okay,' I said, anxious to make it short because Dickie was in the same room. 'See you then.'

As I hung up, I expected Dickie to shout at me and tell me Hilary shouldn't have phoned in the first place, but she didn't. I turned around and to my utter amazement, she was crying. I stood there like a lemon, not knowing what to do.

'She's such a nice girl,' Dickie blurted out. 'She asked about the children and how they were.'

I was feeling really uncomfortable by now. Something in me wanted to comfort her and yet since that limp lettuce handshake she'd given me the day I'd arrived in the nursery, I'd never touched her. How would she take it if I was nice to her anyway? I had a feeling there was a boundary line here and she had just crossed it. I was still on the other side and too unsure of her reaction to respond to her tears. She blew her nose noisily.

'That business about her sacking was so awful,' she went on. 'It was terrible for me too. You have no idea what I went through, going to County Hall every day.'

All at once I felt a sense of indignation rising within me. Awful for *her*? She'd been the one who had insisted on Hilary getting the sack and in effect she had ruined my friend's prospects for years to come. And yet, here she was, trying to make me feel sorry for her!

'Is she still working with that family?' Dickie said, dabbing her eyes.

'Yes,' I said, 'but she's just handed in her notice because she's got a much better post.'

'Oh, good,' said Dickie, looking down at the floor. 'I wish her well.'

I hovered for a while not knowing what to do. 'You can go now,' she said. I never told anyone what had happened in the office that day but I think she must have thought I had. She was particularly unkind for the next few days, throwing all my clothes and bedding all over the floor again and picking fault with everything I did.

We never invited friends to the nursery because we felt Dickie would do or say something unpredictable. She probably wouldn't but somehow we all thought she would. We weren't allowed visitors when we were on duty anyway but one evening Joe from North Africa called with something I had left behind at a friend's house. Dickie walked passed as we talked in the hallway and when he'd left, she accosted me in the corridor.

'Does your mother know you go out with *coloured* men?' Innocent question but not when it's said with an obvious look of disapproval and with a strong emphasis on the word 'coloured'.

'Oh, yes,' I said. 'She's met him and he came home with me.'

As she lumbered off it was a good job for me that she didn't turn round suddenly. I'd stuck out my tongue to her receding back. She was no judge of character anyway. There was a teacher who worked in the village and several of the girls had been out with him. He was quite good-looking and Matron Dickenson thought he was wonderful because he buttered her up every time he came to the nursery to pick up his date. But without exception, every girl who went out with him only did it once.

'He's got about eighteen arms,' one complained after she'd been to the pictures with him. 'I was too busy fighting him off I didn't even get to see the film.'

'He even tried it on at the bus stop,' another complained. 'He had his hand up my skirt and was pulling my knickers down before the bloomin' bus came!'

'What, go out with him?' I heard a third girl say. 'Not bloody likely – the man's a sex maniac!'

I told Hilary what had happened with Dickie after her phone call. 'Silly cow!' she giggled. 'I only asked after the children because I knew she'd say no if I asked to speak to you first.'

Our daily duties were much the same as they had been in the previous nursery with the exception that the girl on 'Lates' had to put coke in the boiler during the winter. The boiler man came in every day to stoke it up and rake away the ash, but it had been agreed that we should put the last bit of fuel in for the evening. I hated that job. The boiler room was downstairs and the cockroaches used to jump at your legs as you went down. It terrified me that I had to open this furnace and tip the contents of the coke scuttle inside. The heat was fantastic and, as I have a vivid imagination, I could always see myself falling over something and banging my head on the boiler or something. Fortunately nothing like that ever happened although one time when I was down there, I was staggered to realise that Barbara Field, the little deaf girl, had followed me to the stairs. She had been having a tantrum in the playroom and managed to dart out when the staff nurse wasn't looking. She had run blindly but seen the stair door opening and charged down. Everyone was shocked to think what might have been if I had not been there to stop her going any further and almost immediately a two-way high bolt was put on the boiler-room door. It meant you could lock it by turning it on both sides. It was the right thing to do, of course, but it only added to my loathing of the place because now the girl on 'Lates' had to lock herself in the boiler room while she filled the boiler.

Barbara was always one step ahead of us. After lunch, the children were expected to have a rest. We put them on stretchers and covered them with a blanket. They only took off their shoes. The playroom curtains were drawn and we spoke in whispers. Most children were ready to sleep and soon nodded off. The older ones were allowed to quietly look at books and those nearly ready for school sat in the book corner.

Barbara had the propensity to lie on her stretcher and make silly noises. This meant that the other children couldn't get to sleep, so Staff Nurse said Barbara should be left in the children's dining room on a stretcher to sleep. That worked for a couple of days but there came the day when the staff dinner gong went and Barbara was still wide awake. Of course, she was running around the room as soon as we'd gone. Staff Nurse got one of us to put long tapes on a liberty bodice (an old-fashioned sleeve-less bodice made of a warm, fleecy fabric). We put the bodice on Barbara and then tied her to the stretcher. She could sit up but she couldn't get off. That worked for a couple of days too, until she discovered that she could rock her body in such a way that the whole stretcher moved along the highly polished floor. We came back into the room some twenty minutes later, having left the 'sleeping' Barbara, only to find she had scooted to the cupboard and emptied a couple of packets of baby rice and a bottle of concentrated orange juice all over herself.

I suggested that we fix the stretcher to the radiator (it wasn't on – this was late spring) and everybody thought I was pretty clever to come with the idea. When we got back to the dining room, Barbara had done a huge poo and posted it in between the slots on the radiator. Guess who was given the job of cleaning it up!

Of course, these days the idea of a child being strapped to anything is abhorrent, and quite rightly so. After that incident, Dickie decided to have Barbara in her office at lunch time, so that solved the problem.

It was around that time that I had spent the whole of one morning in the laundry, washing nappies. As I took a very large basket of nappies outside to hang up to dry, I put my foot on the iron grating by the door and the whole thing moved forward. My leg went from under me and I landed painfully on my bottom. The nappies I was holding went all over the place. Some were on the floor and some were even flung onto the low roof of the laundry. At exactly the same moment as it happened, Dickie appeared by the back door. Scowling with disapproval, she said in her sing-sing voice: 'Really, Nurse! Now you'll have to do them all again.' Then she turned away and walked back into the house. I got up and rubbed my sore backside. Miserably, I picked up the nappies and took them back in the laundry to rinse them all again. I thought some pretty dark thoughts towards her as I did it. How could she be so callous? She hadn't even bothered to ask if I was all right.

I'm not sure why the Matrons were as they were. I'm sure none of them started out like that, and yet somehow, years of institutional life had made them vindictive, insensitive and very often needlessly cruel. It was less than twenty years since the end of the war, and perhaps they'd suffered in some way. People were never encouraged to talk about things, so although it doesn't excuse them, these women may have carried a lot of inner pain or maybe it was simply because they had no life of their own outside the nursery. Perhaps they were bitter because life had dealt them a bad hand, I don't know. I thought they were all like that but years later I was to meet one Matron who was entirely different. She'd worked in children's homes all her life and yet she was kind and caring and a real champion for the children in her care.

There was sometimes a conflict of interest between what we were being taught at college and what was actually happening in the nursery. Both nurseries I'd worked in thus far had divided the children into three distinct age groups. Babies, Tweenies and Toddlers was now considered 'old fashioned'. The new thinking was to recreate a family group. The idea was to have fewer children together (maybe only six or at a push eight) with their own carers. They would retain the playroom for the older children and the nursery warden but everything else should be done in the family group. The big advantage would be that brothers and sisters at the moment separated by age would be able to stay together. It would also help with child development if the younger children could learn from the older ones. The older children would gain confidence and a feeling of generosity towards the little ones they helped. It would foster a feeling of belonging, especially for children who had been taken into care some time ago and might have lost the continuity of family life. The disadvantage might be that the older children could feel frustrated if the younger ones disturbed their play time, or a smaller child may feel overwhelmed by a boisterous, bigger one.

It was all academic for us anyway. Matron Dickenson frowned on the idea and dismissed it out of hand without even bothering to give it a try. She and the nursery warden decided 'it wouldn't work'. We students were frustrated as well. Maybe she was right and it wouldn't have worked but we would have loved the opportunity to give it a try.

People working with the council I worked for really were beginning to understand the importance of the family unit. If children were available for adoption, they were starting to try and keep siblings together. Much has been written about brothers and sisters being separated, sometimes sent as far away as Australia and Canada in what turned out to be a mistaken idea that they were giving the children a fresh start and the chance of a better life. Terrible mistakes were made out of sheer ignorance. The country was still struggling with the aftermath of World War Two. My own childhood in the Fifties was a happy one but my parents didn't have it easy. When Dad was laid off because of the bad weather it was tough. He had no money and there was no allowance he could claim. Yes, councils shipped children abroad. And yes, it did save the ratepayers from having to keep children in expensive long-term care, but the child care officers honestly thought they were sending the children to countries where they would have a better life.

Marion and Monica made it difficult for the new policy of keeping family together to work. They were twins but they hated each other. The animosity in their relationship would rival that of Jacob and Esau in the Bible. As soon as they saw each other, they would begin to cry or to snatch the toy the other was playing with. In fact, the only physical contact between them was a punch or a kick. They were supposed to be together in the Tweenie room but quite often the girl in charge would swap one of them with someone in Toddlers, simply for a bit of peace and quiet. The girls had little chance of a new life in a real family. If they were to be kept together, who would want to adopt or even foster such female warriors!

Attitudes and ideas were changing but new ideas take time to catch on. An American paediatrician called Dr Benjamin Spock had brought a whole new way of thinking into childcare. He had published a book in 1946 and by 1958 onwards his message started to filter through the British childcare system. The girls I trained with and I were part of the first wave, I guess. The way Matron and the nursery warden worked was fast becoming 'old school', which was why they found it so hard to adjust. Dr Spock was the first person to actually study children and the dynamics of family life. He taught parents and child carers to be more proactive with the children in their care and to treat them as individuals. He also changed the focus of the family from the provider (i.e. the father) to the child. The former was an excellent idea but I didn't agree with everything he taught because I think by making the child central in everything, we created a very self-centred and greedy generation. The world is desperately trying to put right the wrongs that generation has done. On the plus side, he made us realise how precious childhood is and that we should guard it for our children in whatever way we can.

Chapter 9

If I've made it sound as if we had a terrible time, all the time, we didn't. There were lots of laughs along the way. I made a good friend in a girl called Evelyn. A very neat and tidy girl, she was the sort that never had a hair out of place. She was well respected, efficient and loving towards the children. I've forgotten her surname but she moved to Wimbledon when we left the nursery. I nicknamed her 'Evil', which rather horrifies me now, but it was all done and taken in good fun.

It was while I was at the nursery that I met a boy called John. I can't remember how we met but for our first date, we had a very romantic day out on the River Thames in a punt and I fell hopelessly in love. He was a bandsman in the Army and went abroad. We dated all the time and I used to visit his parents who lived nearby and they were lovely people. I had high hopes that John and I would marry one day but obviously he didn't feel the same. I was very miserable for a few weeks when I realised he had come home on leave and not bothered to contact me but then it was time to bounce back – and the best person to help me was Hilary.

Hilary and I did some mad things and it was a wonder that we didn't put ourselves in danger. Soon after John dumped me, she and I both had a day off together. It was the day of the Oxford and Cambridge Boat Race. We met somewhere near Hammersmith Bridge but decided that was too near the start so we walked along the river towards Barnes Bridge. It was magic. People in the huge houses along the river were having champagne parties and for the first time in our lives we could see how the other half lived. I hardly remember the race itself except that Oxford won (1963) but then we walked through the crowds. At one point we met some Greek boys and we were in effect 'picked up'. That makes it sound rather sordid, but we had a fantastic time. When I say we did stupid things, we got into their car and drove into central London with them. It never once occurred to us that they might not take us into London or that we risked being driven somewhere lonely where we couldn't get help. It obviously didn't occur to them either. There were already five boys in the car when we squashed in (no seat belts back then) and they took us to a Greek restaurant. The driver had the unlikely name of Caroli Bambos and Hilary liked him a lot. I was a bit of a gooseberry but the restaurant was wonderful. They gave us a meal and the men did some amazing Greek dancing. We ended the date by driving to Heathrow Airport in the middle of the night to watch the early flights. No one had thought of hijacking back then so you could go up on the roof and watch the planes. It didn't cost anything and there were no security checks. All you needed for a great time was the occasional cup of coffee to help you stay awake all night. Tired but happy, the Greek boys drove us back into central London and we caught the early train back to Hilary's house. Life was good again.

In the summer of 1963, I went on holiday to Hemyock in Devon with an old school friend. We visited my Auntie Laura, whose son still lived in a prefab. They were never intended to be more than a temporary stopgap to help with the acute housing shortage after the war, but nearly twenty years after they were first put up, people still lived in them. It was a cosy little house – much better, I felt, than my mother's two-up, two-down cottage, which was riddled with damp and still had no main drainage. Mum and Dad had their toilet at the bottom of the garden. It was only a bucket under a wooden seat and Dad used an earth closet for disposal. That's a polite way of saying he dug a six-foot hole and when the bucket was full, everything went in it. Unbelievably, they stayed in those conditions until 1970, when I got in touch with their MP, the Medical Officer of Health and their GP. With a letter from their doctor, they were finally able to have proper facilities. In the nursery, for all its privations, I was used to proper toilets and hot baths whenever I wanted them.

We also stayed with my friend's aunt in Sidmouth. I don't think we did anything very exciting, the most eventful occurrence being the time I accidentally knocked her aunt's picture off the wall. When we picked it up it said, 'Turn from evil and do good', which gave us both a laugh. The Swinging Sixties was still a London-based thing which had only just got started. It took a while to reach the sleepy backwaters of Devon.

1963 also stands out for the world events. On the whole, we were all too wrapped up in the day-to-day workings of the nursery and our own limited off duty to be bothered about what was going on around us but there were some things which made an impact on our lives. It began with the Great Train Robbery, an audacious theft of £2.6 million (£40 million in today's money), which took place in August. Then came the Profumo Affair, which opened a huge can of worms for the Government.

We had only just stopped talking about that when President John F. Kennedy was assassinated in November. It was hugely scary at the time. It was upsetting that he had died, but somehow the event made the whole world seem a very unsafe place to be.

'Do you think it was the Russians?' was the question on everybody's lips.

We were bewildered and unable to believe what had happened. The death of Diana, Princess of Wales in 1997 had the same kind of impact as far as the grief went, and although we in this country didn't line the streets or place banks of flowers in public places when Kennedy died, there was that same sense of loss and confusion. My roommate had come to West Moors for the weekend but it spoilt it a bit. When I met her off the bus, she already knew. Someone at Southampton coach station had got on the coach and told all the passengers and the local bus from Ringwood was agog with it all. The television schedule was ditched and we had wall-to-wall Kennedy, going over and over the same grainy pictures of nothing in particular. Somehow Jackie Kennedy in her blood-stained suit said it all. Marilyn and I did go to Bournemouth the next day and later to the pictures but our thoughts were dominated by the events in Dallas, Texas.

Back at the nursery, the Christmas of 1963 was a lot better. I was dreading it because the previous year had been so awful but Matron Dickenson pulled out all the stops and we had a good time. In the run-up to Christmas, I spent my off-duty hours with the other girls, wrapping presents for the children. We would put a pillow case at the end of their beds and during the night, the night nurse would swap the empty case for a full one. The toys were marked with their name once the children opened it. It was a much better arrangement than before and the powers that be were beginning to understand the need for personal things. Each child had a 'Christmas outfit', a completely new set of clothes from central stores which he or she could wear straight away. On Boxing Day, while the festivities went on around us, a couple of us girls were scratching names onto tape and sewing them into the jumpers, trousers or a dress they'd worn the day before.

I was used to looking after children from deprived backgrounds so it came as a surprise to encounter someone with a double-barrelled name – three actually. Georgie, Dawn and Diane Maxwell-Hayes had accents a cut above the rest, or at least Georgie did. He was nearly five and the twins were nearly two. Georgie was a supremely confident child, used to demanding and getting his own way. He apparently knew everything before you even told him and according to him, he was the toughest kid around. The twins were slightly bewildered, but they had each other. They came to the home just before Christmas. Their parents had been arrested for some sort of fraud and because the authorities were afraid they might abscond, they were likely to be in jail for some time. I suppose their extended family were too appalled to want to help so the children were placed in care until a more suitable solution could be found. So while the child care officers worked behind the scenes, Georgie and his sisters spent their first and only Christmas in a children's home.

The nursery was wrestling with the same perennial problem. We needed a man. Nobody cared what he looked like but every member of staff was asked to find one. We had the costume but we didn't have a Father Christmas. I didn't even have a boyfriend I could call upon and everybody else's men were unavailable.

But how could we have Christmas without Father Christmas? At the very last minute, Sister Hemmingway volunteered to do it. She had no Wellingtons and the Father Christmas tunic ended at her knees. The trousers were far too big and too long and there was no time to do any alterations. We gathered the children in the hallway as we heard the sleigh bells (a set of hand bells from the music corner) on the roof. Everyone was fixed on her face as she came sweeping down the staircase with a loaded sack. She certainly looked the part, with her long flowing beard and the hat pulled down over her forehead. She even sounded the part with lots of 'ho-ho-hos' although they were perhaps a little too high-pitched. The children didn't seem to notice and she was very convincing. So convincing in fact, that Georgie took flight. He ran into the playroom and hid behind the rocking horse, refusing to come out even when his name was called.

'Father Christmas has brought you a lovely present,' I told him. 'He wants you to come and get it.'

'*You* go and get it,' he told me, and I could see he was visibly trembling.

All my reassurances were to no avail. I had to collect the present on his behalf.

Eventually, the sack was empty and Father Christmas went back upstairs on his way to the roof and his waiting sleigh. His back view was even more stunning than his front view. The large cushion stuffed up his tunic had lifted the hemline at the back. The children were busy with their new toys but the staff had more than a glimpse of Sister's stocking tops and suspenders as she 'ho-ho-hoed' and lumbered back up the stairs.

Georgie and his sisters left the home in the New Year. Two sets of relatives had agreed to take them in until the court case was settled. They were to be separated, the twins with one family and Georgie with another, but the child care officer had exacted the promise that they would meet up on family occasions.

That Christmas was a lot more fun for both the children and the staff. The children had a great day and their presents had been better thought out. We ate a scrumptious meal – roast turkey and all the trimmings – and we pulled crackers and the table was buzzing with lively conversation. In the evening I organised a show in aid of the Save the Students Fund and out of politeness I sent Dickie an invitation. To our amazement, she wrote an acceptance and came. We spent several evenings working hard on our show. We looked for talent and discovered girls who could sing or 'do a turn'; we also did the tramp's sketch. Four people on a park bench, along comes a tramp. He sits on the end and begins scratching. He gets out a paper and starts to read, but one by one the people leave until at last he has the whole bench to himself. Then he spreads out the newspaper, covers himself and lies down to sleep. It was probably an old music-hall sketch and I don't know if Dickie had ever seen it before but she laughed heartily. We also sang songs. I changed the words to the pop song 'Bobby's Girl' by Susan Maughan,

109

which was in the charts at the time, making a joke of how much we all wanted our NNEB:

> Each night I sit at home
> Hoping Fox-T will phone.
> But I know she's got somebody else,
> Still I will hope and pray
> That soon will come the day
> When I can be a staff nurse myself . . .
> I want the NNEB,
> I want the NNEB
> That's the most important thing for me
> And with the NNEB,
> with the NNEB
> What a fabulous staff nurse I will be!

Matron was enthusiastic about the show and we all relaxed. Perhaps now she would be a little different in the coming year? We could but hope, but our expectations were quickly dashed as her mean-spiritedness quickly returned. Several times I returned to my room (as did other girls) to find the contents of every drawer, my wardrobe and my bedding in a huge pile in the middle of the room. It was worse when she did it on a day off. If you'd been looking forward to doing something, you were faced with wasting two and half hours of your precious off-duty time tidying your room before you were allowed to go out. Once you'd tidied your room, you had to find Matron and ask her to come and see if she was satisfied with your efforts. You had to wait outside the closed door until she came back out again and pronounced that your room was now tidy. Once when she did it to Marilyn, the poor girl spent ages making it right again only to find that Matron wasn't happy with something and had done it all over again! How soul-destroying is that? Marilyn was so upset that the girls who were off duty helped her do it all a second time. There was no rhyme or reason why Dickie did it, but I wonder if she'd had some sort of army training. We were always tidy because we knew what would happen if we weren't, but it made no difference. She did it anyway.

Suzanne, a student who came a year after we started, introduced us all to Radio Caroline when it began in 1964. Suzanne idolised Dusty Springfield. She copied her hairdo and her make-up, and played her record, 'I Only Want To Be With You', endlessly on her record player.

People don't realise what a fantastic thing it was for young people when Radio Caroline began. We followed the tussle between the station and powers that be, namely Ernest Bevins, the Postmaster-General who did his best to prevent Radio Caroline from broadcasting. The government appealed to the International Telecommunications Union, the body which regulated frequencies and transmissions throughout the world, but it was to no avail. The ship was three miles off the coast at Felixstowe, just outside territorial waters. The first record they played on air was The Beatles' 'Can't Buy Me Love' and for the first time in our lives, we had wall-to-wall pop music all day long. Bliss . . . It was a good time for music as well. 'Surfin' U.S.A.' by The Beach Boys, 'Rhythm of the Rain' by The Cascades, 'He's So Fine' by The Chiffons, 'It's My Party' by Lesley Gore, 'If I Had A Hammer' by Trini Lopez . . . Of course The Beatles were still big and the Stones, Roy Orbison, The Four Seasons, Ray Charles . . . I could go on and on. Brenda Lee, Sam Cooke, Johnny Mathis, Johnny Cash . . . Radio Caroline played them all. Mine wasn't the only nursery to be hit with Radio Caroline fever. My friend from my nursery assistant days, Evie Perryer, told me of an occasion when the Matron of her home was going on holiday. As soon as she'd gone, off came the lisle stockings and on came Radio Caroline. They had it blasting away when ten minutes later, there was absolute panic in the nursery because Matron was coming back up the drive. She'd missed the bus!

As the year wore on, it was getting closer and closer to the time when I had to take my final exam. I had worked hard; I couldn't bear the thought of failure.

According to the NNEB syllabus, during my two-year training period I had to be taught about the health of the young child, including his development and signs of good health in general. I should know how to feed him, stimulate physical activity, give him adequate rest and sleep, ensure he had plenty of outdoor life and that he wore good clothing and footwear. I was taught about good personal hygiene habits for children and the care of nurseries and their equipment. I was given a rudimentary knowledge about infection and infectious diseases and a solid understanding of public health bodies and the medical services available. I was also taught about the education of the young child at home as well as in the nursery or nursery school setting. Above all, I was taught how to be observant so that the children in my care would be happy and healthy. My training involved taking copious notes, end-of-term tests and keeping diaries on the children in my care. I also had to make a child's dress with smocking, knit a jumper and create a dossier containing all my college work and nursery observations. I completed everything except the smocking. My Auntie Betty was much better at smocking than I was! One of the girls in the nursery discovered a lucrative way of making money with her new-found talent of smocking. The White House, an exclusive shop in New Bond Street, sold smocked romper suits and dresses to the rich and famous, and they paid good money to skilled workers. She could get twenty pounds for garments that would retail at fifty to a hundred pounds.

My exam was held on 1 July 1964 and there were two papers. I had two and a half hours to answer five questions. I began with, *What are the special points to be considered when buying (a) a cot and (b) a perambulator for a baby?* In the afternoon I had another two and a half hours to answer the second paper.

One question was: *A baby aged three months has sore buttocks. What might cause this condition and how should it be treated?* And another was, *How can the year-old child be helped to share in family meals? Describe a suitable menu for the midday meal.* I was fairly confident but we had to wait five agonising weeks for the results.

There were one hundred and twenty failures that day but I was one of the 1,211 candidates who passed and my registration number was 28115. I had done it at last!

In her final report, Matron Dickenson had some kind things to say but still managed a last few unfairly hard criticisms. She said I was withdrawn and still needed to assert myself more. (And remember I was the one who had organised the Christmas show and written most of the sketches and songs.) In fact, she saw my shortcomings as a failure on her part. It hurt me for years to come, probably because I only saw one word . . . failure.

Looking back at it with a more mature and detached eye, it is so obvious that she never really knew me. My friends have laughed at the idea of me being withdrawn about anything. I enjoy a good laugh and I'm not ashamed to say I love being at the centre of one. Having said all that, looking at it now, it's not such a bad report and I wonder if her erratic behaviour was the reason I walked away with such a jaundiced view of myself and my own capabilities.

Chapter 10

I had contracted to work as a staff nursery nurse for a year after my training. Whenever we were upgraded from nursery assistant to student nursery nurse and then on to staff nursery nurse, we had to move to another nursery. This was so that we wouldn't be put in the position of having to tell people who had once been our friends what to do. I arrived at my new nursery on the last day of August 1964 knowing that in exactly one year I could turn my back on nursery life for good. I enjoyed being with the children, but the restrictions were beginning to get to me. The fact that you never knew your day off until the Sunday of the same week, the difficulties of getting an evening off, especially a specific evening, the low pay, the strict routine . . . I longed for less restraint and more freedom. My new matron, Mrs Harrison, was about five foot tall with square hands and a totally authoritarian manner. She shared her accommodation with her family but they kept well away from the nursery.

Since passing my exam, I had joined the ranks of the elite. I was now an NNEB, but I still had to share a room with two other girls, Nurse Judy Crawford and Nurse Rosalyn Taylor. Judy was very large, blonde and passionate about Avon Topaz. She had the talcum powder, the perfume, the bath oil, the soap . . . everything, and I can never think of her without remembering that smell or think of Avon without remembering her. Ros was a gentle and loving girl and we became very good friends.

I worked in Tweenies and to my absolute delight, Evie Perryer came to work there as well. She was a little bit embarrassed that she had actually failed her exam but the council had given her a second chance. It was obviously a case of exam nerves because she re-took the exam again in the autumn and passed with flying colours. Because the three of us got on so well, Judy moved into a single room and Evie, Ros and I shared a room near the top of the house.

We spent some time swapping stories and told Evie that we had heard how the Matron in her nursery had taken her up to the attic and held her legs out of the window while she was made to clear the leaves from the gutter. Apparently it wasn't quite like that. Evie had indeed gone up to Matron's room and been told to clean out the windows on the outside. She was standing outside on a flat roof cleaning the corner windows when Matron obviously forgot she was there and shut the window. To Evie's horror she was stranded and she had to attract the attention of somebody in the garden before she was let back in! 'It was perishing cold,' she told us as we sympathised. It was still a horrific story and it's a wonder to me that Evie wasn't emotionally scarred by the incident.

Once again the regime in the nursery was very strict and the children were looked after with the same divisions centred around their ages; Babies (up to a year), Tweenies (one- to two-year-olds) and toddlers (three- to five-year-olds). Miss Forest, the nursery warden, was a very caring woman and I think the children in her room were genuinely happy. It was light and airy, she had a piano and the walls were full of colour. She also had a cat and the children loved him.

We had the same sort of duty and off-duty times but of course I had to forfeit my monthly weekends at home. For now on it was one day a week, the occasional weekend and two weeks' holiday a year, however I had in effect a huge pay rise. The council was no longer docking monies for my training so my wages went up from six pounds, four shillings and five old pence (six pounds, twenty-two pence in today's money) to nine pounds and ten shillings (nine pounds, fifty pence) a month. I was rich!

In the Tweenies, there were eight children in my care, all between the ages of one and two years old. One child was dear to all our hearts. Little Kieran lived in a world of his own. He had some sort of glucose deficiency and had to be given medication every day but so long as he had something in his hand which flipped when he patted it, he was happy. A piece of paper, a leaf, a floppy toy, he would spend hours patting it with the back of his hand. In this day and age there would have been a deeper diagnosis, perhaps with experimental care thrown in, but back then, as long as a child wasn't disturbed in any way, they were left pretty much to themselves. Sadly, long after I'd left the nursery, I heard that Kieran had died. He was about four years old.

Miss Forest liked to do things a little differently so that in autumn, the girls in the Toddler room made pretend harvest loaves with the children. They created a harvest corner where they put their field mouse decorations and they talked about harvest time and gathering in the crops. Later on they sung harvest songs around the piano. As everyone turned to leave, one child looked at Miss Forest with a puzzled expression. 'Please, Miss, what is Harvey's Vegetable?'

I settled down and I was fairly happy but in truth I was living out my time there, longing for the day when I could leave the confines of council nurseries. During my twelve months there as a staff nurse, I had only one serious brush with the Matron and that was when I was on night duty. The routine was that we gave the children a tiny drink of orange squash when they got up in the morning, just to freshen their mouths. I went to the kitchen only to find that the orange bottle was nearly empty. Looking in the larder, I found another bottle and used it. I left a note on the kitchen table saying something along the lines of 'Dear Matron, There wasn't enough orange squash for the children's morning drink so I took a new one from the larder, signed Pamela Cox'. When I had poured the drinks, I left the empty bottle and the opened bottle on the kitchen table beside the note.

When I gave Mrs Harrison the night report at 8.30 a.m. I could tell that she was annoyed about something. Her lips were pursed and she kept clenching and unclenching her fists. While she was doing her best to control her temper, I was racking my brains to think what I had done. What could have been so awful to put her in this mood? As soon as I'd finished my report she hurled herself at me. 'Who gave you permission to go into my larder?' she barked.

I was startled. She'd made it sound as if the larder were her own personal property.

She glared at me angrily. 'I will not tolerate a thief.'

'But I didn't take anything for myself,' I protested hotly. 'It was for the children.'

'The children,' she declared unreasonably, 'will have water rather than you go into my larder.'

I couldn't believe what I was hearing. We argued heatedly but she would have none of it. As far as she was concerned, I was a thief and that was that. I managed to hold on to my dignity until I left the room, but when I got upstairs to bed, I hurled myself onto my bed and cried myself to sleep. I woke up thinking how ridiculous the whole thing had been. I had just given myself a headache by crying over two inches of orange squash. We hadn't cottoned on to the phrase back then but the feeling was 'get a life!' When I came on duty I was astonished to find that she had gone to the ridiculous expense of sending for a handyman, who had not only put a lock on the larder door but there was also a padlock and chain around the handle!

The routine was still very strict, but somehow life was easier in that nursery than it had been in the other two. At Christmas we managed to persuade Matron to let us have a party but we were faced with the same old problem . . . where to find some men. The International Friendship League was still going but we wanted men in bulk. Somebody managed to get a few trainee doctors to come along and I fell for a chap who was the spitting image of Dave Buckley from The Ivy League. Their song, 'Funny How Love Can Be', was high in the charts in February 1965.

Occasionally I used to stay at Hilary's place on my day off. Her mother always thought I was a really bad influence and did her best to discourage our friendship. If she had but known *I* was the restraining influence on her daughter! There were many occasions when Hilary was cross with me because I wouldn't do something she wanted. Like the night she and I and her younger brother played with an Ouija board until I was too scared to go on. We had made our own board with each letter of the alphabet in a wide circle and two cards in the middle, Yes and No. Then we had asked the spirit of the glass some simple questions like, 'who died this week?' It must have been around January because it spelled out Churchill. Indeed, Sir Winston Churchill, the man who had led the country through the Second World War, had died a few days before. We stuck to known subjects until Hilary accused one of us of pushing the glass. That's when it got scary because we asked questions that none of us could possibly know the answer. Hilary's sister was pregnant. 'Will she have a boy or a girl?' we asked, and it spelled out B-O-Y. The questions became more personal and then I wanted to stop. In the end, I refused to do it anymore and they couldn't do it with just two of them. Hilary's parents were upstairs. They were deeply religious Methodists and I often wonder what they would have said if they'd known what we were doing in their lounge.

I used to go to London to have my hair done. That may sound posh but there was a hairdressing school near Baker Street and you could get your hair done by one of the students for less than a pound. It was great. If I had my hair cut, there was always an experienced teacher on hand to make sure the student didn't make any ghastly mistakes, and a couple of times I was looked after by a student who was weeks or even days away from working in an upmarket beauty salon. I was paying pennies for a hairstyle by someone who would charge a lot of money in the days ahead, and they loved doing my hair, which I wore long and flicked up at the sides. It was the days of the bouffant and getting the deep wave I had falling slightly over the right side of my face just right was a work of art. After a hairstyle, it was time to go window shopping. Sometimes I'd meet up with Hilary or one of the other girls and we'd head for Carnaby Street or more likely C&A to try and occasionally buy. By 1964, London was at the forefront of the Swinging Sixties.

The gardens at my new nursery were large. The children had a few big toys. There was a climbing frame and a Wendy house and some baby swings. On warm days we would get the paddling pool out and they would have great fun. At one time, Tony was sitting in the paddling pool when I added a little more warm water to it.

'Don't put in too much,' he said. 'I'm scared of heights.'

With the rise of children from ethnic backgrounds coming to live in the nurseries, we had to learn new methods of care. For example, we used to try and brush Afro hair with Western hairbrushes until an agency nurse from Nigeria pointed out that we needed to use a comb with long teeth in order to give a satisfactory clean. Nobody bothered much with suntan lotion back then. The children all had calamine lotion on their skin but generally, we avoided being outside when it was very hot and if we were outside, there was plenty of tree cover in various parts of the garden.

Having been in two places which were isolated in their own grounds, this nursery had neighbours. One particular day we heard two of our neighbours having a humongous row. It went

119

on for ever and finally we could hear crockery being smashed. We all giggled and enjoyed it but I suppose it was a salutary reminder that even if you had a home of your own, it wasn't necessarily a happy one.

I was still a dab hand with the sewing machine and I often made my own clothes. It was possible then to make a dress for less than half the price you would pay for a shop-bought dress. I even had a go at making a coat. Sadly, I was no tailor and I had an inflated belief in my own skills. It was in white light-weight wool and fitted at the waist. The skirt was made up of several panels and the top had a low-necked Peter Pan collar. I lined it as well and when I put it on, I thought I looked wonderful. It was getting near my time to leave the nursery and I wore it for a job interview. I didn't get the job, and on my way home I had to walk under a footbridge near a fish and chip shop. There was a man eating his fish and chips out of news-paper at the far end of the bridge and I couldn't avoid walking past him. As I drew level he said, 'Hello, ducks. How much do you charge?'

I was so mortified that when I got back to the nursery, the coat went into the bin!

It was late at night. Mrs Thompson wasn't a nosy neighbour but she was very concerned. The baby next door had been crying for far too long. She could hear his little brother running about but she couldn't hear any adult voices and she was increasingly convinced something was wrong.

'They won't thank you for interfering,' her husband warned. 'Keep out of it.'

On her wedding day, Mrs Thompson had made a promise to love, honour and obey, a vow she took very seriously, but this time it was different. It had been a couple of days since she'd seen the children's mother. She wasn't very friendly and Mrs Thompson didn't approve of the way she looked after her kids.

Richard and Eddie never looked clean. Half the time Eddie's nappy hung between his knees, foul-smelling, obviously very wet, but his mother seemed uninterested.

Mrs Thompson bridled at the unfairness of it all. She and her husband had tried for a baby for years with no success at all, and yet there was the woman next door with two lovely boys who were neglected.

The child's wail wafted through the walls again and Mrs Thompson knew she would get no sleep tonight. She'd be lying there, listening and worrying. Little Eddie's cry was definitely weaker now and besides, he hadn't moved out of the bedroom all day. And what was Richard doing, still running around at this time of night? His mother usually screamed at him if he was naughty, but Mrs Thompson heard nothing.

'Something's wrong,' she told her husband again.

'For God's sake, woman, give it a rest will you?' Mr Thompson wasn't a bad man but he was tired. He worked hard all day and when he came home he valued his bit of peace and quiet. He wasn't a man to make waves and his motto in life was 'keep your head down'. Besides, he remembered what had happened to the woman across the road. She had reported another neighbour when she saw her dishing out an extreme and dangerous punishment to her child. The NSPCC had gone round and the young inexperienced officer had accidentally let slip which of the neighbours had contacted them. As soon as they'd gone, the woman knocked on the informant's door. As she answered, a fist smashed into her face and she was sent reeling backwards. She'd made a full recovery but Mr Thompson didn't want the same thing to happen to his wife. Richard and Eddie's mother looked perfectly capable of doing far worse.

Mrs Thompson lay awake in bed until her husband dropped off to sleep and then ran down to the phone box on the corner.

When the police broke in they found a terrible state of affairs.

Eddie was still in his cot with two empty feeding bottles. He was desperately trying to get some nourishment from the teat and when the WPC gave him some plain water, he couldn't get it down fast enough. The children had head lice and body lice too. Richard had been trying to look for food: the rubbish bin in the kitchen had been tipped out. The place stank. Eddie's cot sheets were grey with dirt and wet with urine. Richard hadn't fared much better. He wore no nappy but he was far from toilet trained. After a check-up at the hospital, the two boys were sent to the nursery.

It was 11.15 p.m. and I was asked to get up and help the night nurse get them cleaned up and put to bed. If I close my eyes I can still heard poor Richard's plaintive cry as we bathed and deloused them. It had to be done. Head lice spread like wildfire in nurseries and we had to protect the other children as well. We began by combing the boys' hair over the sink. Some of the lice fell into the sink and we washed them away down the plug hole. They weren't always easy to see because head lice adapt their own colour to the colour of the hair. The nits, or eggs, cement themselves to the hair and their favourite place is around the ears. After we'd got rid of as many as we could, we washed their hair using soap. We didn't rinse it but tied it round with a towel for about ten minutes while we gave them each a bath. This gave the nits a chance to swell.

Eddie had been wearing a stinking nappy and a vest full of holes. I was about to bin them when the night nurse stopped me.

'They'll have to be boiled.'

I couldn't believe it. Why? They weren't even fit for the rag bag.

'He can't possibly wear them again,' I protested. 'I wouldn't even put them in a dog basket.'

'When the case comes to court,' she said curtly, 'the child has to appear exactly as we found him. It won't help his case if we take him clean and well dressed. The judge has to see the state he was in.'

'Thank goodness we don't have to keep the body lice too,' I retorted.

Once they'd had their baths, we set to and combed their hair to get rid of the lice. We used a special steel comb for the purpose and parted the hair, combing down from the scalp to the ends. We found plenty of nits and a few adult lice which had escaped the soaping. We rinsed their hair and then put a little Suleo-M onto their heads and thoroughly massaged it in. The Suleo-M didn't actually kill the nits but any remaining nits which hatched out would feed on the scalp and die of Suleo-M poisoning.

The children were exhausted, traumatised and hungry. As quickly as we could we did what we had to and by the time we'd finished, the brothers were changed out of all recognition.

'Who's a handsome little boy?' I asked Eddie as I gave him a cuddle.

He was too. He had blond curly hair and periwinkle blue eyes. His brother had straight hair but I was willing to lay odds on the fact that he looked more attractive in his nursery issue pyjamas than he had done for many a long month. After a light meal and another drink, Eddie cried himself to sleep even though Richard was in the bed right next to him. They were such lovely boys, it was hard to believe what had happened to them. It was a good job Mrs Thompson acted on her instinct. Had she left it much longer, the boys might have been irrevocably damaged by lack of fluids.

About three weeks later, it broke my heart to dress Eddie in that same holey vest and brown nappy again. They were thoroughly clean now, but he looked awful and young as he was, he knew it. Richard had come to the nursery in a shredded tee-shirt and no underwear. The child care officer took him in a pair of trousers to spare his dignity but he had to be presented to the court exactly as he was taken into care. At the end of the hearing, the children's parents were to be prosecuted for child neglect so Eddie and Richard came back to the nursery. My life was full of expectation but their lives seemed bleak. Eventually, the brothers were fostered, long term, by a loving couple. When I look at photographs I took of them playing in the garden together, I can only hope they have no memory of their terrible start in life.

In June of that year, Hilary and I went to Lido Di Jesolo, Italy, on a package holiday. No one bats an eyelid to go on one now, but in 1965 they were still a relatively new innovation. We travelled for two days by coach because I was too scared to fly. Our coach drivers were Herman and Alberto and our courier was a man called Georgio. He thought he was God's gift to women and spent his time flirting with a buxom blonde in the group. Most of our party were what we termed 'old people', but probably they were no more than fortyish. We travelled for almost forty-eight hours, taking regular comfort stops on the way – there were no facilities on the coach – and when we were nearing our destination, Georgio passed round the hotel brochure, saying, 'Please, English people, do not pull the chain in toilet too hard. A little touch, little, little or it doesn't work, eh? You may be in the hotel, or you may be in the annex.'

There was a little worried murmuring. People looked at each other anxiously. Nobody had said anything about an annex. When we arrived, our worst fears proved to be correct. We were in the annex! It had been built as staff quarters and was satisfactory as such, but as hotel guest rooms it was totally inadequate. Hilary and I had booked a twin room with a shower. Our beds were foot to foot with no room at all on either end. We had a shower but if you used it, Hilary's bed got soaked and to open the wardrobe, you had to walk right into the room and then open the door because it got wedged against my bed. I had long hair and hadn't been able to brush it for almost two days so more than anything else I wanted to get my hair-brush out of my suitcase.

We were annoyed by the accommodation and talked about complaining. The rest of the coach party were furious. As we unpacked, the volume of noise in the corridor rose to an angry crescendo.

'I've been married to my husband for twenty years,' one woman was shouting at Georgio. 'I've never slept foot to foot with him, and I'm not going to start now!'

'We demand another room, in the hotel, now!'

In the distance, we heard a loud clanking sound and then someone shouted, 'And the bloody toilets don't work either!'

Georgio, overwhelmed by angry guests, promised to do his best. He said he would call the Overland rep, but by now it was 11.30 p.m. and everyone was too tired to put up much of a fight. To add to the problem, it seemed none of the rest of the hotel staff seemed to speak English.

As Hilary and I lay exhausted in our beds, we decided not to let the terrible room spoil our holiday. After all, we hadn't come all this way for the room, we'd come for the sun, the sea and the boys! That night, to compound our misery, there was a terrific storm. It was so awful, I was convinced we were going to die there, sleeping foot to foot in a hard Italian bed but when morning came and the sun was high, everything looked a lot better. A few of our fellow guests managed to change their rooms but the majority of us stayed where we were. We later discovered that the management had overbooked. Every other week a party of German tourists came and to ease the situation, the Overland coach party was put in the annex.

'When the English peoples come,' one waiter confided in us, just before it was time for us to leave for home, 'we no speak-a the English.'

Now at last we understood why it had been so difficult to get things changed when we'd first arrived. The hotel itself was built right on the beach. It was a tower block and seemed very impressive. Although we were in the annex, we were allowed to use all the hotel facilities and the food was wonderful. However, in 1967, just two years after we were there, the hotel hit the headlines when it had to be evacuated. A massive crack had appeared in the building and eventually it was deemed too unsafe to remain. It was less than three years old when they pulled it down.

Hilary and I found the boys and had dates aplenty. In ten days, we had more than fourteen dates. Sometimes we had to dodge one group to go out with another. We had never been so popular or had so much fun.

We never saw Herman and Alberto again until it was time to start the journey home but we saw quite a lot of Georgio. He had a habit of taking an early morning swim before he took up his duties . . . or at least, that's what we all thought until I saw what I saw. I wished I had a movie camera but they were luxuries the likes of us could never afford. There were no mobile phones to take short videos in those days either, more's the pity. It happened one morning when I was on the beach. Georgio came out of the hotel in his swimming trunks. I watched him walk towards the water. He looked around to see if anybody was watching but he didn't notice me. Then I saw him bend to the water and wet his hand. He flicked a few water droplets onto his chest and then strutted back up the beach towards a group of pretty girls coming out of the hotel. So much for his early morning swim!

The Italians were deliciously outrageous. When I refused his advances, one waiter told me, 'Tomorrow, Roberto, he getta the sack.'

'Why?'

'Because tomorrow, the 'otel guests complain, the soup it is watery because Roberto, he cry in the soup . . .'

Another date insisted on called me 'Ham', which sent Hilary and me into peals of laughter. 'Do not fight me, Ham, kiss-a, kiss me.'

Our 'steady' dates were two Italian airmen called Raoul and Gianni. They took us to hideaway bistros off the tourist track and best of all, they paid for us! Needless to say, we both fell hopelessly in love. I was with Gianni, who was very handsome, but a bit vain. On our last night we all went to a dance and on the way home we lingered on the beach to say our goodbyes. Hilary and Raoul wanted to be alone, which left Gianni and me together. He wanted to make love but I refused. I was convinced that a holiday romance wasn't such a good idea. After all, I'd never see him again. He immediately fell into a huge sulk and almost in tears he asked, 'You no like-a my body?'

'No, no,' I protested. 'It's not that.'

'What wrong my body?'

What indeed? He was gorgeous. 'There's nothing wrong with your body.'

'Then why you no like?'

How could I explain that in a day or two, he and Raoul would be courting other tourists without a second thought for us? Our parting was soured by his bad mood but up until then, I had had the best time.

As our holiday came to an end, I knew I would have to go back to the same old, some old and yet I had grown up a lot in Italy. I had enjoyed being romanced and although I knew a lot of it was only flannel, I felt different about myself. I was a nursery nurse. I had proved myself and succeeded, but I was also attractive and fun to be with.

Some of our coach party had a miserable time. They had allowed the dreadful rooms to spoil everything for them. On the way back, they even tried to get us to sign a petition in the coach. The petition demanded a full refund. While Hilary and I agreed that the accommodation was far from what we expected, our holiday had been so much more than a hotel room. We had been to Venice and had a gondola ride. We'd visited beautiful churches, we'd danced the night away and we'd sampled food we'd only ever read about in books. Life in the nursery had taught me to forget the things I couldn't change and make the most of every opportunity to enjoy life. Above all, I allowed plenty of space to have a laugh and some fun.

Chapter 11

Jackie Jordan was a lovely little boy although perhaps not the brightest. His mother was what people called 'tuppence short of a shilling' and was herself living in a home. Before the birth of her son, Jackie's mother had a certain amount of freedom in that she was allowed to go outside on group outings. On one such outing, she disappeared for a while in a large park. After searching and calling for ages, it was with great relief that the staff eventually found her, apparently none the worse for her experience. However as time went on, they noticed she was putting on more and more weight. A doctor's examination proved that she was pregnant. She had no idea what had happened to her and her labour was difficult because she was frightened and upset. Even after she'd had baby Jackie, she didn't apparently comprehend that he was hers. My friend Ros was very fond of Jackie and even though making special relationships with children was frowned upon, at Christmas she went all the way to Hamleys toy shop in Regent Street to get a special teddy bear for him.

The child care officers had horrendous caseloads, so when a child like Jackie Jordan was in a home, well looked after and safe, he was a long way down the pecking order. They would of necessity have to spend their working days helping children in far more hazardous situations, so children like Jackie had little hope of being adopted. Besides, there was too much going against him. He was mixed race and his mother was in a mental institution, unaware she had even had a child. Jackie might be lucky enough to be fostered but with a background like his, he was more likely to spend the rest of his childhood in a home. It seemed grossly unfair and of course, it was. Perhaps if the child care officers had had a lighter case load, or people adopted a child for who he or she was and didn't look into the background too closely, things might have been different, but in saying that, it's obvious that neither of those things was likely to happen. Jackie's mother had been taken advantage of through no fault of her own and prospective parents have every right to have all the information available to make an informed choice about the child they want to adopt. For children like Jackie, things did look bleak but he had a loveable personality. I have no idea what happened to him and feeble as it may sound, I can only hope that despite his circumstances, he made a go of his life. I wasn't to know back then but because the child care services were moving into a new era, there was every likelihood that Jackie would be fostered, and because he was such a charmer, I'm sure he would have made the best of every opportunity.

Life was varied to say the least. We all had a terrifying few weeks in May. The night nurse reported footsteps outside one of the bathroom windows in the middle of the night. No one took much notice until a few days later, when someone else reported the same thing. Now we were too scared to go on night duty. A contingency plan was drawn up in case of a break-in or an attack and the police mounted extra patrols of the area. I was on night duty at the time. Occasionally I'd see a torch in the grounds late at night, and after the initial panic, I'd be relieved to realise it was only a police officer walking the grounds. But things went from bad to worse. After several nights when I reported footsteps, they stopped altogether. Life returned to normal . . . until they started all over again.

Night duty was always very busy. We began at nine and there

were baby feeds to do at ten. The washing had to be sorted out. Anything left in the dryers had to be taken out and folded. There was ironing and pressing to do on the upstairs landing. I was once so tired, I nodded off as I was using the presser and touched the side with my forearm. I was certainly wide awake then and I bore the scar of a long burn on my arm for several days to come!

At around midnight it was time for a meal. The day staff left the night nurse a dinner on a plate but it was often inedible. After hanging around all day, the only way of heating it was on a plate over a saucepan of boiling water. Sometimes when I saw the congealed gravy and the grey potatoes, I almost lost the will to live. I hate wasting food, but it had to go down the toilet. If I put it in the bin and Mrs Harrison saw it, there would be hell to pay.

After my meal, I would have the mending to do. That was the worst, because if you nodded off then, you could run yourself through with the needle. I had plenty of puncture wounds because it was too hard doing close work at that time of night. One night a child had woken up and wanted to go to the toilet. I sat her on the potty and after she'd been and was back in bed all tucked up, I went downstairs to the sluice room to empty the pot. I knew the police were in the area so I wasn't unduly worried but when the sluice room door closed behind me, I heard the footsteps and my heart rate went through the roof. It was only as I stayed to rinse the potty that I realised they were getting louder and yet staying in the same place. It was raining very hard and the doorbell rang. Someone was out with a late pass. I hurried to let her in and although she was soaked and wanted nothing more than to get to her room and change, I persuaded her to come to the sluice room with me. We listened and it didn't take a rocket scientist to realise that what we heard wasn't footsteps at all. We opened the window and timed the 'footsteps' with the drips of rain from a broken guttering onto a part of the corrugated iron roof. What a relief and what a laugh, although I don't think anyone wanted to admit what had happened. We told the other members of staff and Matron but I don't think she informed the police. Too embarrassed, I suppose. Anyway, after a couple of nights, the police eased off their patrols and nothing more was said.

I had been used to a pay phone at my first nursery and no phone calls or visitors at all where I trained. Here we had the use of the phone on Tuesday and Thursday evenings. I don't recall that we were allowed to telephone out but we could give the number to someone and ask them to call us. Matron Harrison was very strict about phone usage. It went out on the jack outside her office at 7.30 p.m. and she took it back at 9.30 p.m., but oh, it was bliss to be able to talk to a friend! My mother still didn't have a phone, so we relied on letters, but Hilary quite often phoned me, and the odd boyfriend or three did as well.

I usually met them at dances or on my days off. Nothing serious, but I enjoyed being taken to the pictures or for a meal. Occasionally I would be taken out for the day. Johnny comes to mind. He had a wicked sense of humour. We once ate lunch in Bentalls' in Kingston upon Thames. I can't remember what I ate, but he had something with salad. He ate half the meal and then complained that he had found a dead caterpillar on the lettuce. There was a terrific hoo-ha and he got another lunch and didn't have to pay for the first one. Of course, you've guessed it: the dead caterpillar was his! He'd found it on a leaf on the way into the restaurant. Johnny and I split up when he went to university.

Then there was Humph. His name was Humphrey and he had a small sports car. He was quite attractive until his sports car had to go back because he couldn't keep up the payments! How heartless we are when we're young . . .

Maureen had a phone call one Wednesday night. Matron was rather annoyed and told the caller to ring back the next night.

She hung up. The caller rang back immediately and said she was Maureen's mother and insisted that she speak to Maureen. We were all watching TV when Matron came in to tell Maureen she had a phone call.

'Tell your mother,' Matron snapped angrily, 'that you are only allowed telephone calls on Tuesday and Thursday. I can't imagine why the silly woman can't understand that.'

The telephone was still in Matron's sitting room (she hadn't put it outside on the jack) and her television was blaring. Maureen struggled to hear what her mother was saying. It was only as she broke down that Mrs Harrison turned around and realised something was wrong. She switched her television off. It turned out that unexpectedly Maureen's father had just died. At least Matron had the decency to apologise and Maureen was immediately sent home.

When we heard what had happened we were very upset.

'Pity the poor man couldn't have waited until tomorrow,' one girl remarked dryly when Maureen had gone home, 'and then his daughter might not have got into trouble.'

Sometimes we heard stories about other nursery nurses on the grapevine. One such girl was Wanda. Her father had died when she was still at school and she had two other younger siblings who were struggling with health issues. When she moved to the nursery, it was over a hundred miles from her home and as time went on, her mother was finding things increasingly difficult. When Wanda went home for a week's holiday, they discussed the problems and it was agreed that she would give in her notice when she returned to the nursery.

At first Matron was very angry and accused her of wasting a two-year training course which someone else could have taken. Wanda painstakingly explained the situation and Matron reluctantly accepted the special circumstances, but by way of 'punishment' she was immediately put on night duty to work out her one month's notice. It's worth pointing out that Wanda was only seventeen years old and in anybody else's book, an absolute heroine giving up her opportunity for a qualification because of her loyalty and love for her family!

The day Wanda left the nursery, she went into Matron's office to say her goodbyes, wearing her Guildford College scarf.

Matron snatched it from her neck. 'You're not entitled to wear that!'

Wanda had paid good money for it. They cost thirty-five shillings (one pound, seventy-five pence in today's money) which was quite a chunk out of our meagre wages so she took it back and walked out of the office. As she walked down the long drive leading to the nursery, Matron came to the front door to see her off the premises. It was a bit of a mystery as to why she did this but as Wanda shut the gate, she turned around, put down her case and carefully put her college scarf back around her neck. Matron's shoulders heaved with indignation and she took in a deep breath. Wanda waved and Matron's hand moved slightly. Clearly she was unsure of what to do but then Wanda picked up her case and stuck her tongue out before turning to leave, with her head held high! We loved to hear stories like that.

It was when I was at this nursery that I took the first tentative steps towards something which was to change my life forever. I used to go to church every once in a while, and although I was often bored by the services, I felt the need to show my face. I found a church with six old ladies, the vicar and me, and whenever I was at a loose end, I would go there on a Sunday evening. One very cold night, the snow was on the ground and I still had about half a mile to walk when I passed a Baptist church. It sounds corny but as I went past the gate, the door opened and two people went inside. They were bathed in a yellow light and I heard someone say, 'Come in. Welcome.'

I walked on for a few steps but then something drew me back.

I went in and received the same warm welcome. The place was very full and as I sat in my seat, everyone rose to sing. I had never heard such singing – they sang as if they meant it! They were so enthusiastic. I remember little about the rest of the service but I know I enjoyed it. I began to go regularly and I met a couple, who invited me for meals at their house and took time to befriend me. I was impressed by their lifestyle and their commitment and although I wasn't yet ready to make the same decision, at long last my friendship circle was widening and I had interests outside the nursery.

It was July 1965 and my time in the nursery was almost at an end. I could have stayed on if I had wanted to, but I was desperate for a change so I began to look for another job. I would miss Evie and Ros but we promised each other that we would keep in touch. By this time Evie had met the man who was to eventually become her husband. A little later on Ros began going to the same church that I had been going to and became so close to the pastor and his wife she was almost an adopted daughter. I joined a nanny's agency and after a brief stay in York with a friend, all my savings were gone, but it didn't take me long to find my first job in my career as a private nanny.

I went to London for an interview with a Mrs Bancroft. She had a little boy called Rupert who was not quite old enough for kindergarten. According to the job application, my duties would solely be to look after the child. Mrs Bancroft had a housekeeper, Ruth, to do all the cooking and housework. I would live 'all found' and she would pay me eight pounds a week, a fantastic wage at that time. I was told to take a taxi from the station and I found myself in a very posh neighbourhood in North London. The house had white stone steps up to the front door and the housekeeper showed me into a luxurious sitting room on the first floor. Mrs Bancroft was charm itself. An elegant woman, she was in her early thirties, still beautiful and wore very expensive-looking clothes. She'd been widowed at a young age. She had a cat called Blackie who sat on my lap throughout the whole of my interview. I was used to pets – we'd always had a dog at home – so as we talked, I sat and stroked Blackie's back. Much later Mrs Bancroft told me that it was her cat that got me the job.

'A cat is a good judge of character,' she said. 'When he sat next to you all that time, I knew you were a good person.'

Mrs Bancroft asked me about my experience and qualifications and eventually I met Rupert. He was a rather plain child, which surprised me considering what a beauty his mother was, but we took to each other and I was delighted when Mrs Bancroft offered me the post. After four years, I had finally reached the pinnacle every nursery nurse talked about. Working in private was supposed to be the best kind of job you could get. Good wages, privileged living and the chance to travel the world at someone else's expense; the contrast from working in cash-strapped council-run nurseries couldn't have been more marked. The day I went to work there I unpacked my suitcase and I felt as if I had finally arrived. I was a private nanny!

It turned out to be a very lonely occupation. I had peaches out of season in November (they had more food than they knew what to do with) and I was living in the lap of luxury but Rupert was spoilt and could be difficult. He was just a toddler but I was the eighth nanny he'd had. For all that luxury, he displayed some of the same symptoms I'd come to recognise in a deprived child and demanded attention all the time.

The house was beautiful but it wasn't really a suitable place to bring up children. There was no outdoors and the living space for two adults, one child and a pet was small. The lounge was huge, with oak panelling and a massive stone fireplace. Mrs Bancroft had two long settees with what seemed like hundreds of little cushions on them. There was a drinks table, which was well furbished, and a round table under the window. There was always a large floral decoration on the table and someone came in every week to replace it. The kitchen was large as well. There was an Aga cooker and the biggest fridge I had ever seen. The housekeeper, Ruth, kept the place looking pristine and cooked the occasional meal, but most days Mrs Bancroft went out for her meals. Ruth was married, so she often left with what she had cooked in her shopping bag. It was far too much for Rupert and me and I hated to see a lamb roast or a chicken pasta going into the bin.

Just off the kitchen was a small sitting room which doubled as my room and Rupert's playroom. There was a television and two comfortable armchairs. Upstairs there were only two bedrooms, so I had to share with Rupert. Not ideal, but we managed. The bathroom was straight out of a glossy interior design magazine and I had never before seen such a place. It was fabulous, with mirrored tiles and a creamy thick carpet. I had to use Fenjal bath oil when I bathed Rupert and whenever I smell it, it takes me back to that bathroom. I had my own bathroom downstairs in the utility room next to the kitchen. It wasn't as beautiful as the one upstairs, but it was warm and nicely decorated.

The room belonging to his mother was dominated by a king-sized bed and Mrs Bancroft had a walk-in wardrobe for all her beautiful clothes. Apart from a small wine cellar off the stairs leading to the sitting room, there was no other space.

We lived not far from a lovely park. I settled on a routine which meant that Rupert and I went into the park twice a day. I got to know some of the other nannies who walked there. Most of them were Norland nannies, easily recognisable by their distinctive tan coloured uniform and white gloves. The whole ensemble could only be bought at Harrods and it cost in excess of one hundred pounds. Their salaries were an eye-watering one thousand pounds. The Norland nursery was in Berkshire and the nannies' parents were usually well-to-do because it cost a lot of money to train there. For all that, none of them were snobby and they recognised Rupert. I gained more than a little sympathy when they knew who my employer was, which was a little disconcerting. I tried fishing to find out why, but they wouldn't be drawn. There was one nanny known as Nanny Alexander, who was apparently an absolute saint. She remained faithful to her families for years but she had only worked for Mrs Bancroft for ten months.

'If Nanny Alexander couldn't stick it, it must be hard,' someone told me sagely.

I quite enjoyed meeting the others in the park because I was hungry for friendship. For all its faults, the council-run nurseries were full of girls like me and I missed the fun we had had.

Blackie ate only best steak even though it cost twelve shillings sixpence a pound, and he had the most appallingly bad breath as a result.

'You can tell her,' my dad said when I told him, 'I'll come and miaow for a week if she'd like to give me best steak.'

Rupert used to go to music and movement which was held in a school hall a short walk from where we lived. It was run by a woman who had once taught the mothers of the children who came. I admired her greatly because she treated all the mothers, grandmothers and nannies alike. She would come in halfway through the lesson and walk along the walls where we were all seated, bidding us 'Good afternoon'. The classes were actually taken by her daughter and I sometimes saw the children of TV stars and famous singers.

Rupert was usually difficult when it was time to go home. He often played up, refusing to put on his shoes or his gloves or making a scene about something. When the class ended, the children would stand in a long line, the boys making a deep bow and the girls a curtsey. One day as they lined up to say goodbye there was a small scuffle between the children about who was going to hold the teacher's hand. Rupert managed to get there first and as we got ready to leave, for once he was as good as gold. I noticed that one child was very upset and I thought it was because Rupert had managed to hold the teacher's hand and she'd been disappointed.

On the way out, the instructor called me into her office. As soon as the door closed, she said in a stern voice, 'Rupert, you pinched that little girl, didn't you?'

I nearly died of embarrassment. I apologised and the teacher made it very clear that she would not tolerate such behaviour in her school. Rupert was completely unrepentant and seemed to have no idea why this kind of behaviour was unacceptable. It was only as we were on our way home that he realised the full import of what he had done. He casually said, 'You won't tell Mummy, will you?'

When I explained that I would have to because his teacher was going to telephone his mother anyway, he threw a tantrum and screamed all the way home.

Needless to say, Mrs Bancroft was not best pleased, although thankfully she didn't heap all the blame onto me. I knew some mothers had the tendency to keep all credit when things go right but at the slightest hint of something unpleasant and it was all Nanny's fault. Rupert was scolded and then the incident was put behind us.

A week later when we went to music and movement class, I was accosted by a woman in a large fur coat and dripping with diamonds. 'Your little boy pinched my little gel,' she announced.

I apologised and with great difficulty managed to get Rupert to apologise as well. I still felt dreadful about it. Even after a week the poor child had a pinch mark on her arm which, although it had changed colour, was still clearly visible.

Rupert's mother spent a lot of time doing her own thing. Rupert was sometimes visited by his uncle. Mr Valentine was in his mid-forties and had a reputation as a ladies' man. He didn't have much experience with children and it showed. Once when Mrs Bancroft was away and the three of us spent the whole day in my little sitting room and I recall feeling increasingly awkward as the day wore on. I remember encouraging him to hold Rupert on his lap and setting up some game so that he could play with him. Rupert had a favourite story about a giraffe with a short neck that made friends with a bird that couldn't fly. When the giraffe got his head stuck down a hole while playing hide and seek, the bird flew to get help. The other animals pulled the giraffe until his neck grew long and then his head popped out. I knew he would sit still and enjoy the story so I persuaded Mr Valentine to read to Rupert. Although he did, he seemed awkward and embarrassed.

To my mind, my employer did some very extravagant and crazy things. She once ordered a new car and took her favourite nail varnish with her to the showroom and asked them to spray her car the same colour.

Mrs Bancroft loved practical jokes. A friend of hers turned up one day and was very eager to give Ruth a present. 'Open it!' he said. As she did, it gave out a farting noise and Mrs Bancroft thought it was hugely funny. Ruth didn't, but what could she say? They practised the 'trick' on everyone, including me, and when they all went out to a restaurant that evening, they took the 'present' with them. The next day, Mrs Bancroft told me that they had used it in the restaurant and that her friend the Baron had even given it to the waiter. Apparently the waiter and the management took a very dim view of it and they were asked to refrain. I know I was expected to laugh along with her but I simply couldn't. It really wasn't at all funny, and Ruth and I had discussed the matter and how humiliating it was. It all seemed very childish and embarrassingly so.

The doorbell never stopped ringing, nor did the phone. Mrs Bancroft had open house and people dropped in all the time. Occasionally she would send for Rupert and I would have to take him into the sitting room. The poor child must have felt like he was part of a peep show because after a few 'oooh's' and 'aaaah's', everyone lost interest in him and he was sent to find Pamela. Her mother could never part from him without some word of criticism. 'Why did you put those socks with these trousers?' or 'Tell Pamela to brush your hair'. In the end, I had to say something. I had to explain that by saying it in front of Rupert, her son was constantly being told that he didn't measure up, or that he was a failure. We agreed that if she had any complaints, she would tell me and me alone. It worked for a short while.

One of the most fascinating characters Mrs Bancroft entertained was Webster Diggory-Clements.

To all intents and purposes, Webster Diggory-Clements was the archetypal perfect English gent. Always immaculate, he dressed in Savile Row suits and had a fresh carnation in his button hole. Webster was an old Etonian and was seen at only the best places, like Royal Ascot, Hurlingham and even the occasional garden party. He didn't always have an invitation, but he was always in the best company. I honestly believed he hadn't got a penny to his name and that he'd lived on his charms for years.

I was once returning to the flat with Rupert from an afternoon walk when Mr Diggory-Clements stepped out of a taxi. I let him in and he swept into Mrs Bancroft's sitting room with a large bottle of champagne. 'Jennifer, my darling,' he announced to Mrs Bancroft just before the door closed. 'I was just passing one of those new wine shops when I saw this in the window. My dear, I'd swear it tapped on the glass and cried out, "Buy me. Buy me for Jennifer." How could I resist? This comes from an excellent vineyard and deserves only to grace the lips of an exquisitely beautiful woman like you . . .'

I hid my wry smile behind my hand and ten minutes later, he left, blowing kisses and smiling happily. The unopened bottle remained on her sitting room table.

A week later Mrs Bancroft had invited a few hand-picked guests to have drinks at the house before they left for an outrageously expensive restaurant in Knightsbridge, where she had booked a table for lunch. Uninvited, Mr Diggory-Clements, in his usual effervescent mood, swept into the room just as the party was about to leave and almost immediately spotted his champagne. No one had remembered to put it in the wine cellar.

'My God!' he cried. 'Just look at that! It'll be ruined. It should be in a cool, dark place.'

'I'm sorry,' Mrs Bancroft told him, 'It's my fault. We'll take it to the cellar right away.'

'But it's been standing on this table next to the window with all the traffic thundering by for days. It will be undrinkable.'

They argued but he was having none of it and insisted that he take it away. Some twenty minutes after they had gone, he knocked on the door again. Ruth told him that Mrs Bancroft's party had already left for the restaurant so he climbed back into his taxi. When she got back home, Mrs Bancroft told us that some fifty minutes after he'd first arrived at the house, he'd turned up at the restaurant with an even larger bottle of champagne. Everyone was so impressed and so of course, Mrs Bancroft felt obliged to invite him to stay for a meal, although the restaurant charged them more than the price of the bottle for corkage.

A month went by and the post arrived with her usual invoice from the wine shop. To her absolute horror she discovered that she had not only been billed for the Magnum of Champagne but the Jeraboam as well!

There was an illegible signature at the bottom of the page, followed by 'Purchased on behalf of Mrs Jennifer Bancroft'.

Chapter 12

In 1965, as part of the agreement to work for Mrs Bancroft, I managed to get home to West Moors for Christmas for the first time in five years. It was part of an unwritten agreement that no one in the home had Christmas Day off duty. It was irksome but it was fair. It meant that there was plenty of staff on duty to ensure that all the children had a good time and it prevented petty squabbles about who should have the day off. If someone was given Boxing Day off, she would have to work on New Year's Eve and vice versa. As there was little point in asking for the day off because I wouldn't have enough time to travel all the way to Dorset and get back in one day, I hadn't been home for Christmas since 1960.

As my last duty before I caught the train, Rupert and I had spent a happy time in Harrods looking for a present for his mother. We bought earrings for his mother and we enjoyed wrapping them up when we got back home. Mrs Bancroft let me go, albeit reluctantly, but she sent me home with a huge pile of presents. I had a beautiful jewellery box and a bottle of expensive perfume. Mum had a pair of doe-skin gloves and my dad had a very expensive-looking tie. I think when he saw the tie, he was glad she hadn't taken up his offer to be the pet for a week.

We didn't do much as I remember but it was wonderful to enjoy my mother's roast chicken with all the trimmings.

Chicken was considered a luxury back then. We toasted each other in beer (Dad's choice), ginger wine (my choice) and cherry brandy (my mother's favourite Christmas tipple), pulled crackers and wore silly hats. Our entertainment was the telly, especially listening to the Queen's speech. On Boxing Day we went to see my Auntie Betty and did the same thing all over again.

Back in London Mrs Bancroft had ordered some clothes for Rupert from a very refined clothes shop on New Bond Street. Although they had them, they didn't usually sell 'off the peg'; they were reserved as Sale items. You choose the style and a colour and whatever you liked was made-to-measure. These jackets were fully lined but whoever had cut out the pattern had made a serious mistake: the lining was far too small. As a result, the jackets pulled at every seam and Rupert looked a bit like the Michelin man. As Mrs Bancroft had spent a lot of money on the outfits, she decided to send me back to complain. I went everywhere by taxi – it made me feel like somebody when I could stand on a street corner and just wave my arm, especially when someone else was paying the fare! However, I was soon taken down a peg or two. When I got there, I was taken to a Miss Lyons. Apparently Mrs Bancroft was her client. She examined the jackets and then, looking down her nose at me, said very haughtily, 'Well, Nanny, it's the way you've washed them. I cannot be held responsible for that.'

I had never washed the clothes and I told her so but she was so rude, eventually pushing the clothes into a bag and walking off to serve another customer. I went back with my tail between my legs. Mrs Bancroft was furious. She got onto the phone immediately and demanded to speak to Miss Lyons.

'When I send my nanny,' I heard her say in ringing tones, 'I expect her to be treated as if she were myself.'

I was duly sent back in another taxi to a very frosty Miss Lyons, with the demand from my employer that we either be given the money back or some other outfits. Embarrassed, I tried to placate the woman.

'I would greatly appreciate it if you would help me, Miss Lyons,' I smiled. 'You know Mrs Bancroft's tastes perhaps a little better than I do.'

But she was having none of it. 'I'm afraid the decision must be entirely yours, Nanny,' she said stiffly.

After some deliberation, I finally returned with two complete outfits: a blue shirt with coral stitching and matching corduroy trousers, a brown dogtooth check suit which had short trousers, a Kashmir jumper and a pair of socks. The bill was an unbelievable ninety pounds! Fortunately for me, Mrs Bancroft was delighted, especially with the suit.

Rupert had some very expensive clothes. HIs best coat was double breasted and closely fitted, and with real mink on the collar. It cost the unbelievable sum of eighty pounds and Rupert looked very sweet in it. I spent a lot of time with his wardrobe. Everything was either handwashed or went to the cleaners. I made sure he wore the right socks with the right trousers and ironed everything very carefully.

When I had taken the job, as a very new Christian I had extracted the promise at my interview that I would be allowed time off to go to church. That had happened in the first week of my employment but the next Sunday my employer was busy and the following one she was out all day. I wanted to go, so I decided to take Rupert with me and he loved it. The children went into a Sunday school and the teacher was particularly gifted. Better still, Rupert was mixing with other children his own age and as a result, he talked about it incessantly. He loved the songs and he came back home with a book of stickers. The problem was, my employer was Catholic and back in those days, there wasn't the mixing of denominations we now enjoy. Christians of different persuasions kept very much to their own kind, sometimes even crossing the street to avoid someone from another church. However, Mrs Bancroft was willing to offer a compromise, and I was asked to take Rupert to his church one week and to my own church the following week.

The Catholic church was huge and I was totally unfamiliar with the order of service. We sat in the pew and once I had taken off his coat and gloves and he'd looked around, Rupert was bored. I did my best to keep him interested in what was going on at the front of the church, but he was a bright child and knew exactly what to do for attention. His questions became louder and louder and as soon as he became difficult to keep under control, I decided we were spoiling it for others who had come to worship, so I made our escape. The only problem was, as I had gathered up his things and we'd stepped out into the aisle, the rest of the congregation was making its way to the altar rail for Communion. We found ourselves going against the flow and I quickly realised that with a small child behind me, I couldn't simply barge my way through. I turned back and went with the people until we reached the rail. Of course now I realise that as non-Catholics we could have knelt there with the others and received a blessing but because I knew Rupert was too young for Communion, I walked past the rail and headed towards what I thought was the door I had used to come in.

By this time, Rupert was throwing a complete wobbly because he wasn't allowed a drink (Communion wine) and the wails were growing ever louder. I reached the door and did my best to turn the huge round handle. It rattled and shook but it was only as I looked up that I realised I couldn't possibly have come in that way because it was bolted somewhere near the high vaulted ceiling.

By now I was desperate to get out. I found another door and wrenched it open. In my efforts, my elbow shot back and knocked over a tall flower display behind me, which landed with an almighty crach. As the whole congregation gawped, I felt a sharp tap on my shoulder and a priest beckoned me and led us both out of the church.

When I confessed to my employer what had happened, she thought it hugely funny.

Rupert had every single toy in the book but few friends. We had our routine which included daily walks in the park and meeting the children with other nannies and of course, the music and movement classes. If he was ill or the weather wasn't good, Rupert and I didn't see another child for days on end. This to my mind wasn't good. His mother loved him dearly but her social calendar didn't include meeting other parents with children. I was desperate to find a way of helping this child to socialise, so I took him to the places where he might have the company of other children. I met up with girls from the nursery and we'd go skating or to the zoo together. I even took Rupert home for a weekend with my parents, although quite what he made of their humble surroundings I don't know. He was used to living in the lap of luxury whereas my mum and dad didn't even have a bathroom or inside toilet and my dad had a penchant for wandering around in his string vest. The one thing I do know, Rupert loved being with them and playing with my cousin's children, who were a little older than him, but more than willing to accommodate him in their games.

We all went to Bournemouth and played on the beach together. We had tea in Bobby's, a large department store, and that was when I learned the value of paying immediate attention to your charge. Rupert was in the habit of interrupting adult conversation and I was talking to my friend as we sat down at the table.

'Palifar,' he began. He couldn't say Pamela and so Palifar had stuck.

'Just a minute, Rupert,' I said firmly. 'I am talking.' I carried on with my conversation but eventually I gave him my full attention. 'What was it you wanted to say, Rupert?'

There was an old woman riddled with the most terrible

arthritis making her way through the tables. I had noticed her sitting at the table in the corner some time before and I'd hoped and prayed my small charge didn't make any ringingly loud remarks. By now, the woman was only a handshake away when Rupert said in a booming voice, 'Is that the wicked witch?'

I was mortified. The dear soul looked at me with a twinkle in her eye and that only made me feel worse. 'No,' I said gently. And as the woman made her way slowly and painfully to the door, how I wished I had answered the child's question before she was within earshot.

Soon after we got back to London, Rupert was ill with whooping cough. I nursed him but the poor child really struggled to breathe at times. His doctor came from Harley Street and in my humble opinion, he wasn't all he was cracked up to be. I was so concerned and at one point I felt that Rupert was so ill that he should be hospitalised, but the doctor would have none of it. Thankfully, he improved and before long we were back to the old routine. I taught him nursery songs, which not only helped to strengthen his lungs again but also impressed his mother.

'That boy knows every nursery rhyme in the world,' Mrs Bancroft told her friends proudly. Rupert enjoyed anything with a strong rhythm and especially songs with humour in them.

> Doctor Foster went to Gloucester
> in a shower of rain.
> He stepped in a puddle right up to his middle
> and never went there again.

Rupert had never been shown finger plays either. It took a while for him to get the right finger involved as we said the rhyme but he mastered them eventually. *Five Little Froggies* was his all-time favourite and at last Rupert could do something which pleased his mother. He enjoyed showing off his new skills when he was called in to meet his mother's friends.

Rupert also loved the *Dark, Dark Wood* story. It made him feel deliciously afraid and he would beg for it again and again.

> *In a dark, dark wood, there's a dark, dark house.*
> *In the dark, dark house, there's a dark, dark room.*
> *In the dark, dark room, there's a dark, dark cupboard.*
> *In the dark, dark cupboard, there's a dark, dark box.*
> *In the dark, dark box, there's a BOO!*

I would start the story in a normal voice and let it get quieter and quieter until on the last line I was whispering and then I'd shout BOO!

A few weeks after I had started the job, my old friend Hilary came to see me. She had popped in as a surprise although I think I was the one who was the most surprised. She was five months pregnant! I knew she was seeing someone and that it was serious, but by this time they had split up and she hadn't told him about the baby.

'But he loves you,' I protested. 'He'd be really chuffed to bits to know you're carrying his child.'

By the look on her face, I clearly shouldn't have interfered. She became openly hostile, took an immediate dislike to Rupert and made no secret of the fact that she thought my job was rubbish. I was sure it was only sour grapes because we were about to leave for the South of France and I was busy packing.

'How will you get there?' she eventually asked.

'We're flying,' I gulped as I remembered that I had refused to go to Italy on our holiday because I was scared of flying. She gave me a disapproving glare and we had a rather prickly parting.

It was early spring when we all left for the South of France. Mrs Bancroft had been telling me for a week that the air would be so much better for Rupert's health after his cough. We flew from Bournemouth, so Mrs Bancroft invited my parents to have an evening meal in the hotel where we were staying the night before we left. My father chickened out, but my mother came. Mum had a taxi both ways because Mrs Bancroft wouldn't hear of her coming on the bus and she paid the fares. She was very generous that way. My mother was a bit bemused by it all, but it was good to see her and say goodbye because I had no idea how long I would be gone.

The airport at Hurn was very low-key in those days and we flew in what felt like a rust-bucket. It was very noisy and there was only the three of us on board. When we landed at the airport, Mrs Bancroft's brother was waiting for us on the tarmac. I hadn't realised that he lived in that area. He was filthy rich, with an amazing house overlooking the sea.

Mrs Bancroft had rented a cottage in a beautiful area and at last Rupert and I could enjoy a different walk and the seaside. The weather was pleasantly mild but not yet warm enough for us to go out without a coat. The cottage was fairly isolated, with our nearest neighbour about half a mile away. It had its own grounds although the only thing in the garden was a swing. The cottage itself was white with dormer windows. There was a large kitchen, with two other rooms downstairs. They had been knocked into one, with double French doors to separate them, if necessary. Rupert and I shared a room which had two single beds. He was thrilled to have a grown up's bed. The wallpaper was floral and matched the counterpanes on the beds. There was a kidney-shaped dressing table with a mirror next to the window, with a curtain in the same material as the counterpanes.

The biggest drawback was that we were both friendless and lonely. Mr Valentine had hired a young housekeeper called Judy but, although she spoke English, she and I had little in common. We had little time to get to know each other either because she lived out.

* * *

It was Judy who fixed me up with a blind date. He was English, living in the South of France while working in the area and going to take me for a meal in a restaurant when I had the day off. I gave myself some serious pampering, a hairdo and a new dress. I also tried a face pack. I'd bought some Fuller's earth from the chemist and pasted it all over my face. Horror of horrors, I'd obviously got the time wrong because he turned up half an hour before I expected! Judy gave him some coffee in the kitchen while I rushed around upstairs, getting rid of the face pack and slapping on some lipstick. He was a nice man and we were getting along famously. In the restaurant he told me something funny and as I laughed I put my hand up to my face. To my horror I could feel a distinct line of Fuller's earth along my jaw line. What he thought of it I have no idea but it was so predominant I had to excuse myself and go to the Ladies for another face wash. Sadly, he didn't ask me out again.

I took Rupert out as much as I could but he was very lonely. Back then, we didn't have the social support system we enjoy now. There were no Mother and Toddler groups and because the whole place was geared to the summer and tourists, nothing was open in February. We spent our time on the beach dipping into rock pools, or travelling into town on the bus.

My employer was beginning to do things which I found unacceptable. Rupert was scared of water, so I had been taking it very slowly. We had walked beside the sand for a while then when he was confident enough, we ventured a little closer to the water. As time went on, he was happy to look into the rock pools, so long as the tide was a long way out. He didn't realise that, over time, I was gradually getting him closer to the water's edge. I told Mrs Bancroft of our progress and she was very pleased. She was planning to spend the summer in Spain at an exclusive club and so she was keen for her son to enjoy the beach. I had a day off and she looked after Rupert. When I got back, I was horrified to hear that she had taken Rupert to the swimming pool and grabbing his hand, had made him run towards the water. The poor child had had become hysterical and the doctor had to be called. Thankfully, he recovered but from that moment on he refused to even get on the bus if it was going near the seaside. We were even further back than square one.

Mrs Bancroft also wanted Rupert to have a spoonful of multi-vitamins every day. They were quite a new thing in the Sixties. Mrs Bancroft bought the plain ones and I wasn't allowed to put any sugar in it. Actually Rupert quite enjoyed them until the morning when his mother came into the breakfast room and said, 'Oooh! Let me have a taste.'

Rupert loaded his spoon and her mother ate it but at the same time pulled a face and shuddered. From that moment on, taking the vitamins was a battle and although I tried to persuade him, after the way Matron made poor Flora eat her carrots I didn't have the heart to insist he ate it.

As April approached, I was coming up for twenty-one and Judy told me that Mrs Bancroft was planning to give me a car as my birthday present. Although it would have been handy to take Rupert out and about, the whole idea frightened me to death. If I accepted such a generous gift, I'd be beholden to her for at least a year and already I was having concerns about her as an employer. One evening Judy and I were trying to watch a good thriller on the TV when Mrs Bancroft came in, wearing a new ball gown. We admired it but she wouldn't move from in front of the screen, apparently oblivious to the fact that this was our off-duty time and we were engrossed in the movie. It was annoying and we couldn't tell her to get lost. Eventually I said something cutting to her. A lot of nasty things were said and we never did see the end of the thriller.

I was also frustrated by Mr Valentine's attitude. He kept giving me 'would-you-just jobs' and I resented it.

'Oh Nanny,' he would say in an off-hand manner, 'would you just iron my shirt while you've got the ironing board out?' 'Nanny, while you're washing that shirt for Rupert, would you just rinse my swimming trunks and the towel?'

I did some jobs, mostly with a bad grace, but his attitude towards me was changing as well. I never liked him but I was beginning to feel uncomfortable about the way he was looking at me. 'Leering' would have been a bit more accurate.

The day he made a joke about my breasts was the last straw. We'd been having trouble with the door knocker on the front door and one afternoon it finally fell off. Mr Valentine handed it to me and said, 'When you go into the village buy us a new one, Nanny. You're the expert. After all, you've got a lovely pair yourself.'

I knew he was joking but I was furious, though I chose to adopt a higher tone. 'How dare you!' I snapped. 'I am employed by Mrs Bancroft to look after Rupert,' I said haughtily. 'I'm sorry, but my duties do not include me doing a million and one jobs for you, nor listening to your snide remarks.'

With that, I stalked out of the room. He had gone way too far and as far as I was concerned, it really was time for me to move on.

I knew I'd have to have a really good reason if Mrs Bancroft was going to let me go with a decent reference. If I let them, they would talk me out of it, so I thought of several different reasons why I had to leave.

When I had taken the job I had only just become a Christian. I knew it was important to nurture my newly-found faith and so it was important to me to be allowed time off to go to church. Back in London, Rupert and I alternated between churches but his parents became upset when he enjoyed mine more than his. After the incident when I couldn't find the exit, going to church was brought to an abrupt halt. Because of my employer's social calendar in France, it was proving to be impossible for me to go at all. My day off sometimes dwindled down to half a day. If Mrs Bancroft had been up late the night before and didn't rise until noon, I couldn't go. Today's private nanny has a clearly written contract which has been agreed upon by her employer and herself. If I had had such a thing, it would have made life a lot easier. As it was, they constantly took advantage. I had managed to get to the occasional mid-week meeting at the Baptist church but I had only gone to the Sunday service once. Beginning with the church thing, I gave in my notice and just as I had predicted, I was immediately promised a weekly opportunity to go. It was time to use my second reason for leaving.

My dad was ill. He was only fifty-five but from that time, although he lived until he was seventy-seven, he never worked again. I told Mrs Bancroft that I needed to be nearer home for my mum's sake. Immediately I was promised that if needs be, they would get me on the first flight home but I stuck to my guns.

I was put under great pressure to stay. Judy kept telling me about the car, little realising it was the promise of a car that had freaked me out in the first place.

'It's a lovely little red Mini,' she would tell me. 'I've seen it. I wish someone would give me a red Mini.'

I was unimpressed so they tried another tactic. Mr Valentine took Mrs Bancroft, Rupert and I over to Spain for the day. It was supposed to be a special treat but I hated it. He had no idea that by trying to make himself look good in his nephew's eyes he was actually making me look a fool. I nearly died of embarrassment in the restaurant because I couldn't understand the menu. I felt even worse when he gabbled a translation in a superior tone as he eyed Rupert to make sure he was listening to his perfect Spanish translation. By the time he had finished, I'd forgotten the first thing he said and still didn't know what to eat. I felt so uncomfortable I wished the ground would open up and swallow me. 'I'll have what you're having,' I said feebly.

When we got back to France, he insisted I go back to the

cottage in his car. Within sight of the cottage, he pulled up and began to pressure me to stay.

'I know what it is to be a Christian,' he said. 'I'm a Christian too. I gave fifty pounds to charity the other week at the golf club. Mrs Bancroft needs you. If you leave you'll be doing a very unchristian thing.'

There was no point in arguing with him so I said nothing. When we got back to the cottage, I put Rupert to bed and then rang the pastor of the church. It was late in the evening and luckily he spoke good English, but bless his heart, he came out to pick me up. By the time we reached his home, I was in floods of tears. He and his wife calmed me down and then they brought some rational thinking into the situation. 'Giving money,' he said gently, 'even as much as fifty pounds, to charity is no proof of being a Christian. You want to go to church and you also want to honour your parents. Now that's good thinking.'

I worked my notice and left a week before my twenty-first birthday.

Chapter 13

I had a small 'do' for my twenty-first birthday on 19 April 1966 at my home. The only people there were Mum and Dad, my Auntie Betty and Uncle Bob, Elaine, three schoolfriends and Hilary. We ate egg sandwiches and cake. My greatest coup was getting two brothers called Michael and Rafe Tunnicliff to come. They were the local talent (think James Dean), both public-school educated and absolutely gorgeous! Having them in my house was as good as dying and going to heaven but I'm not sure why they came. They didn't appear to fancy any of us, so I rather suspect that they were having a little laugh at our expense but who cared? They made my day and they were FAB!

As soon as I got back home, I applied for and got a job working in the premature baby unit at the local hospital. Employing nursery nurses in the hospital situation was quite a new innovation. It was always difficult for the nursing staff to juggle the needs of the patients when there were tiny babies to feed until someone had the brilliant idea to introduce nursery nurses onto the wards. Because we were trained in the care of healthy babies, we could take up the slack, leaving the Midwives, SRN and SENs to care for the sick children and their mums. We were given responsibility for the care of healthy babies, making sure the feeds were prepared and doing other duties, like helping the mothers to learn how to bath their baby. As time went on, however, we were asked to do much more than we should have done and certainly we were not trained to do some of the tasks demanded of us. If we had plenty of staff in the unit and the mums were fit enough to feed their babies, we might be asked to sit with someone in the labour ward. We never actually nursed them, but having someone in uniform hanging around in the room during the long hours of labour (fathers didn't go in to see their babies being born at that time) was comforting for the mother. If one midwife was trying to cope with two deliveries at the same time – babies never understood the concept of being patient in a queue – we could at least keep the mum who had a long way to go calm.

The hospital building was old but the maternity unit had been purpose-built later on. It was an oblong shape with individual rooms along the two longest corridors. Each room held two beds and could be totally private if the wooden shutter bearing the words 'No Entry' was thrown across the window in the door. At either end of the oblong were two nurseries. The one nearest the labour ward held the most premature babies and the babies who were very ill. The unit had two main nurseries in which the cots were against the walls. On the other side of a corridor, there were three isolation cubicles and a room which was sometimes used for medical procedures. Sister's desk was at one end and the clean milk kitchen (where the babies' feeds were made up) and dirty milk kitchen – with its washing sinks, where the feeding bottles were washed before sterilising – were opposite. The nursery at the far end of the oblong was for healthy babies, although it too had two isolation cubicles. All the walls in both units were made of glass.

Nursery nurses fed the long-stay babies, those whose mothers had gone home to look after older siblings. We also fed the babies with mothers who were sick after their delivery and we were responsible for taking the rest of the babies to their mothers at feeding time. The system of care was very different back then. If a baby had been a normal birth, as soon as the next time for feeds came around, he would be taken to his mother. If he had been a forceps or a breech birth, or he was a caesarean then he would be 'rested' for a few hours. It wasn't until much later that doctors realised how dangerous this practice was. The babies could so easily become hypoglycaemic and in the most serious cases that could result in seizures and even (in rare cases) brain damage. These days, as soon as a baby is born he is put to the breast.

The hours of duty were nowhere near as long as they had been in the nurseries. A typical day would be a 7 a.m. start until 2 p.m. or 2 p.m. until 8 p.m. or a split shift. No one liked the split shift, which was from 8 a.m. until 12 noon, then 4 p.m. until 9 p.m. Night duty was from 9 p.m. until 8 a.m. in the morning. We wore a uniform which was very similar to the nurses'. They wore blue, but the nursery nurses wore a peach coloured dress and we had an apron and a plain cap with a red band on it. I lived in the nurses' home, which adjoined the hospital, and for the first time, I had a room to myself. We shared a communal bathroom and toilets but the home had a cleaner, so we didn't have to worry about housework. I made friends with one of the cleaners called Rose. She treated me like royalty and I went to her house a few times for tea. She once let slip that she and her husband made love every Friday night and it because a long-running joke just between the two of us. If I saw her grinning, I would look at the clock or at my fob watch and say, 'It's not Friday, is it?' and she would fall about laughing. We all ate in the staff canteen although we were allowed to have a kettle and make tea and coffee in our rooms. Right from the start, I loved it. I had longer off-duty times and I enjoyed the company of the other girls. Best of all, I was close enough to home to be able to go back for my days off and my grandmother lived within walking distance of the hospital so I was able to see her every week.

We would congregate around Sister's desk when we came on duty so that we could hear the reports. Sister Baker was an excellent nurse and I liked her a lot but she was a little sparse with her reports. She read slowly and deliberately in a sing-song voice, 'Little Baby Harris, satisfactory, Baby Cook, satisfactory, Baby Wright isn't feeding very well, Baby Swift satisfactory, Baby Vaughan has a scratch on her face and is wearing gloves but apart from that she's satisfactory . . .' With upwards of thirty babies in our care, sometimes it was hard to stay awake!

Once the report had been read, we were allocated our duties. Depending on how many staff were on duty, we might be asked to look after the babies in the bottom nursery, the one furthest from Sister's desk, or to stay in the premature baby unit itself and tube-feed some of the very tiny ones. Tube feeding wasn't part of the nursery nurse's training but we had been taught how to pass a nasogastric tube down the baby's nose and into his stomach, how to ensure it was in his stomach and not in his lung, and how to use it. Some of the babies were so tiny, the smallest being only as long as the width of my hand, and yet on the whole they were born survivors. No matter how tiny the baby was, a good nursery nurse would apply her training. Babies need to *feel* loved, and so that touch of the hand or stroke of the face and simply talking to them as we cleaned them up or tube-fed them was so important.

If there was no breast milk available, Sister fed them on Carnation milk. It made them very solid but it put on the weight quickly and that meant they could go home. The normal calculation for feeding a normal baby was 3oz milk (60 calories) per pound of body weight per day. It was believed that a premature baby needed eighty to a hundred calories per pound of body weight per day. These small babies required three-hourly feeding rather than four-hourly. The ratio of Carnation milk to water was half and half. All other babies were fed on SMA. The babies would have to be at least five pounds, seven ounces before they were deemed to be strong enough for the home environment. With the very tiny babies, that could mean spending as much as the first three months of life in hospital. Although it was difficult for the mums, it did mean that we nursery nurses could form some sort of bond with the babies in our care. I would encourage that first smile and bath times with a growing baby were always fun. We gave some of the stronger babies a bath even if they were still in the incubator because the nurseries were kept at a constant 80°F (27°C). Of course as soon as they were up to the required weight of five and a half pounds, they would go home, but until then it was good to have an alert and happy baby on my arm. Their mothers were encouraged to come in as much as they could, but that wasn't always easy, especially if they had other children at home or they lived a long way away from the hospital and had to rely on public transport.

Some of the mothers wrestled with guilt. They were torn between the baby they had to leave behind and the needs of the other siblings at home. The midwives were caring people but it was often the nursery nurse sitting alongside her feeding another baby who had the time to listen to her concerns and encourage her. She usually only needed someone to tell her she was doing her best and succeeding under very difficult circumstances and then she would be fine again.

The nursery nurses were responsible for making up the feeds, although Sister and the doctors stipulated what was actually required. We were also responsible for looking after the dirty milk kitchen as well. That meant we washed the bottles under cold running water after use and then, using a bottle brush and hot soapy water, cleaned them thoroughly. After the bottle was rinsed again, it was put into a Milton solution (a liquid used to sterilise the baby's feeding bottles) for at least one and a half hours. The Milton was diluted to one part in eighty (two ounces of Milton to one gallon of water), and it was completely changed every twenty-four hours. The teats were rinsed in cold water, then rubbed thoroughly with salt to get rid of all the milk. They were then submerged in the Milton solution in the same way as the bottles. We had to take great care that the bottle and the teats were completely covered in Milton solution. The bottle should have no air bubbles and the teats were held down by a weight. This was to avoid cross infection and contamination when we made up the feeds next time. For the same reason, the teats had to be covered at all times when they weren't actually in the baby's mouth.

When we were on general duties, we used to take the babies out to their mothers for feeding. One day I put a baby in one woman's arms. She looked at it and said, 'That's not my baby.'

With a quick apology, I whisked the baby away and took it back to the nursery. I had taken him from the cot with the mother's name on it but the baby had kicked his label off his leg. When I looked in, it was still on the sheet. I told Sister and we were vigilant with all the other babies, checking their labels very carefully before we took them to the mums. No one else had a label missing and the only baby left was the baby I had taken to her once already. Sister put on a new label and I took the baby back. My heart was in my mouth as I handed the baby to her. She smiled lovingly at the child and said, 'I knew that first one wasn't mine.' And giving the baby a kiss, she added, 'You're my little darling, aren't you?' I walked away, heaving a sigh of relief.

These days babies have two labels, one on a left arm and the other on a right foot. It would be a very unlucky baby who lost both labels at the same time!

Our routine was the same every day but every day felt different. We would feed the babies at 6 a.m., 10 a.m., 2 p.m., 6 p.m., 10 p.m., and 2 a.m. if they were on four hourly feeds. If they were on three hourly feeds it was 6 a.m., 9 a.m., 12 noon, 3 p.m., 6 p.m., 9 p.m., 12 midnight, and 3 a.m. Each child had a feed chart, which was religiously kept up to date. We also had to write in how much of the feed the baby had taken. As we fed the babies we chatted amiably and I got to know some of my colleagues very well – like Thelma – who was married, with two growing girls. A small woman with her hair pulled tightly back in a French pleat, she had been one of the first nursery nurses ever trained, gaining her certificate in 1946. Then there was Nancy, who made us roar with laughter and got us into trouble for bad behaviour when she told us about her little girl, all grown up now, who had upset the family at a wedding. She had been told she was going to see a beautiful bride who would look just like a princess. When the bride appeared, she had a dress made of feathers (highly fashionable) and trimmed with swan's down. While every woman in the church took in her breath with admiration, Nancy's little girl was horrified. 'But Mummy,' she protested in a very loud voice, 'she looks just like a duck!'

We fell about laughing and Sister came into the unit to tell us off. 'This is a hospital,' she snapped, 'not a musical hall.'

We looked dutifully remorseful. 'Yes, Sister, sorry, Sister.'

As Sister hurried away, we started to giggle again. 'If only she had said a swan,' Nancy sighed ruefully. 'Half of my family are still not speaking to each other.'

I say the days were different because the babies were constantly moving on and moving in. Confinement lasted ten days for the first baby and five for the second and any other subsequent babies a mum might have. Unless the baby or the mum was ill, the turnaround was quite quick. Sometimes if we were short of beds, the mums would be allowed home a day or so earlier. Most mums were eager to leave, but some of the more seasoned mums enjoyed the enforced rest away from family.

As time went on, I remembered some of the returning mums. Mrs Coxall lost her little girl the first year I was on the unit. She was a good weight at birth but sadly she had a serious infection. Despite being put on penicillin, the baby eventually had a fit and died. Mr and Mrs Coxall were broken-hearted but that didn't stop them coming to find me and thanking me for all the help I had given their baby. I kept it together until they had gone and then I went into the linen store to have a weep myself. Fifteen months later, Mrs Coxall was back to have another child, this time a boy. It was a bittersweet moment but this time she went home with a beautiful healthy baby.

There was one lady who during my time in the hospital came in almost every year. I saw her with baby seventeen and eighteen, and then she missed a year. However, she was back with baby nineteen the year after. 'Hello darling,' she beamed as I appeared with the new baby. 'I weren't 'ere last year. Did you miss me?' We discovered that she had lost her husband (he had died) but she had remarried someone else before starting all over again. Her new husband was very tiny but she was very large, which had posed a few problems in the labour ward. One doctor had a problem locating the baby, but his mum produced him all the same. The council had knocked two council houses into one dwelling for her ever-increasing family and I'm sure there was lots of laughter in her home. She seemed a very easy-going, jolly sort of woman.

Occasionally we would have an occurrence which was outside of the usual parameters. Elsie Peterson and her friends decided to take a coach trip to the seaside. They booked the coach and from the minute they stepped on board they were having a high old time. All her pals were married women but Elsie was single. She'd looked after her parents until they'd died and the years had flown by. She envied her friends with their families and in some cases their grandchildren as well. Sometimes Elsie felt that life had passed her by. She had nothing to say when they all grumbled about their men folk.

'My Jack never lifts a finger in the house. I have to do everything, the lazy sod!'

'Lucky you. My Harry thinks he's bloody Barry Bucknell!'

(Barry Bucknell was a DIY expert on TV and in his heyday his programme *Barry Bucknell's Do It Yourself* attracted some seven million viewers.)

'I can put up with Tony's bodgit jobs around the house. What I can't stand is his dirty socks. I swear, they're so strong the dog passed out the other day!'

Elsie and her friends laughed uproariously.

'Count yourself lucky, Elsie. You've got a nice tidy house and you can keep it just how you like it.'

Elsie smiled and sighed inwardly as she listened. Yes, she had a nice house but she wished she had a man to grumble about.

When the coach parked up and they all filed out, the parking attendant winked at Elsie. He was no spring chicken but her heart beat a little faster and as she walked by him, he winked again. 'Have a nice time, love,' he smiled. 'And don't forget, I'll be here in the coach park all day if you need anything.'

Elsie and her friends did everything you're supposed to do at the seaside. They took their shoes off and walked along the sand. They had a little paddle and ate an ice cream. They walked into town, had a look around Woolworths and found a nice café with red checked tablecloths on the Formica table tops and had fish and chips. Her friends wanted to go to the pictures but Elsie had other plans: it was time to take a chance on a little happiness. She made an excuse that sitting in the pictures gave her a headache and that she'd prefer to sit in the gardens with a magazine. She almost blew it then because one of her mates wanted to stay with her – 'You can't be on your own, ducks.'

'No, no, I insist,' said Elsie. 'I'll be fine. You go on and enjoy yourselves. I'll meet you back at the café for a cup of tea afterwards.'

Eventually she persuaded them and the friends parted. Elsie hurried back to the coach park. If the attendant was surprised to see her, he didn't let on. Before long, they were together on the back seat of the coach and in a fumbling way, Elsie was losing her virginity. He wasn't a tender lover. Perhaps he was inconsiderate or maybe he was afraid someone would catch them at it before he'd finished. Whatever the reason, the experience was hurried and rough but Elsie didn't mind. She'd done it at last! She'd had her go at life. She'd had a good day out. The man was shocked to find that she'd never done it before and even more shocked when Elsie didn't stop bleeding. In the end it was so bad, he called an ambulance.

There was a little bit of a muddle at the hospital because Elsie was brought up to the labour ward. The duty doctor examined her and repaired a tear in her vagina. Soon after she was admitted, I was called to the labour ward because it was the late shift and they were short-staffed. I was told to wait for the baby to be brought up and then take it straight to the unit. I'm not sure why the ambulance men couldn't take the baby to the unit themselves but after ten minutes of hanging around, the baby still hadn't materialised.

'Where's your baby, dear?' asked Sister Williams.

'With any luck it'll be along in nine months,' Elsie grinned wickedly.

Sister gave her a disapproving stare but Elsie blinked back shamelessly. The whole incident was treated as a bit of a laugh by some and a shocking indictment on the morals of the day by others. Although we were in the middle of the Swinging Sixties, the old ideals and prudishness were reluctant to go. Friends of mine working in antenatal clinics would tell me that a few of the older nurses would take every opportunity to 'shame' their unmarried patients. They knew better than to say anything directly, but when an expectant mum was called for examination, they would shout her name in ringing tones, 'MISS Jackson . . .', thus making sure that every woman in the waiting area knew she wasn't married.

Although more unmarried girls were keeping their babies, it was nowhere as easy or socially acceptable as it is today. With the advent of the pill, getting contraception was becoming easier but it was still a big deal. Contraceptive clinics had yet to evolve and it meant a trip to the GP, which could be embarrassing for a girl. She couldn't get away from the nagging fear that he might tell her mum. For people like Elsie, she felt that life had passed her by. By today's standard she was still a young woman and maybe that trip to the seaside changed her life in more ways than one. I hope she found someone to love her.

The nursery nurses not only fed the babies round the clock but we also helped with other duties. If there was a lot going on in the labour ward, we would walk around with breast pads or cream for the mothers' nipples. We never examined the mums, that wasn't our job, but we could do the routine stuff to help out. One day I walked around with breast pads and cream. At every door I asked quite clearly, 'Do you have enough breast pads? Do you need any cream for your nipples?' and dished out whatever was required.

I enjoyed the contact with the mums. Somehow I found out that I was pretty adept at getting a reluctant baby to breastfeed. The midwives had been taught how to help the mums but I seemed to have the knack of persuading a cross, hungry baby to latch on and suck lustily, and it wasn't long before I was being called upon to help the mums. It wasn't part of my job description but I was happy to do it. The mums were grateful, the baby was well fed and I felt a little glow of achievement. Good news all round!

Most of the mums were excited by the birth of their babies and it was hard not to join in with their pleasure. Occasionally there were the sad times, like when a baby died or was born with a deformity. I am slightly squeamish but I knew the importance of never letting a mother see how I felt, so whenever we had a report that a deformed baby had been born, as soon as the reports were finished, I would immediately go to look at the child. It wasn't because I was ghoulish, far from it, but once I had had that initial look, I could become matter-of-fact about it, which gave the mum some feeling of security. It was always sad to see a terribly deformed child and we did our best to help the parents come to terms with it.

Baby Thomson had Hydrocephalus, the build-up of too much cerebrospinal fluid in the brain. Normally, this fluid cushions the brain but if you have too much, it causes harmful pressure. Now that we are in the twenty-first century there are effective treatments but back in the 1960s, all we could do was give the baby bed rest and drugs to help ease any pain. Baby Thomson's head was the same size as an adult and increasing. His reedy cry was enough to break your heart and so when he died a couple of days later, everyone felt it was a merciful release. His parents were broken-hearted but a little over a year later, Mrs Thomson came in again. Of course, now we realise that she would never forget her first child, but everyone on the staff went out of their way to make this delivery a successful one and we were all delighted that this baby had no problems.

There was a story from the labour ward which could have been a disaster but turned out well. Mrs Smithers' baby was very flat when she was born. She was blue and not breathing. The doctors had her on the resuscitation trolley and were doing their best to revive her. We had a very old nurse working on the ward at the time. She was probably in her sixties and her only son had been tragically killed in a car crash. As a result Nurse Myers became a devoted Catholic. She was in the labour ward when Baby Smithers was non-responsive after her birth. Nurse Myers glanced at the mother's notes and saw that she and her husband were Catholics too. She realised that the teaching of her church meant that it was vitally important that the baby was baptised. If no priest was available, the nursing staff could do it, but it seemed everyone's attention was on getting the baby to live. Nurse Myers whispered in one doctor's ear, 'The baby is Catholic. Baptise the baby.'

He ignored her.

The other doctor was Italian. Nurse Myers didn't know his religious persuasion but knowing he came from a Catholic country was enough for her. Surely he would understand the importance of baptising the baby? She filled a kidney dish with cold water and took it to him. 'Baptise the baby.'

The doctor looked at the kidney dish and nodded. Nurse Myers relaxed. The doctor took the dish and threw the cold water all over the baby. There was an instant reaction: the shocked baby shuddered and then opened her mouth and let out a furious cry. I'm not sure what they wrote on the baby's report, but she certainly wasn't ready for the next life just yet.

One afternoon I was asked to fetch all the mums who had had their babies within the last two days and to bring them up to the nursery. The midwife was going to show them how to bath their babies. We had several baths in the unit so the midwife was going to bath someone's baby and then all the mums could sit at their own bath and do their babies collectively. The midwife made it look easy but all the mums were nervous. She showed them how to test the water with their elbow.

'If it's too hot for your elbow,' she told them, 'it's too hot for baby.'

The baby the midwife was bathing seemed to enjoy the water and looked content as she splashed him a little, talking gently all the time. She showed the mums how to take the baby out and how to dry him while he was lying on his tummy on their laps.

'He's much less likely to roll off your lap if you dry him this way,' she said, stretching out his arm. 'Make sure you dry all the little creases.'

The baby was dressed in a gown and put back in his cot to

sleep. So far, so good but everyone thought their child was made of glass and they were terrified that they'd break. Mrs Brown was visibly shaking as she put her baby girl into the water. The baby baths were facing each other. The midwife was one side and I was on the other. All at once Mrs Brown realised that her dressing-gown sleeves were getting wet. Without thinking, she let go of the baby and began to roll them up. Fortunately I was right beside her and managed to grab the baby up as she slid under the water. The poor woman was mortified and hysterical because of what she had done and it took an army of nurses to convince her that she wasn't a terrible mother who should be locked up for life. The baby was fine – in fact, I think it was all so quick it didn't even faze her.

We used terry nappies in the nursery. They were bulky and had to be fastened with a nappy pin. Folding the nappy and pinning it together in such a way that you didn't harm the baby was a learned skill. I loved the time spent teaching the new mums how to do it and especially the bit where you had to stab the pin in the nappy with your own hand behind it so that it didn't touch the baby. The tiny babies had muslin nappies – their little bottoms would have been swamped by the terry towelling ones.

I had been in the nursery for about three months but I still hadn't actually seen a baby being born. Sister Williams called me into the office one day and asked if I would like to.

'I certainly would,' I told her.

A little later that day they called me into the labour ward, where a woman was in the end stages of her labour. I was given a face mask and told to stand in the corner, out of everybody's way.

'If you feel faint,' Sister Williams told me, 'go outside – we don't want you cluttering up the floor in here.'

I nodded. The woman screamed and shouted, and finally it was time for the baby to be born. For me it was an emotional experience. As soon as I saw the baby's head appear I thought to myself, this is a living human being coming into the world. With the next pain, the baby slid onto the labour ward bed and began to cry lustily. She was so perfect and there was a lump in my throat as I watched the skilled midwives wipe her clean. Call me sentimental but I could have been looking at a future Wimbledon tennis champion, Britain's first woman Prime Minister or the nurse who would look after me in my old age.

'You've got a little girl,' they told her mother.

The woman burst into tears. 'Oh, a little girl. How lovely! I wanted a little girl. I've got a little girl!'

I'm terrible when it comes to other people crying. If someone is crying, it makes me cry too. The more excited and tearful the woman became, the more emotional I felt. By now the tears were running down my face and into my face mask.

'Outside if you're going to faint,' boomed Sister Williams and grabbing my arm, she propelled me unceremoniously out into the corridor.

I felt a little miffed. I should have liked to have seen the whole procedure, but never mind. I had seen my first baby born and the mother and I were thrilled that she had got what she'd wanted.

As time went on, although I still found the birth of a baby a wonderful thing, I learned to engage in a more professional way with the mums. Most of all they wanted reassurance – someone to convince them that they were doing well and would be able to cope with the huge responsibility of bringing up a baby. But not all mothers were easy to talk to, and some had trouble understanding us. We had an American woman on the ward and she became very frustrated because she kept saying that the nipple wasn't big enough. I told the midwife, who went to see her. She gave her a long talk about the benefits of breast feeding and said that baby would be fine, only to find out that the woman was bottle feeding her baby! The midwife came back to me and complained that I had wasted her time.

The next time the feeds went out, as I gave the woman the bottle for the baby she said, 'I hope it's got a different nipple on it today.'

For a second, I was flummoxed and then I realised she was talking about the teat!

The same woman was rushing down the corridor one day shouting, 'Where's the bathroom? Where's the bathroom?'

Someone pointed to the bathroom but when she got there, she said very crossly, 'I want the bathroom, not the wash room,' and we realised she was actually looking for the toilet.

If I was tempted to feel superior, I soon found out the consequences of not making myself clear. A few days later I was back doing the breast pad round. 'Do you have enough breast pads? Do you need any cream for your nipples?' I asked as I pushed the laden trolley from room to room.

'Hello nurse,' said Mrs Light.

'Breast pads? Cream for your nipples?' I smiled.

She shook her head and as I was going out of the door she called out, ''Ere, nurse, that toothpaste you gave me last time ain't half funny!'

Chapter 14

I made some good friends at the hospital. Letitia was a nursery nurse like me. She and I used to go dancing at the local Hippodrome ballroom, which was just around the corner from the hospital. Although night life was changing, some of the old ways of doing things clung on. The ballroom had two dance floors. Upstairs there was a room where they had a pop group. It was loud, hot and very sweaty. Downstairs they had a live band that did things in the same way they had done when my mother was young. The band would play three dance tunes and then everyone would clear the floor for the next three. The waltzes were most popular because they were a slow dance. A boy would walk up to a girl sitting at one of the tables around the dance floor and ask her to dance. If she accepted, they would enjoy three dances. I imagine it must have been soul-destroying for a boy who couldn't manage to persuade any girl to dance with him. It was certainly embarrassing for any girl who was left sitting at the table while her friends were on the floor with some dishy blokes. I enjoyed the spontaneity of the pop room but most of all I loved the music in the lower ballroom. My all-time favourite was 'The Shadow of Your Smile'. It was a song that just about anyone who was anyone had recorded . . . Connie Francis, Brenda Lee, Tony Bennett, Perry Como and of course, the great Frank Sinatra. Slow and smoochy, it was especially delicious in the arms of a good-looking boy.

We had an unwritten rule that if your friend was with a boy when the dance ended, you would make your own way home. Back then nobody was scared to walk the short distance to the hospital on their own. Sometimes a girl would strike it lucky and a boy would offer to take her out for supper. Near the centre of town were any number of bistros, where you could sit at tables with checked coloured tablecloths and eat your meal by candle-light. The candle was stuck in the top of an empty bottle of Mateus Rosé, a popular brand of medium-sweet wine which came from Portugal.

Letitia was the sort of girl who always found herself a date, so it was no great surprise when she met me in the cloakroom, having retrieved her coat and told me she was off out again. What was surprising was the fact that when I caught a glimpse of him, he looked really old.

'How did you get on?' I asked the next day at work.

'You're not going to believe this,' she began.

'Go on,' I said cautiously.

'He's a millionaire.'

'Oh yeah, and my name is Sandie Shaw,' I grinned.

It took a while to convince me but she was adamant. She had met the gentleman on the dance floor and enjoyed his company. He'd asked to take her home and told her he would meet her in the Rolls by the entrance. Nobody could have been more surprised than she when sure enough, there was a Rolls-Royce waiting by the kerb with the gentleman in question at the wheel. He had taken her for supper (a sure winner) and had asked to see her again.

'My friends are never going to believe this,' she told him.

'Then come to my house on Sunday,' he said, 'and bring your friends too.'

When she gave us the invitation, that's when we knew she was serious. The next Sunday, Letitia and another friend, Stella, and I set off for the New Forest and his house. It turned out to be three farm cottages, which had been knocked into one dwelling.

The furnishings were plain but expensive. He had a cook house-keeper, who had prepared us a meal but we were disappointed when, instead of the lavish cuisine we had been dreaming of all week, she cooked shepherd's pie, with lemon meringue pudding afterwards. It was nicely cooked but we had expected a lot more.

It turned out that Letitia's friend had won the football pools some ten years ago. He'd used the money to buy a string of garages and then made another pile by selling them on. He was hardly love's young dream. An East Ender, with a full-blown Cockney accent, he particularly enjoyed farting. Letitia was keen to foster a good relationship with him but she had a rival in the form of a local farm girl, who had already set her sights on him. After our day out, Letitia used her week's holiday to be with him on the farm while they got in the harvest but her rival had already seduced him with her charms and she came back a disappointed woman.

It makes me shudder to think about it now but I used to hitchhike everywhere. I never felt in any real danger but of course I was taking one hell of a risk every time I did it. I met some interesting people, including the impresario who ran the aqua-swimming team in Bournemouth. They did two shows a day in a swimming pool built next to the pier and attracted holidaymakers and locals by the score. Mum and I had been to see the show several times and we loved it. The girls wore pretty bathing costumes and they'd swim in forma-tion while coloured lights danced across the water. Think synchronised swimming in the Olympics and you have some idea how entertaining it was. There was a stage at each end of the pool and in between the shows, magicians and acrobats would perform variety acts. The impresario was keen for me to audition for the show but considering I couldn't swim a stroke, I never went for it.

On one of my spells of night duty there was an 'incident'. We were very short of nappies on the unit so at about two in the morning, Sister sent me to the labour ward to ask if they had some to spare. Sister Garfield, who was in charge, was in her office. I asked for some nappies and she told me to help myself from the labour ward cupboard. I was just on my way out when a bell sounded. Sister Garfield looked up and her face paled.

'That's the antenatal bathroom,' she said. 'Who is likely to be having a bath at this time of night?'

I shrugged. It was certainly very odd because the toilets were in another area entirely. It wasn't as if someone could have made a mistake. Sister glanced at the pinboard. 'There's nobody down there,' she frowned.

The antenatal beds were kept for patients who had to be on complete bed rest until their babies were born. Anyone else was upstairs with us.

'Come with me,' said Sister, taking her torch.

My heart was in my mouth as I followed her torch beam down the stairs and along the dimly-lit corridor towards the antenatal ward. The place was in darkness and the two two-bedroom units were empty, with their doors wide open. Yet further down the corridor there was a light on in the bathroom.

Sister Garfield flung the door open and cried out. There, standing in the bath, was a naked man! He had an unkempt beard and wild-looking grey hair. He was drying himself with the bath mat. Clearly, he'd come in for a bath (there was little security in those days) and he must have touched the emergency bell with his bottom as he stood up to dry himself. I'm not sure which one of the three of us was the most shocked. The fellow obviously meant no harm because he apologised and held the mat in front of him to cover his modesty.

'You'd better get dressed again,' said Sister tartly. 'I've already rung for a porter to escort you off the premises.'

She made a sign to me behind her back and I raced back to her office to tell them to do just that. We couldn't leave Sister on her own with him so Staff Nurse came back with me, but she was still outside the door and the man was in the bathroom, dressing himself. His clothes were most likely louse ridden and remembering poor Eddie and Richard, the brothers who had come to the nursery in the middle of the night, I couldn't help wondering what was the point of having a bath if he had to put the same unwashed clothes back on again. The porter came and the man was escorted away.

'Shut that bathroom door and put a notice on it,' said Sister when he'd gone. 'I don't want any of our mums going in there until it's been thoroughly cleaned.'

We were halfway back to the labour ward when the porter returned to check that we were all right. 'I heard this was the antenatal ward,' he chuckled, 'but I didn't think you went that far back!'

You would have thought that security would have been tightened up after that but we were far more trusting back then. The whole incident was treated as a 'one-off' and nothing more was said or done.

I never have liked night duty much but there were a few things which made up for having to do it. If we got down to the canteen before 12.30, the cook would do us fresh fried egg and chips. Believe me, they are much more delicious at that time of night than any other time. Outsiders would turn up in the canteen as well. Usually they were policemen, who were patrolling the quiet streets around the hospital. The girls in the accident department were always getting the beat policemen dropping in for a cup of tea. One night, one of the nurses had some cream cakes. It was her birthday and they were all looking forward to a slack time when they could enjoy them together. They had invited the policemen to join them but that particular night, their sergeant turned up too. He had had a report of some of his men hanging around and making a nuisance of themselves with the nurses. The cops managed to keep out of sight until he was on his way again and then they hurried out, but not before one of them was seen stuffing his cream cake under his helmet as he left. Funnily enough, although the hospital had an open door principle, we never felt vulnerable and I never heard of anyone being physically attacked by a member of the public. There was a kind of admiration and respect for doctors and nurses.

Mrs Wallace was looking forward to having her twins. It was her first pregnancy and she and her husband couldn't wait. They'd bought two of everything and they'd gone for yellow and white so that it wouldn't matter if they had two of the same sex. The labour was protracted but it went without a hitch. At 3 a.m. Mrs Wallace was delivered of a baby boy. He was small, but he had a lusty cry. About ten minutes later a little girl came along. Mrs Wallace was delighted. Her family was completed, all in one go. Her husband had elected to wait outside rather than going home to wait for a phone call so now that it was all over, she asked the nurse to call him in. His wife had another contraction as he walked in the door.

'Oh,' said the midwife, examining her again, 'there's another baby.'

There was a loud crash and Mr Wallace landed in a heap on the labour room floor. Nobody had time to worry about him and he wasn't bleeding so they left him there while they dealt with a second little girl.

The Wallace triplets were a sensation in the premature baby ward. Everyone was thrilled to have them around and I for one couldn't wait to have a turn at feeding them. They were sturdy babies and made it to their going-home weight without a problem. Their mum looked especially radiant in the pictures of the family which appeared in the local paper. The other nursery nurses and I crowded around to look and grinned.

'It was such a shock,' she'd told the reporter. 'We thought we were only going to have twins.'

Her husband was nowhere to be seen. He had made himself

scarce as soon as we knew the press photographer was on his way. He'd decided to stay in the background and who could blame him? He was still sporting such a large black eye!

Mavis McGowan had always wanted to get married but somehow it had never happened. She'd watched her friends become wives, mothers and grandmothers but now in her early forties, she was still single. Then she joined a dating agency and met a kind, gentle man about her age. He had devoted his whole life to his career but now that he too was in his mid-forties, he was lonely and wanted a wife. They had a cosy courtship and were married.

After a year of marriage, Mavis discovered she was pregnant. There couldn't have been a happier couple in the county. Mavis enjoyed her pregnancy, showing off her bump in a way which scandalised some of their more strait-laced neighbours.

'Disgusting,' they said. 'Flaunting herself like that! The woman should wear a proper smock.'

Back in the 1960s people didn't even mention the 'p' word. When it was obvious a woman was having a baby, it was whispered that she was 'in the family way' or 'expecting' because that encroached less on people's sensitivities. Pregnant women were almost non-existent in the media as well. They were not often shown on advertisements and if they were, they were with their husbands and their bump was concealed by a loose dress. The A-line dress was at the forefront of maternity fashion (such as it was) because it hung from the shoulders, flaring straight out to the hem. Because it completely ignored the waist and hips, the pregnant woman could conceal her condition.

Mavis' pregnancy was flawless until the actual birth. There were complications and it was deemed necessary for her to have a caesarean birth. Her baby, a little girl, had what we now call Down's Syndrome, though the term in the 1960s was much more abrupt and unsympathetic: 'mongol'. When she was told, although

179

Mavis was devastated, she handled it fairly well at first but then the baby had to be rushed to a specialist hospital because she had a severe heart condition. Her father went with her in the ambulance and Mavis was left to rest in her room, with the nursing staff keeping a close eye on her.

Normally after a woman has a caesarean birth, she is reluctant to move. Just to make small movements, such as shifting up the bed, means she will probably need something or someone to hold onto. Also, it will hurt to cough or laugh – after all, a caesarean is major surgery. But during that night, Mrs McGowan found the strength of ten men. She began by getting out of bed and ringing for the police on what she didn't realise was an internal telephone. When a midwife came to see what was happening, she verbally abused her. I was in the premature baby unit and the sound of her voice carried to where we were looking after the babies. Our Sister from the unit went to see what was going on. The next minute, someone came rushing in to tell us to get the duty doctor.

All the babies were fed so after I'd rung for the doctor, I went outside into the corridor, where the shouting had reached an alarming level. Mavis McGowan was still in the corridor, fighting the staff who was trying to get her back into her room and into bed. Sister was knocked out cold on the floor – Mavis had thumped her so hard she'd banged her head on the wall. Another nurse was attending to her. Somehow or other they got Mavis back into her room but by now a great many of the other mums were gathering in the corridor and becoming very upset by what was going on. I took it upon myself to reassure them and send them back to their beds.

The doctor came to sedate Mavis but she was determined not to go to sleep without a fight.

'You'll all burn in hell for what you did to my baby!' she was screaming.

Staff tried to reassure her that everything possible was being done for her child but in her confusion, she seemed to think that the baby's condition was their fault. 'Call yourself a doctor? Look at you! There are five of you around this bed and you still can't hold me down.'

When Sister recovered, she rang for Mavis's husband and by the time he came, Mavis was back in her room but still agitated and upset.

'I can't give her any more,' the doctor said. 'She's had enough to knock out a horse.'

The drugs seemed to have little effect but the effect her husband had on her was electric.

'Now, now, my dear,' he said soothingly as he walked through the door. 'What's going on here?'

She quietened down immediately and sobbed in his arms. Everyone was shell-shocked by the whole thing. Fortunately, Sister made a full recovery, as did one of the doctors who had been kicked in the chest. Of course in the morning they arranged for psychiatric help for Mavis and several months later we heard that she had made a good recovery. Despite the way she had treated the people who were caring for her, we were all desperately sad for Mavis and her husband when their baby daughter died. It is a well-known fact that older mothers are at greater risk of having a Down's Syndrome baby but perhaps this was never fully explained to Mavis during her antenatal visits. These clinics weren't as informative as they are today and the midwives could do little more than check the baby's and the mother's health. It would take a further revolution in healthcare to bring them up to today's standard, where dads are included in the process as well!

Christmas on the wards was wonderful. We spent our off duty in the days running up to Christmas painting Disney characters all over the glass in the baby unit. As in the nurseries, with a picture to copy we had everybody from Cinderella to Bambi smiling down at the babies. Someone got the decorations out and although they were a little tired, they brightened the place up no end.

On Christmas Eve the nurses came through the wards singing carols. They had their red and black cloaks on and they carried torches and a lantern or two. Each little baby was given a special present, only a tin of talcum powder, but we put a little tinsel around it and the mums were so thrilled you would think it was the best Christmas present ever. On Christmas Day the Salvation Army band came onto the ward and played. Just for a lark, one of the nurses peeled a lemon as they blew into their instruments and the poor men left puddles of saliva behind on the floor. She thought it was hugely funny until Sister told her she should be the one to get the mop and bucket!

An empty room was set aside for the staff. When we took our meal breaks instead of going down to the canteen, we could go into this room and enjoy plenty of Christmas fare. There were nuts, crisps, sandwiches and cakes, even wine and beer although everyone was very cautious about how much we had!

Babies don't know it's Christmas and so we had several Christmas Day births. The first baby to be born was put into a special crib, which was covered in white lace and had a blue ribbon tied at the top. If the Christmas Day baby had been a girl, Sister would have tied a pink ribbon there. Once, the local press turned up to photograph the baby for the next issue and everything seemed very cosy. Fortunately, or unfortunately as the case may be, the pressman had gone home when visiting time started. That's when the lady's husband and her boyfriend had a bundle in the corridor over the baby! It seems both of them thought he was the father.

I made friends with some great people and I was having the best time. Letitia and I were as different as chalk and cheese but we got on really well together. Most of the time, we went dancing.

Letitia was always smartly dressed and she attracted men. She had a failed marriage behind her but she was a fun-loving girl. She met a sailor and after they'd had a bit of a fling, she was pregnant. When she was born, her little girl was beautiful.

Jemima was a laugh a minute. Ours was the sort of friendship that if we hadn't seen each other for ages we could pick up where we left off. I liked that. She was an attractive girl with thick wavy hair and a strong West Country accent, which she would emphasise whenever she wanted to make people laugh. We used to go on camping holidays along with Stella, the girl who had come with Letitia and me to meet the football pools' winner. Stella, who had a car, was well-groomed with a short, tidy hairstyle. She was business-like in her work and she smoked. She spoke slowly and deliberately and her witty understatements often had us in stitches. We were never really cut out for the outdoor life because the first time we went, we arrived at the campsite as it was getting dark and pitched the tent. When we woke up in the morning we discovered we'd pitched facing a drainage ditch and not only that but we'd somehow ended up with a bit of pole which didn't seem to go anywhere. In the daylight we could see that it was part of the upright pole and our tent was three foot at the front and six foot at the back! Stella's deadpan statement, 'I don't think we got that quite right . . .' only added to the hilarity. Nobody could be bothered to alter it, so it stayed that way. We also gave the people on the campsite a bit of a laugh when we emerged to go out for the day. Everyone else was in slacks and tee-shirts. We came out in our glad rags, complete with high-heeled shoes and handbags, and then we had to push the car because it had got stuck in a rut.

On another occasion, Jem and I decided to go for a picnic in the New Forest. We met in Ringwood and went to a cake shop for more supplies. The queue was long and we were talking so Jem was a bit distracted as it came up for our turn.

'Two Bum Rabas,' she said. The assistant hesitated.

Jem was irritated. 'Two Bum Rabas,' she repeated.

'I think you mean Rum Babas,' I suggested, and we had the whole shop laughing.

When we arrived at our chosen picnic site, we got the food out.

'Oh, that was a quarter of ham,' said Jem, pulling two greasy-looking pieces of paper apart, 'but I was feeling rather peckish last night.' A bit later on she said, 'Ah, now I did have two pork pies, but I got up too late for breakfast.' Luckily there was more than enough in my bag to make up for her depleted supplies.

Another time we were in a pub. 'A Drambuie and lemonade,' said Jem.

The barman wrinkled his nose. 'A Drambuie and lemonade?'

'Yes,' snapped Jem crossly. 'A Drambuie and lemonade . . . er, no, I mean a Dubonnet and lemonade, please.'

As well as good friends there were other girls who were a little harder to get along with. Nurse Hartley was an SEN. A bit of a loner, she lived with her mother and father and didn't appear to have much of a social life. She had completed the three-year SRN training course but had failed the final exam. She could have tried again but I think she knew that she really didn't have it in her. Besides, being an SEN carried far less responsibility.

Night duty wasn't exactly hard work but it was non-stop. The mums would feed their babies at 10 p.m. and then we would let them rest all night. That meant the girls on nights fed the babies on four hourly feeds as well as those on three hourly feeds. In other words, we spent nearly all night feeding babies! Whenever Nurse Hartley was on night duty, instead of going to the canteen for some of those wonderful egg and chip meals, she would eat her sandwiches and do some embroidery, although there was little time to achieve very much during her break time. I think it was a peacock on the cushion cover but the trouble was, she had been doing it for so long (at least three years, according to someone else) that it stank to high heaven and it was filthy dirty.

One year, I was on night duty the night the clocks went back. On this particular night I was with two other girls, who decided to go for their tea break together. We had all been swapping spooky stories and then I was left alone in the nursery. I was a bit jumpy and then at around 5 a.m. I looked up and there was Nurse Hartley. I nearly jumped out of my skin. Was she real or a ghost? As she put her sandwich bag and apple under the desk, I realised she was real after all.

'You're keen,' I joked as I came up behind her. 'It's only 5 a.m.'

It transpired that instead of putting her clock back an hour, she had put it forward an hour. 'I'll have to go back home,' she said. 'I've left my mother cooking the breakfast!'

Chapter 15

When you're young, you not only feel invincible but immortal as well. In the hospital, we did encounter the occasional death but usually it was a baby who was badly deformed or born with an obvious problem. If they were very premature, the lungs hadn't had time to properly form and so the baby would be in distress from the word go. In other words, it was very sad when someone lost their baby but it was not unexpected, and it usually meant an end to suffering. I learned how to be sympathetic and yet professional in my dealings with broken-hearted parents. I hope I did it with compassion but I had never experienced a loss myself.

I had my greatest shock when I was twenty-three. I had kept in touch with some of my school friends but there were several whom I hadn't seen since school days. We would exchange Christmas cards but even the birthday cards had dropped off by the time we'd all reached twenty-one. I still sent a Christmas card to Angela Kingston but apart from a cursory promise to 'write a letter in the New Year', she and I knew little about each other. We had been part of a foursome at school. The other three were far brainer than I, but I think because I was the joker, perhaps that's why they hung out with me.

The patients would often give us their newspapers once they had read them, so you can imagine my surprise when I saw a front-page story with Angela's picture in her special

186

constable's uniform. I found a quiet place and read with mounting horror that she had been in hospital having a routine appendectomy when she'd suffered a blood clot in the lung. Ironically it had happened the day before she was to be allowed home and the hospital had arranged a mercy dash to Southampton Chest Hospital. Even that was not an unusual occurrence but the reason why it had become a newsworthy item was because that same ambulance on its return happened upon a serious accident in the New Forest and the medics on board had performed some lifesaving procedure before getting the second patient to the general hospital just in the nick of time.

As soon as I came off duty, I rang Angela's mother. Apparently my friend was seriously ill but not without hope. I expressed my concern and asked if I could ring back later in the week. It dominated my conversation on the ward and I realised for the very first time how fragile life is. It only takes one thing to go wrong and because we all live on a knife edge, it can have shattering results.

I waited for four days and then rang Angela's mother again. I was so expecting her to say, 'Oh, she'll be coming home tomorrow or next week,' that I bounced into the conversation. There was a long pause and then she said, 'You obviously haven't heard our sad news.' Angela's condition had been critical – she had died the day before. I was devastated that I had been so jolly when I rang. All I could do was say how sorry I was and what a wonderful friend she had been.

I shed my tears and posted a card of condolence to her family. The next day on the ward I told the rest of the staff but instead of the reaction I was expecting, I noticed that they were all looking at one another.

'What?' I said.

'We saw it in last night's paper,' someone said. 'We thought you would see it too.'

'But why didn't you say something?'

'Nobody wanted to be the one to tell you. We didn't want to upset you.'

That upset me even more. To spare my feelings they had withheld the information and all I could think about was how much I must have hurt my friend's mother with my innocent and cheerfully optimistic telephone call. I told my colleagues what had happened and everyone agreed it had been a genuine mistake. I don't do that 'not speaking to you' stuff, so it was enough said.

People handle 'news' in all sorts of ways and sometimes the reactions of the fathers when their babies were born would surprise us. We expected joy, tears, smiles and the occasional overreaction but Mr Clapton's reaction was in a class of its own.

Mrs Clapton had been in labour for twenty-two hours. Husbands were not required on the labour ward so Mr Clapton had gone home to sleep the night away. He turned up first thing in the morning to see his wife. His little daughter was already in the baby unit.

Mrs Clapton looked deliriously happy. 'Have you seen the baby yet?' she sighed.

Mr Clapton lifted her hand and kissed her fingers tenderly. 'Not yet. I came to see you first. Oh, darling, you've made me the happiest man alive!'

'You don't mind that it's a girl?'

'Absolutely not. I'm sure she's beautiful.'

'Oh, she is. She's got such a lovely face and the dearest little ears. Her hair is jet black and her eyes are blue.'

Mr Clapton felt dizzy with happiness. Ten minutes later when he came into the ward and asked to see his baby, I showed him where to stand and staff nurse pushed the cot against the glass. He pressed his cheek onto the cold glass as staff nurse pulled down the covers. Baby Clapton screwed up her face under the bright light. Mr Clapton's face fell. 'Flippin' Norah,' he gasped, 'she looks just like a bloody coconut!'

I mentioned earlier that we nursery nurses were sometimes asked to do things when we had no training. Jaundice is a condition which can develop in the newborn, causing yellowing of the skin and conjunctiva of the eyes. If the liver is immature and doesn't function properly, jaundice is the result. Jaundice can also make babies very sleepy, which in turn can lead to poor feeding. That compounds the situation because the baby is then in danger of becoming dehydrated.

If a baby was severely jaundiced, the doctors would perform an exchange transfusion. That, put simply, meant that a large portion of the baby's blood was exchanged for new blood. There was a room in the unit, kept separate for just such a procedure.

As nursery nurses, we were trained in the care of healthy babies but had no nursing experience. We were not called upon to listen to a baby's heartbeat through a stethoscope or to give injections. One day, the doctor wanted to do an exchange transfusion on a baby but there were few trained nurses on duty. He came to Letitia and me and asked one of us to be his assistant. Letitia was a lot stronger than I. She simply said, 'I'm not trained to do that,' and walked away. That left the doctor looking at me.

'This baby really needs this,' he said. 'Without it, she will die.'

What could I say? I agreed. He explained very carefully what I was expected to do and it was mostly to keep a careful track of what he was doing. He would use a three-way exchange tap and I had to write down ten millilitres of blood out, followed by ten millilitres of blood in, until the majority of the baby's blood was healthy blood. I had a crash course in using a stethoscope and how to write up the charts. Thankfully, there was no need for injections and to be perfectly frank, there would have been no way that I would have agreed to that anyway. That really was a step too far, but all he could think about was giving this much-loved and wanted baby a chance at life.

This treatment is virtually obsolete now. Jaundice is treated by phototherapy, which is done by masking the baby's eyes and placing her under a special blue light for a few days. Apparently some doctor in South Africa had noticed that babies put outside in the sun (not directly!) were less likely to develop jaundice. By the time I left the hospital, this 'new' form of treatment was normal practice. Happily, after the exchange transfusion the baby made a full recovery. After it was all over, I caught up again with Letitia.

'Why didn't you help? How could you walk away like that?' I accused.

'This hospital is full of fully qualified nurses,' she said firmly. 'You were the one in the wrong. You had no business doing medical procedures you're not trained for and you shouldn't have let him blackmail you like that. What if something had gone wrong? Who do you think would have got the blame?'

I had to admit she was right. It was a sobering thought and although there never was a next time, I would have been far more sensible if I was ever asked to do it again.

As I have already said, the other skill I developed which was not part of my nursery nurse's training was getting the baby on the breast. I seemed to have a knack for success. Of course, that made me a bit unpopular in some quarters. One midwife in particular called me a 'presumptuous little cow', but others increasingly would pop their heads around the door and ask Sister if they could 'borrow' me for a minute. I was also able to show the mums how to express their breast milk. Whenever possible, we fed the premature babies on breast milk but as they were too small and too weak to suck the breast, the milk had to be expressed and then given via a feeding tube. We didn't have suction pumps on the ward. These were hand-held pumps which covered the breast and the mother squeezed a rubber bulb on the side of the contraption, which in turn squeezed the breast and made the milk go into a glass bottle. Because we didn't have any, expressing breast milk had to be done by hand, which could be both frustrating and very tiring if you can't get it right. We showed the mums how to lean over a sterile aluminium tray and squeeze her breast in such a way as to get the milk.

One girl I made friends with had a very unusual name. Ursula Greedy had put up with years of sniggers and jokes about her name and I admired her because she seemed to take it all in her stride. Her favourite story was the one about her mother ordering a new bed from a big department store. As she was arranging to have the bed delivered, the girl asked the inevitable, 'What name is it?'

'Mrs Greedy,' said Ursula's mother.

The girl froze, her pen still hovering over the page. Then she looked up and gave her customer an embarrassed smile. 'Do you know,' she began, 'for an awful minute, I thought you said Greedy.'

'I did,' smiled Mrs Greedy.

It was Ursula who, after a particularly busy night on duty, caught the bus home to her parents. She was dog-tired and at that time they had just changed the design of the double decker buses. As you walked into the lower deck, there was a long seat under the driver's cab, which faced the rest of the bus. It was the only seat available and Ursula sat down wearily. She had a bag on her lap and the next thing she knew, the conductor was shaking her awake. She had fallen asleep and gone right past her stop. The bus was now back at the depot.

'I wouldn't have minded too much,' she told us as we all fell about laughing, 'but I had my legs wide apart, showing all next week's washing and the bag had fallen to the floor. The contents were everywhere.'

We all laughed some more.

'And if that wasn't bad enough,' she went on, 'I had a huge

191

dried-on dribble going from my mouth right down the front of my coat!' By the time she'd finished telling us, we were helpless with laughter.

She wasn't the only casualty who fell asleep when she shouldn't. One Sunday when I was on night duty I got up early to go to church. The service was at six-thirty and it was warm in the church. I had been struggling with my eyelids for some time. I sat in the pew, hoping that I looked religious rather than sleepy, but it was when we said prayers that disaster struck. I decided to kneel. That would keep me awake, wouldn't it? No. The prayers droned on and on, and finally my head jerked forward and I bashed my cheek on the pew in front. Several people were distracted, and I tried to make light of it. Unfortunately by the time I went on duty at 9 p.m., my right eye was several shades of black and blue.

'Whatever happened to you?' Sister cried in alarm.

She was totally speechless when I told her it had happened in church.

There was only one death of an adult patient while I was in the hospital. We sometimes had a sick mother, but never one quite like Mrs Binney. She had suffered from severe depression with her first two pregnancies and she was on the ward with her third baby. Had she been around today, she would have been able to have an abortion in the early weeks but back then, it was much more difficult. However, if several doctors had agreed, it was still possible and she was a prime candidate. The medical staff were not only thinking of the mother and her unborn child when they offered her a termination, but also of the two little girls already in the family. The doctors explained to Mr and Mrs Binney that to have another baby would be extremely detrimental to her mental health but Mr Binney wouldn't hear of an abortion. It was against his beliefs, he told them. In truth, it felt like they were on the horns of a dilemma, but what happened next raised all sorts of unanswered questions.

Mrs Binney had round-the-clock care. Her baby was born, another girl, and everything seemed perfectly normal for a while. But as the time went on, her mental state became more precarious. For her own protection, she was put in a room by herself and a midwife had to sit with her twenty-four-seven. She talked incessantly about 'doing away with herself', although I don't think she made any real attempt.

Mr Binney hadn't yet visited her, nor his new daughter. One afternoon as the visitors came streaming onto the ward, Mrs Binney looked at the glass panel in the door and said, 'Oh, I think that was my husband. Does he know I'm in here?'

The midwife knew that her husband hadn't been to see her, so she was anxious that, if he had finally turned up, his visit would be hassle-free. She went to the door and looked into the corridor, but turned back immediately when she heard a slight sound behind her. Mrs Binney was on the windowsill! The midwife scrambled back into the room, shouting for help. She managed to hold onto one of Mrs Binney's legs as she fell, but the woman was too heavy for her and even as help came running into the room, the poor girl couldn't hold on any longer and she felt Mrs Binney slip through her fingers. The maternity rooms were on the third floor.

When the medical staff reached her three floors below, it was too late to save Mrs Binney. Mr Binney didn't show interest in caring for the baby and eventually a child care officer came to take her into care.

We felt very sad about it all, but baby Wilson's father became the stuff of story-telling for an entirely different reason. I have always been amazed at how quick-witted some people are. I can never think of anything witty to say until I'm either half a mile down the road or the thing which gave rise to a clever remark happened ten minutes ago. Not so Mr Wilson. His baby had been admitted to the premature baby unit. He was a healthy boy but small for his dates. Nurse Blundell was looking after him.

She had her gown and mask on to prevent cross infection. Mr Wilson pushed open the door and began to walk into the isolation room. Nurse Blundell, who was writing up the chart, swung around.

'You can't come in here,' she said tartly. 'You're not sterile.'

Quick as a flash, the father replied, 'Nurse, if I was sterile, I wouldn't be here!'

I was coming up to my twenty-second birthday and it seemed as if all my friends had steady boyfriends or were getting engaged and married. I'd had dates and I had gone out with people for a few weeks but it never really came to anything.

Jack was a friend of a friend. He was no oil painting but he was into body-building in a big way. He let it be known to all my friends that he was delighted to find a girl who hadn't slept around and for a time, I was the apple of his eye. However, he couldn't accept that the same rules which applied to others, applied to him too. He was desperate for me to sleep with him and couldn't understand why I wouldn't. We started to argue about it but it wasn't his insistence that I should 'prove' my love for him that made me call it a day. Back then, the shop windows had a navy blue blind which the shopkeeper pulled down on Saturday as the shop closed and raised again first thing on Monday morning. The gilt went off our relationship when I caught him constantly admiring his own reflection as we walked along the street.

Mike could talk for England about his favourite subject – Mike. And as for Edward . . . well, I rather suspected he had another girl or a wife somewhere because he was away an awful lot. All in all, I had reached a point when I was feeling rather miserable and a bit desperate so I wrote to Marjorie Proops, agony aunt of *Woman* magazine, worrying that I hadn't yet met a man I'd really fallen for. I came across the letter she sent me in reply the other day. In it she suggested that I should put the idea of falling in love out of my head for a while. She advised me not to rush into a relationship simply because all my friends were getting married or engaged. I must have complained that I found it hard to relax with a boy and that I didn't always enjoy kissing and petting with someone I wasn't very keen on. She encouraged me to wait until I found someone who meant something to me. In reality, she was telling me there were plenty more fish in the sea, and somehow coming from Marjorie Proops, it was a lot more palatable than when my mother said the same thing.

Her advice seems delightfully old fashioned now and she answered my concerns about love (and sex!) with care and sensitivity. It must have struck a chord with me and obviously meant a lot because I kept it in a box alongside old love letters and other items of sentimental value.

Chapter 16

I loved working in the hospital but I was ready for a change. I was beginning to feel bored by the same old routine and now I wanted a new challenge. I applied for several jobs and eventually went to work in Middlesex in another children's nursery. After our terrible experiences in the training nurseries, my friend Evie Perryer, who was by this time married and with her own children, was horrified. 'How can you bear to go back?' she asked in hushed tones. We both had bad memories of the old nurseries where we had worked when we were young but I was happy to tell her that this nursery was totally different.

The landmark I had to look for was a road called Honeypot Lane and as I set out for my interview, I imagined a tree-lined lane with fields on either side. It turned out to be a fast dual carriageway dotted with huge factories and industrial estates. The nursery, consisting of two large buildings – one a house and the other a purpose-built nursery, joined together by a covered walkway – was tucked away behind the big main road. It was in its own grounds and almost as soon as the door was opened, I liked it. It had a good atmosphere, the Matron was friendly and the children ran up to her when she appeared. In the other nurseries where I had worked, either the children were indifferent or they moved away when Matron came into the room. As Miss Armstrong showed me around, we collected a couple of children. They held her hand as we walked through.

The children were looked after in family groups. It was the model we had learned about in college, the one my Matron and nursery warden in the Surrey County Council nursery were so sure would never work. The girl in charge of the room had up to eight children in her care. Their ages ranged from eighteen months to five years old, although there was some flexibility even with that. When I arrived there to work, I discovered that one room actually had a seven-year-old child who had been allowed to stay until he and his younger brother were both old enough to move together. Kevin went to the local school just up the road.

I was put in charge of the baby room. We had six cots and three members of staff, with two of us were on duty together at any one time. The duty hours were totally different. We had three days off a week. They were taken together, so you might work Monday and have Tuesday, Wednesday and Thursday off. Of course it was never the same day off each week so you might end up with Monday, Tuesday and Wednesday off one week and Friday, Saturday and Sunday off the next. That meant you'd work for eight days on the trot before getting a day off but somehow, it didn't matter. With three days off each week, it meant that we could all have a life outside of the nursery. We worked from seven until seven and there was a permanent night nurse so I didn't even have to do night duty.

The milk kitchen was next door to the baby room, so once again we were a self-contained unit within the nursery. When I started, the walls were plain and the floor was grey and red tiles. We had flowery curtains and there was a small hatch which connected the baby room with the milk kitchen. The room was spacious enough for a playpen and we could also put down a rug for the babies to lie on.

It didn't take me long to get to know the children in my care. Sadly their stories were the same as they had been in other nurseries. Alison was six months old. Her mother was West

Indian and had abandoned her in the hospital where she was born. Alison had a huge hernia on her umbilicus. It protruded about three inches and although it didn't seem to bother her, it was unsightly. As I have already stated, the child care officers would relax when they knew that a child was happy and well-cared for in the nursery because they had far more pressing cases. Time would slip by and a child would sometimes wait until it was too late for whatever was needed, but not in this nursery. This Matron was a real champion of the children; she wouldn't let any child in her care languish or be forgotten. Alison should have had that operation ages ago. Miss Armstrong started ringing up and badgering for something to be done and less than two months later, Alison was in hospital being patched up. When she came back to us, she was a different little girl. She still had a protrusion but it was only slight and although the hernia had apparently never seemed to bother her, now she was more active and eager to be on the move all the time.

The staff wore their own nylon overalls. C&A Modes was the best place to get them, and so we all looked different. I chose a floral one but the girl working with me, Valerie, was in pale blue. She was a rather plain girl, with fair hair swept back in a French pleat and dark-horn-rimmed glasses. The third member of staff was an Irish agency nurse called Maxine. She was Irish and had freckles. She wore a maroon nurse's dress but no apron. Because of the way the off duty worked, I would be working with one of them but we were seldom all together. The routine was much the same as it had always been: we fed the babies, cleaned the room, made up the feeds, took the babies out in the prams, either to a shady spot in the garden or out for a walk, and washed nappies. Our meals were cooked for us in the kitchen by two women who lived out. Win and Rob came in every day at around seven-thirty and cooked us breakfast and a midday meal. We had a bread-and-butter tea and a light supper, which was prepared by another woman who came in during the afternoon.

In just the same way as we had done in the other nurseries, every child had a special tea in their honour when their birthday came around. They would 'invite' all the others to come and we'd have a big birthday bash. We would play games like musical bumps or musical statues and pass the parcel. Everyone clapped and cheered when it came to opening the presents and the staff took photographs. The climax was to sing 'Happy Birthday' and then the cake would come in. Win was an amazing cake maker and when any of the children had a birthday, she would always ask them what sort of cake they wanted. Some of them set her a really hard challenge but she always rose to the occasion. She once created a grand piano with black liquorice piano keys and a chocolate finger biscuit holding up the lid, or it might be hedgehogs with chocolate button spines, or a space rocket and a lady with a crinoline dress. When it came to cutting the cake on Gloria's birthday, the lady with the crinoline dress had to be taken back to the kitchen to be cut up. As soon as the knife was produced, Gloria burst into tears.

'Whatever's the matter?' Matron asked.

'Don't cut the lady's legs!' Gloria sobbed.

Mrs Roberts (Rob), the woman who worked in the kitchen alongside Win, told us she had the same birthday as Elizabeth Taylor. 'I was born on exactly the same day and in the same year,' she said. 'We were the same age until I got to be thirty but she stayed at twenty-five.' So when Rob celebrated her fortieth birthday while I was working in the nursery, Miss Taylor still had five years to go.

I soon made new friends. Sylvia was a pretty Scots girl, who worked in another room. She was madly in love with Nick, who was in prison. Nick had been accused of stealing from his employers. Sylvia protested his innocence and I have to say that we took what she said with a pinch of salt. She and I became friends although we didn't go out together much; she kept to her own circle of friends outside the nursery and I was busy visiting old friends. I had kept in touch with Mrs Bancroft and I often went up to London and spent the day with Rupert.

Sylvia's friends used to go to a club near the airbase where the Americans were stationed there with US Air Forces Europe and she went out with a man they called 'Sky-Hi'. I never met the chap but apparently he was very tall and quite beefy too. He was also a great one for spinning a yarn. He told Sylvia that the US forces were issuing their soldiers with the world's first male contraceptive pill and that it was one hundred per cent effective. Needless to say, Sylvia succumbed to his charms.

Then Nick wrote to say that he had got an appeal hearing in court. Sylvia asked me to go with her because she didn't think she could face it if the conviction was upheld and he had to go back to prison and serve the rest of his sentence. I of course agreed to go with her.

We sat nervously in the public gallery while everybody filed in to their places. It transpired that Nick was accused of going back into the supermarket where he worked, via a small window in the toilet area. The window was accessed by a flat roof and apparently Nick's palm print was found on the inside of the window. The prosecution didn't make a very strong case and the barrister complained that he had only received the brief that morning. He floundered when the judges asked questions. In his defence, the barrister pointed out that Nick had an unblemished character, no money problems but he had ruffled a few feathers in his job by making sure everyone did their work properly. Having heard all that, the judge said that he was appalled that Nick's case had even gone to court, much less convicted him. The case was quashed and he was set free immediately. Sylvia was jubilant.

We all met in the corridor and as Nick and Sylvia walked out with their arms around each other into the sunlight, I was left with his solicitor, and guess what, he dated me!

I should like to say the story had a happy ending but there

was more to come. A week or two later, Sylvia was devastated to realise that she was pregnant. There was no way she could pass it off as Nick's baby (passing a baby off as another man's child was a common practice back then) because he had been locked up when the deed was done. The baby was clearly Sky-Hi's, so either the fail-proof male contraceptive didn't work, or it didn't exist. I favour the latter reason.

After a lot of soul-searching and worry on Sylvia's part, she and Nick did a lot of talking. They resolved the problem for a while when they decided that she would give the baby up for adoption but by the time her son was born, she and Nick had already gone their separate ways.

There was a double standard when it came to morals. If a man was unfaithful he was regarded as a bit of a 'Jack-the-lad' but if a woman strayed, she was cheap. Sylvia was lonely and missing Nick when she succumbed to the charms of Sky-Hi and that one evening cost her dear. I was a little more cautious and I'm glad I was: the solicitor turned out to be married.

Having a special relationship with one particular child was always frowned upon but for the first time in my life, I let my affections get the better of me. I couldn't help myself. Miranda was such a lovely little girl – bouncy, full of fun and a joy to be with. There was a chemistry between us from the word go. She was in the baby room when I started in the nursery but she was moved into a family group when she was just over a year. I shamelessly spoiled her and Miss Armstrong didn't stop me. I bought Miranda clothes; I took her out on my day off and had her in the staff room with me watching the TV when I was off duty so it was hardly surprising that by the time she was fifteen months, we had become very close.

Miranda had been abandoned in the waiting room of a doctor's surgery when she was eight months old. Her mother had gone there to ask if someone could look after her because she was finding it hard to cope on her own. Someone showed her to a seat and told her to 'wait here' but when they came back, Miranda was sitting in her pushchair, quite alone. They had no address and no idea who Miranda's mother was. All they had to go on was a name on a piece of paper attached to her coat: Miranda Green. It took Social Services some time to track Mrs Green down.

I had been at the nursery for a year when I was allowed to take Miranda to my parents for a week's holiday. It was all good experience for her and she loved being spoiled. Miranda was West Indian in origin and because they lived in a sleepy Dorset village, my cousin's children had never even seen a black child before. Miranda was younger than they were but it was interesting to note that she ruled their games and they did everything she wanted. The only comment anyone made came from my cousin's five-year-old daughter. She had long silky blonde hair but at bedtime she asked her mother to brush her hair 'very, very hard so that it would be curly like Miranda's'. The whole time they were together, the children didn't even notice that they had different coloured skins.

When I left the nursery about three years later, I kept up my visits to Miranda. We had some happy days out to the zoo, or to London but just as she turned five, her mother turned up again and wanted her back. I was delighted for her and the social workers arranged for visits so that Mrs Green could get to know her daughter again. Miranda finally went to live with her mother and everyone heaved a sigh of relief. Although I missed her, I was glad she was with her own family and I thought she would have a good life. Sadly, it wasn't to be. Her mother abandoned her again a few years later. I had just got married and so I was at a pivotal period of my life. Should I go and see Miranda or let the past stay in the past? I also had to consider the feelings of my new husband. We had no children of our own. Was it right to ask him to be a foster parent at such short notice and so early on in our marriage?

One of the girls from the nursery went to see Miranda in her new home and reported back that she didn't even seem to know her, nor did she react when my name was mentioned. Everyone was convinced she had forgotten me and that it would be best not to rekindle something which had died. For that reason, I let her go. Looking back, I'm not so sure. It was perfectly possible she had forgotten me – after all, she was so young (only four when I last saw her) – but perhaps she hadn't. I felt sad that perhaps in her eyes I too had been one of the adults who had abandoned her, and I have often wondered if she had tucked the memories of me away because they were just too painful. I wish I had the opportunity to find out.

Like my cousin's child, nobody in the nursery noticed the colour of someone's skin until Miss Armstrong employed a certain agency nurse from the Caribbean. Within days of her arrival, she had single-handedly brought racial tension in through the doors. Whenever one of the white staff told a child off, she would take that child into a corner and tell him, 'She only talk to you like that because you is black.' It confused them and undermined what little security they had. Suddenly every child was suspicious of everyone and before long they were running around giving black power signs. They clearly didn't understand what they were doing because they were only three and four, and everybody, regardless of their colour or ethnicity, was doing it. The same woman was angry with me because I was going out with a white man at the time (I am mixed race myself), and Kevin, who was seven and going to school, told the girl in charge of his room that he didn't want to drink his cocoa at night because it made him black. The whole business made everyone so uncomfortable that we were pleased when the woman, of her own choice, decided she didn't want to work in the nursery any more, but it took some while to help the children regain their confidence.

Our children's heads were always kept scrupulously clean and regularly checked but occasionally the school would report a case of head lice. One day Kevin came back from school and sought out his favourite nursery nurse, 'Maria, can you see my traffic lights?'

Maria was puzzled. 'What do you mean?'

'My teacher said to tell you to look out for headlights in our hair.'

I especially loved the run-up to Christmas in that nursery. We were given real choice about the toys we gave the children and who better to know and understand what they would like than the girls who looked after them every day? It was such fun buying and wrapping the presents in the run-up to the big day. Every child had a completely new outfit as part of their Christmas present. On Christmas morning each girl had a beautiful dress and the boys looked very smart in their new jumpers. Little Chris was thrilled with his brand new tee-shirt. As soon as he saw me he yanked up his jumper and pulled the tee-shirt down to show me the picture on it. 'Look,' he said proudly, 'a piller-cat!'

The children helped with putting up the decorations and they really enjoyed the excitement of season. We had Christmas carols playing throughout the nursery and at midnight, Miss Armstrong and a couple of other girls went around the nursery swapping the empty pillow cases for full ones and leaving them at the end of the beds. When Miss Armstrong got to Kevin's room he sat up and stared at her. It was dark and he was black so all Miss Armstrong could see was two bright eyes as big as saucers watching her. She threw the pillow case with his toys under the bed and said, 'Oh hello, Kevin. I was just checking that your pillow case is tied on properly.' She persuaded him to lie down again but when we got up in the morning, all the children were telling us that Kevin had caught Matron trying to steal the children's toys!

We had the same old problem of no man to be Father Christmas so one of the girls (Maria) and I made a pantomime horse. She was the front end and I was the back. We did it in the staff room in our off duty and made it out of some hessian sacking. It wasn't brilliant and it didn't look much like a horse but hey, it was a pantomime horse! On Christmas day the horse turned up and gave the children presents. At one point, someone spotted Miranda searching the corridor for me because she was worried I would miss the horse. By this time we were giving the children 'rides' on the horse and even when she was put on my back, Miranda never once realised that I was the one underneath her. To keep up the pretence and the fun, Maria and I dashed back to the house to discard the costume and then returned to the small kitchen and did some washing up. The children came running up to us, telling us about the horse.

'A horse?' we teased. 'Are you sure?'

'It's over here,' they cried, 'come and see!'

They dragged us along the corridor, their voices high-pitched with excitement. 'It's ever-so big, right up to the sky. And it had presents on its back and then we all had a ride.'

Of course we were amazed when they told us but even though we searched for ages, we never did find it. 'I guess it must have been a magic pantomime horse,' Maria said eventually, and all the children, wide-eyed with wonder, nodded sagely.

In the evening, after a sumptuous Christmas meal in one of the playrooms after the children were in bed and asleep, we put on a show for Matron and the rest of the staff. Miss Armstrong delighted in telling us how the year before she had had to bring the Christmas turkey from the kitchen in the other house to the nursery in the pouring rain with an umbrella over it. By the time she'd got there, her feet were wet and the turkey was cold. Because of her determination not to allow that to happen again, we now had a purpose-built walkway between the two houses. Though small in stature, she was a giant in what she achieved in that place. She wore glasses and had a slightly receding chin but when she laughed, you couldn't help joining in. I don't think she was a particularly religious woman, she certainly never said as much but her favourite expression was 'Glory!' and she would tug at the hem of her jumper or blouse as she said it.

The first Christmas I was there, I had New Year's Day off duty. A girl from Malta called Renata and I decided to go to the Lyceum Ballroom in London to welcome in the New Year. Renata was a careful woman. She was a lot older than me and she had only a few things but they were all top drawer. At a time when to spend ten pounds on a coat was a lot of money, she bought a black astrakhan Persian lamb coat, which set her back a whopping forty-two pounds. She wore the coat to the dance that night.

When we arrived, we went to the cloakroom. I passed my humble Richard Shops coat over the counter and the attendant gave me a cloakroom ticket in exchange. I explained to Renata that she should do the same, but when the attendant gave her a cloakroom ticket, it was clear that she didn't want to leave her coat behind.

'It'll be much safer here,' I told her. 'No one can take it unless they have the ticket.'

But she was having none of it. She took her coat into the ballroom and of course, being New Year's Eve the place was packed. I found us a table near the dance floor (a miracle in itself) and we sat down. Before long, someone asked me to dance but Renata refused his friend. Someone had to stay behind and look after her coat, she said.

Of course, it put a real dampener on the whole evening. If I was dancing with someone, I was worrying that she wasn't having a good time but even when someone asked her to dance, she only stayed with them for five seconds.

'Why don't you stay a bit longer?' I asked at one point. 'You don't have to come back until you've had three dances with your partner.'

'He was not a Catholic,' she said dourly. 'He could not marry me.'

'Renata, you've come here to dance, not to get married!' I complained.

By the time we saw the New Year in, with all the balloons and Happy New Year wishes, I was feeling quite murderous. I had certainly made a vow in my heart never to ask her out again. She didn't like the noise, she didn't like the men. She thought the other girls were lewd and nobody was a Catholic. She wouldn't have a drink from the bar – they were too expensive – and she even put her coat back on when she went to the toilet.

At twelve-thirty we came out into the cold night air and walked to Trafalgar Square to catch the night bus back to the nursery. Back then, once midnight came, everybody went straight back home, so the Square was almost empty. We waited for the bus and I tried to shut my ears to Renata's continuous complaints that she was cold.

'I thought you said your new coat was very warm,' I said eventually in barbed overtones.

She ignored me and pulled her collar up to cover her ears.

The bus came and the people at the bus stop surged forward. We went inside and found two seats together. Renata settled down to doze during the hour-long journey home. The bus was packed. In fact there were way too many people on it and the conductor rang the bell three times. 'No standing upstairs,' he shouted, 'and only eight standing downstairs!'

I looked around. People were standing upstairs, on the stairs, and we had about a dozen squashed in downstairs. Nobody moved. The conductor repeated his edict, adding, 'If you lot don't move, the bus doesn't move.'

Nobody would budge an inch so the conductor rang the bell

four times and the driver cut the engine. The next hour at the bus stop was the longest hour the good Lord ever made. People were tired, frustrated and angry. We all wanted to go home but because the last people wouldn't get off and wait at the bus stop for the next bus, nobody was going anywhere. After about half an hour, tempers flared. A couple of men landed punches and the language was getting a bit ripe too. One man was being particularly belligerent. He stood beside his seat and bellowed at the people standing in the aisles and then hammered the window to abuse the driver and the conductor, having a fag under the bus shelter. There came a moment when he really got up my nose.

'Look,' I shouted, 'if this bus went around the corner and had an accident and you lost your leg, you'd be the first to complain to the bus company!'

'Well, I lost my leg in the war,' he shouted back, 'so that puts you in your place, doesn't it?'

Almost immediately I could feel my face heating with embarrassment. I swallowed hard. 'No,' I retorted defiantly, 'It merely proves my point.' But I retired from the fight. Of all the people in the bus, I had to pick on the only one-legged man to make my point.

An hour later, the next bus arrived and the people standing where they shouldn't have been jumped off and clambered aboard. Finally, we were underway.

'Next year,' I told myself when I climbed wearily into my bed, 'I shall bring in the New Year quietly and at home!' I suppose I dined out on that story for some time to come but clearly, Renata expected something else when she agreed to come to the Lyceum. We remained friends but we never went out together again.

Chapter 17

Daniel was a highly intelligent little boy, taken into care because his mother, a single parent, was still at school. Even in the baby room, he was the one who worked things out. Every other child smiled and enjoyed looking at the 'baby in the mirror' but Daniel explored behind the mirror first. He seemed to be very frustrated with the limitations of his own body. He would try and get a toy just out of reach but if he couldn't grab it first time, he'd get angry about it. He enjoyed someone playing with him, but hated to be left to amuse himself. His cries were far-reaching and ear-piercing. Although I can't bear cruelty of any sort, whether it's against a child, a beast or a man, for the first time in my life, I could understand how a desperate parent might be driven over the edge by a child like Daniel. I had days off duty to get away from the continuous screaming but a mum would be with him round the clock.

'If I were in a flat with him,' I remarked one day, 'and the neighbours were banging on the walls, I think I'd struggle to cope. It's no wonder some mums do awful things.'

We had an odd job man in the nursery. Mr Reed came in daily and did everything, from putting the dustbins out for the dustmen to the gardening and mending a light switch. He was the sort of person who was very friendly until the day you crossed him. In other words, he was a good friend but a bad enemy. He spent a fortune on the *Daily Mirror* because he bought almost every girl in the nursery her own copy. As I made my remark, Mr Reed was putting my *Daily Mirror* in the drawer.

It took me a while to realise that he wasn't speaking to me, although I had noticed that I was no longer a recipient of the *Daily Mirror*. Then I discovered that if I passed him in the corridor and said hello, he would stick his nose higher in the air and walk on, but I was at a loss to know what I had done. We had had some long conversations in the past. Mr Reed had struggled with long held beliefs, especially when on 21 July 1969 the American Neil Armstrong became the first man to walk on the moon. He stood with his *Daily Mirror* in his hand, reading aloud: 'As he put his left foot down first, Armstrong declared: "That's one small step for man, one giant leap for mankind."'

Mr Reed shook his head sadly. 'I can't believe in him now.'

'Who?'

'God,' he said. 'How can I believe in Him now that a man has walked on the moon?'

I didn't see the connection myself, but we spent times like that discussing the changes in the world. In a way, it didn't bother me that he'd decided not to speak to me again, but it clearly bothered him. He looked so miserable and hurt.

I talked to the other girls first. 'Have you any idea what I did to upset Mr Reed?'

They all shook their heads.

'It might be something to do with what you said about Daniel,' Valerie suggested. 'He thinks you said it would be okay to hit him.'

'*What?*'

I decided to take the bull by the horns and stood in the doorway of his shed one day when he was inside. He had nowhere to go so he was forced to listen to what I had to say. I apologised that I may have hurt him, I told him that I would never, ever, under any circumstances hurt a child, but that I was simply trying to understand the frustrations someone under enormous pressure might feel. I told him if he didn't want to speak to me anymore that was fine, but that I valued his friendship. He stared somewhere into space as I rattled on and said nothing at all, so I left. The next day, there was a *Daily Mirror* in the drawer.

Daniel was put up for adoption. If I close my eyes I can still see him bouncing away in a baby bouncer I put in the doorway. He loved that. It gave him something to do and he could see all the other children and the staff moving around. With his new-found abilities he quickly became a loveable, intelligent little boy. We knew there would never be a dull moment with Daniel around and Miss Armstrong was keen to get the thing moving before he was forgotten. He went to a college lecturer and his deputy head teacher wife. I can't help thinking it was a very good choice.

Susan was what was once referred to as 'spastic'. This was a medical term widely used at the time and referred to people with cerebral palsy. There was even a UK charity called The Spastics Society, which had been founded in 1951. The word was dropped as official vocabulary in the 1980s because it became a particularly unkind term of abuse and even The Spastics Society changed its name to Scope in 1994.

Susan was reluctant to move because everything was such an effort. Miss Armstrong once told me that she hadn't a chance of being fostered because she made no attempt to walk. What could I do to help her? I had been reading that some people with her condition had been helped by swimming. In my off duty, I filled the staff bath right up to the overflow and put her in. Susan loved it. We didn't have a swimming baths near us or I would have taken her there, but in the meantime, she used her limbs as she had never done before. Susan had a lovely nature and we loved her to bits. I last saw her when she was about three. She was still in the nursery but she was very much a part of her family group. The day I visited, she was sitting at the table and began to slip from her chair. I resisted the temptation to rush to her aid to see what would happen. When she reached the point when she felt she would not be able to pull herself back up, she said to Alison (the girl who had had the huge hernia), 'Alison, I'm slipping.' Little Alison jumped down from her seat and gave Susan a hefty shove back into place. I had to turn away in case they saw the tear in my eye.

We used to have quite a few staff who lived out and came into work daily. Some commuted quite a distance. One such person was Ellen. She always looked very glamorous and at the time the big Afro hairstyle was in vogue. I used to wonder how Ellen found the time to keep her hair so beautifully done. It never looked out of place. I soon found out why. One morning in the snow, she got off the bus and fell over. Her hair went one way and she went the other!

I only ever once crossed swords with Miss Armstrong in the whole time I worked at the nursery. I admired her deeply and respected her but I didn't agree with what happened to a boy called Jack. Jack had tight curly hair and a sweet face. He was in the baby room because his mother had a drugs problem. Normally that wasn't reason enough to take him into care and as yet there had been no court case, but he had been removed from his mother's care to a place of safety. He was thriving very well when she turned up again. She wanted to take him with her and there was no legal reason why we should refuse her but Miss Armstrong asked us to string it out as long as possible while she tried to find someone in authority who could stop this from happening. Clearly the mother and her boyfriend were in no fit state to look after an eight-month old child. They were moving about like zombies and their pupils were dilated. When I spoke to her, the mother gave me a blank glassy-eyed stare and yet didn't seem to be paying attention. I packed a case, taking my time, and made up a couple of bottle feeds for Jack that she could take with her. I also packed a couple of packets of baby milk powder because when I asked her if she had any, she looked at me with a blank expression as if she hadn't even thought of it. Miss Armstrong was on the phone to Jack's social worker but frustratingly, she was unavailable. We kept them hanging about for over an hour but in the end, we had to let them go. Most of us were saying a silent prayer as we saw their battered car bumping along the driveway with Jack in the back.

The child care officer found Jack a week later. He was found abandoned, starving hungry, covered in fleas and locked in a shed in a large hippie commune. When Jack was brought back to the nursery, he was terrified of being left. I cleaned him up and Mr Reed burned his clothes. He was deloused but Miss Armstrong wanted him to spend a week in isolation. After two days of pulling at my clothes when he knew I was leaving the room, and listening to his heart-rending sobs on the other side of the door, I could bear it no longer. Jack was back in the nursery. We argued about it, but I was determined to have my way. Shutting him away, in my humble opinion, would do more damage than the risk of giving one of the other children in the nursery fleas. We kept his cot apart from the others and he played on a rug by himself for a few days, but he was happy to see people around him. His child care officer told us that his mother had no recollection that she had even been to the nursery, let alone demanded her son back. She was persuaded to give him up and Jack went for adoption.

The childminder looked at her watch. It was seven o'clock and usually Beryl Collins was here by now. Could something have happened to her? It was annoying that she was so late. Mrs Stephens had planned to go away this weekend. The car was all packed up and her husband was putting the last of the camping gear in the boot. The weather was perfect and Mrs Stephens was looking forward to a lazy weekend with a good book. They always went to the same place and were familiar with the farm and the farmer's wife. Mr Stephens would have a beer in the local pub while she unpacked everything and put everything in its place. But now they were stuck with Adam. He was a good baby and although 'Mrs' Collins (who was a Yorkshire lass) wasn't married to him, Adam's father (who came from the West Indies) loved him to bits. Mrs Stephens looked at her watch again. Where was she?

By eight o'clock it was too late to go camping and there was still no sign of Mrs Collins, so Mrs Stephens rang the police. When they arrived at Mrs Collins' flat they were all in for a surprise: it was empty. Mrs Collins had packed up everything and left without leaving a forwarding address. Baby Adam was taken into care. He had been well cared for and his father had visited him regularly. They had a real bond and it was obvious that the man only wanted the best for his son but the problem was that because he wasn't married to the boy's mother, he had no legal standing.

I was dating Adam's child care officer at the time. Bob Carter had a horrendous case load. He was the child care officer for eighty families, which in itself sounds bad enough but when I realised that some of the families he was helping had anything up to eight children, it gave me an insight into how difficult things were for him. With the influx of new immigrants, they were also having to adjust to new cultures and beliefs, some of which were hard to get your head around. He once told me that an African man had walked into their offices and asked them to take care of his children because he was going to die. Everyone was most sympathetic and the wheels were set in motion. Eventually Bob asked the father how long the hospital had given him.

'It wasn't the hospital,' said the man, 'it was the witch doctor.'

The man was told politely that the office couldn't help him and he was sent away. He was regarded as a timewaster until about a month later when the police called to say that he had been found dead in his bed. There were no suspicious circumstances. The man had simply gone to sleep and not woken up but once the children had been taken into care, Bob was left wondering if the witch doctor really did have the power over life and death after all.

Adam's mother was eventually traced to another part of the country. She wasn't very happy to be found because she had a new love in her life and he didn't know anything about Adam or his father. She signed the papers to let her son go. His father wanted to care for Adam but because he wanted to take him back to the West Indies, where his mother would look after him, Bob found this too hard to take. 'Why?' I asked him.

'The child should be looked after by his parent,' said Bob.

'That's true according to our culture,' I said, 'but you know yourself a lot of West Indian children are born here and go back to be with relatives during their childhood. It's their way of doing things.'

'But he won't be brought up as an English boy,' came the reply.

'So? What's wrong with that?' I said indignantly.

'There are better chances in this country.'

'He's half English, half West Indian,' I said, 'what difference will it make which half he's brought up as?'

I could tell Bob really hadn't thought of that and although I can't say I influenced his decision, eventually Adam went back to his father's homeland and family. I'm sure it was right for him. Father and son clearly adored each other and in my book, that's all that mattered.

Chapter 18

We worked with some interesting people in the nursery. Miss Keen worked in the kitchen. She was coming up for retirement and looking forward to moving into a new flat. The only drawback, so she told us, was that she was going to have to get rid of her grandmother's picture. It had hung on the wall in her parents' home for as long as she could remember.

'When things got bad,' she told me, 'we would say if it doesn't improve by next week, we'll sell Granny's picture.' Somehow, they never had to, but it had been such a comfort to have it there. Now, at last, it was time for it to go. She took it to a reputable dealer but the dealer had bad news: it wasn't worth what she thought it would be. Undeterred, Miss Keen took the picture to two more dealers. They gave her the same bad news: 'The picture is worthless.' It was a bitter blow but she was philosophical about it. 'At least the thought that it might be worth something kept us going all through the war,' she said.

My pay wasn't as bad as it had been in the past but I wasn't exactly flush either. My basic pay was sixty-eight pounds, fifteen shillings and eleven pence a month. Eight pounds and fifteen shillings went on tax, my superannuation (a council retirement pension) was three pounds, seventeen shillings and six pence and my other deductions (accommodation and meals) were nineteen pounds and ten shillings. That gave me the grand total of forty pounds, eighteen shillings and three pence a month. I wanted to go on holiday to Spain in the summer and needed a bit of extra holiday money, so I used a week in the spring to do a bit of moonlighting, and took a job as a maternity nanny. I was really lucky because the baby came bang on time and I had promised to work for one week. I went to look after Simon Silver, the first child of his parents. The week went without hitch and I enjoyed being with them. I got the baby into a settled routine and encouraged his mother to overcome her nervousness when handling him. She and her son soon had a firm bond. I was the one who got up in the night to do the night feeds, which meant that Mrs Silver had time to recover from the birth and to get a good night's sleep.

The family were Jewish and I found their culture fascinating. There were two sinks in the kitchen. One was for washing dairy utensils and the other for anything which had touched meat products. I was curious to know why and they told me it was a tradition which had been passed down through the generations from Moses. We compared notes and they were astonished to see how much of their scriptures were in the Bible. The family had a separate cutlery drawer and separate tea towels as well. I once used the wrong spoon and my employer washed it thoroughly and then stuck it upright in the garden, even though it was silver, for a period of time before having it back in the house again.

At the end of the week the family had a small get together with some relatives and I met a Mrs Hyams, who was expecting her first baby in the autumn. She was very beautiful but not very practical. Someone gave her two boiled eggs and asked her to shell them. We were all talking in the kitchen when Mrs Silver noticed that her friend was still standing at the sink holding the two boiled eggs under the cold water tap. She had the tap on as far as it would go and she was getting wet.

'What are you doing?' Mrs Silver asked incredulously.

'My grandmother told me if you hold a boiled egg under the cold water tap,' said Mrs Hyams, 'the shells come off quite easily.'

I was destined to meet up with Mrs Hyams later in the year. She and her husband had asked me at Mr and Mrs Silver's house to come to their home when their baby was born and to look after him or her in the same way as I had looked after Simon. However, I knew that I had taken a bit of a risk with Mrs Silver. If Simon had been overdue, I couldn't have done the job and Mrs Silver would have been let down big time. I was also a bit scared that if the council found out I was moonlighting I might be in trouble, so I said sorry, but I was unavailable. However, some months later, late one afternoon I had a telephone call at the nursery. It was Mr Hyams and he sounded quite desperate. He had employed his old nanny to look after their baby girl but the baby had screamed for three days and nobody knew what to do about it. He said his wife was close to a nervous breakdown and he was at his wits' end. It just so happened that I had three days off beginning the next day so I agreed to come and made arrangements to cancel what I had already planned to do. He picked me up in his flashy car as soon as I'd finished my duty.

The Hyams' house was amazing. It could easily have featured in *Homes and Gardens* or any other glossy magazine. The dining room chairs came from Italy and cost over two hundred pounds each and the glass top table with its tubular steel frame had been made to order. Everything seemed perfect but as we walked in, I knew I would have to be firm if I was to help them. Half the family was there, giving Mrs Hyams the benefit of their advice. The baby, Chloe, was in an auntie's arms and fast asleep. Mum, who was surrounded by more flowers than you'd get in the Chelsea Flower Show, was almost in tears because this was the first time the baby had slept in hours but Auntie was insisting that baby's feed was due at 6 p.m. and she must be woken up to take her bottle.

'If Chloe hasn't slept for a while,' I said. 'I think it best to put her down until she wakes up.'

But the auntie was having none of it. Everyone was looking from one to the other. I sensed that there were too many different opinions in the room and someone had to take the lead. I turned to Mr Hyams. 'If you want me to help, I am more than willing to do so. If you would prefer someone else to help you, that's fine, but please take me back to the nursery now.'

The baby was thrust in my arms and the auntie out of the door before I had even finished putting her into her cot. I sent her mother, who was clearly exhausted, to have a sleep and asked Mr Hyams if he would tell their visitors to give her a couple of days' breathing space.

It didn't take long to work out what had happened. The old nanny had been used to inferior dried milk products. Mrs Hyams had her newborn baby on full cream SMA and the nanny had advised putting in one and a half scoops of powder to every ounce of water instead of one scoop to one ounce. As a result, Chloe was being given a mixture which was far too rich for her delicate stomach. In short, the poor child had a raging stomach ache. When she cried, someone stuffed yet another bottle in her mouth and made it ten times worse. Once I had worked out the proper feeds for her using a lighter milk formula more suited to a new baby's digestion and she'd had a bit of a rest that night, Chloe was fine.

It made life a lot easier once I'd got everything together. The old nanny had bits and pieces all over the house. The Milton solution was in the baby's bedroom, which was far from ideal when it came to making up the feeds. Instead of keeping all the baby's things together in her own little drawers, I had to hunt the clean nappies down. The soiled nappies had been thrown onto the bathroom floor so I requested a bucket with its own lid, which could be kept next to the changing mat.

After I'd had the Milton bucket moved to a small area in the kitchen, I showed Mrs Hyams how to make up the solution with cold water. Now that it was on its own tray, along with a container containing salt to clean the teats on the bottle, it was a lot easier to keep track of things. She already knew she had to totally immerse everything in the Milton solution but there were still a few things she hadn't got quite right. For instance, she didn't know that she should not put metal spoons in the solution because Milton destroys metal. I also had to explain that she should not rinse the Milton from the bottle before she used it because it would make it unsterile again.

Mrs Hyams wrinkled her nose in disgust. 'But it smells funny,' she complained.

'It's a tried and trusted method of keeping baby's things clean,' I said. 'I promise you, Chloe won't taste a thing.'

I also told her that the tray should be kept away from strong sunlight because it would destroy the disinfectant qualities.

'There's so much to remember,' she wailed.

In the end, I wrote it all down.

Chloe had a strong personality right from the start. When I had demonstrated changing her nappy, I wrapped her in a shawl and gave her to Mum. Chloe began to cry. Her mother was distraught: 'She doesn't like me. What am I to do?'

It happened again at the next feed but I wasn't so convinced that the reason was that Chloe was upset to be in Mum's arms. She was an active baby so I took the shawl away and Chloe was happy. What she hated was being wrapped up; she was much happier when she could do her windmill impersonations.

A couple of days of normal living and Mum was overjoyed. So was Dad. You would have thought the sun shone from my ears and they offered me a full time job at a fabulous wage, but it wasn't for me. I had done that before and the loneliness was too much to bear. About eighteen months later, they tried to tempt me again when their son was born, but once again, I said no.

I did one other stint of maternity nannying the year I left the nursery. Mrs and Mrs Kaplan had a baby boy called Samuel. He was a lovely boy and my stay was uneventful.

The money I had got from looking after Mrs Silver went towards a holiday. I went to Spain with one of the girls from the nursery. We had a great time and enjoyed ourselves very much. During my holiday in Spain I had several pictures taken. One was of me with my head thrown back and laughing. Someone remarked about the lump in my neck. I couldn't see it at first but when I pressed Sylvia, she pointed out that everyone was talking about it, but nobody knew how to tell me. 'It was just a trick of the light,' I told them, 'a bit of fat in my neck, that's all.' I went to the doctor, convinced that everybody was making a fuss about nothing, but three weeks after my visit to the GP, I was in Charing Cross Hospital having a goitre removed from my neck. In view of my speedy treatment, I have often wondered if the medical profession had suspected something more sinister. They never said and I never asked. Happily for me I made an excellent recovery and needed no further treatment. It was, however, the beginning of the end of my romance with Bob Carter. We spent most of our dates rowing about something or other and yet neither of us had the courage to end it. He came to visit me in hospital but the three-week convalescence I spent at home gave me time to think. When I got back, we met for the last time and parted as friends.

Janine was Anglo-Indian and her mother had died when she was only a few months old. She was a beautiful child, with big brown eyes and very thick long black hair. Her hair was right down her back and reached her bottom. It was far too heavy for her and Miss Armstrong wanted to get it cut but her father refused permission. In the summer, the poor child sweated buckets and complained of headaches, but he said he had promised her mother on her death bed he would never have it cut, so that was that. He couldn't look after her himself but he didn't want her to be adopted either. I have always struggled with parents who never make an effort to visit their children and yet resist every attempt to make their lives better. I suppose they feel responsibility and guilt at the same time, but somehow they don't seem to think about the effect their decisions, or lack of them, have on their children.

People are curious to know what happened to the children in the end and I have to say I have no idea. It was a different time back then. Today, everyone wants to know everything about everybody. In the late Sixties there was still a feeling that you didn't pry into another person's affairs. People kept family secrets and you could share a confidence and know it would stay there. Like most of my contemporaries, I have scant knowledge about the children in my care. I was told just enough to be helpful but not enough to invade their privacy. This is probably why people of my generation resent having to 'tell all' when dealing with officialdom. I hope that Janine was fostered or that her father remarried and gave her a new home, but the truth is, I simply don't know.

Charles' mother rang up to say she was coming to take him out. We got him ready and he was very excited. He wanted to wait by the front door, so Miss Armstrong let him. He waited there all day. She never turned up and his heart was broken. She rang a couple of days later to say she was sorry but she'd got held up. Miss Armstrong was pretty annoyed with her on the phone and told him how disappointed Charles had been. She promised it wouldn't happen again, so Miss Armstrong agreed that he could go out with her that afternoon. This time, nobody said anything to Charles. 'I think we should leave it as a surprise,' said Miss Armstrong. 'It won't take long for you to get him ready, will it?'

It was a good job she did that. Charles' mother never did turn up.

Janine began having terrible stools. They were very dark and smelly. The carer in her room took her to the doctor and he asked for a sample. When the results came back, she was quite poorly and already in hospital with severe stomach pains. As her mother had died of cancer, Janine was put through a barrage of tests. She gradually improved and although the source of her problem was never discovered, she was sent back to the nursery.

Before long, the terrible stools and the severe stomach cramps were back and she was once again taken into hospital. This time Miss Armstrong was summoned to meet the doctors for a consultation. 'One of your staff is feeding her large amounts of iron,' he told her.

Miss Armstrong was furious. 'There's no way any of my staff would do such a thing,' she said. 'Run the tests again.'

Janine made a good recovery and she came back to the nursery a third time but it didn't take long before she was exhibiting the same symptoms.

'This is very serious,' the child care officer told Miss Armstrong. 'I think the hospital want to make it a police matter.'

It was a real puzzle. Unless someone was deliberately targeting Janine, there was no way she could be getting the vast quantities of iron the hospital was talking about. They said she was drinking a whole bottle of iron tonic mixture every two days. That sort of medicine tastes foul anyway, so it would be nigh on impossible to make a three-year-old drink such quantities without someone in the nursery being aware of it. None of us could work out what was happening. We were all told to watch her like hawks.

Miss Armstrong had an open door to her office. The children could go in at any time to see her and show her a picture or tell her their 'news'. When Janine came into the office to tell Miss Armstrong something, she noticed that the child had dirt around her mouth. Miss Armstrong cleaned her up but later that day noticed more dirt around her mouth. At the same time she saw one of the girls with a dustpan and brush sweeping a shelf. Someone had knocked over a pot plant and spilled the soil. It seemed that Janine had been eating the dirt. It was almost unbelievable but the fertiliser around the plant was made up of nitrogen, phosphorus, potassium and iron. What was even more surprising was to discover that Janine was addicted to it. The pot plants were removed and yet she still kept producing these awful stools. It kept happening until the nurse in her room discovered Janine had hidden a large quantity of the soil under the false bottom of a dolly's pram. She might have appeared to be innocently playing in the Wendy house with the dolls but she was secretly eating more soil. Once the source was entirely removed, her body reverted to normality and the craving ended.

Charles' mother ended up in prison. The authorities explained that her little son could easily be adopted by a loving family. He had everything going for him: he was blond, blue-eyed and a lovely little boy. She was facing a very long term in prison followed by an uncertain future. Gone were the days when people were coerced or bullied into giving up their children. Nobody wanted to go back to that, but the authorities pointed out that Charles was destined to stay in a home for a very long time, if his mother wasn't around. It took a long time, but Charles' mother finally agreed to let him go when he was six. Sadly for Charles, by then it was far too late. Most people adopting a child back then wanted someone under four years old. Because there are so few babies waiting to be adopted, people will adopt an older child now. The only trouble is, an older child is far more likely to have been damaged by their experiences and may take a long time to adjust to new surroundings. Real life isn't like the Hollywood version, where after being placed in a good home, everyone lives happily ever after. Adoptive parents may be in for a bumpy ride and although today's Social Services help them with long-term support, it's still not easy. In the 1960s it was a case of sink or swim and few parents were willing to take a chance.

One of the most radical changes Miss Armstrong brought to the nursery was the way it was decorated. Normally the building would have been re-painted in a maximum of two colours. In my first nursery it had been mismatched wallpapers and blue paintwork, whereas the nursery where I trained was still stuck with dark browns and the occasional splash of canary yellow. Miss Armstrong had very different ideas. She met with a howl of resistance and horror when she told us what she'd planned and I know that it raised more than a few eyebrows at County Hall, but she stuck to her decision.

There was a long corridor which went through the whole building. The walls were bare brickwork and apart from the occasional cupboard to break it up, mostly it was painted in the same old magnolia. The corridor had two right-angled turns and one left so she proposed making each turn an entirely new experience. As I put it down on paper, it will seem as shocking as it was to us at the time, but the amazing thing was, it absolutely worked. The ceiling in one area was black and the walls were a peach colour, with a slightly lighter shade for the cupboards. As you turned the corner, the ceiling changed into a light blue with yellow walls and duck-egg blue cupboards on the third bend; it was teal walls with a darker blue on the cupboards. Every now and then, instead of the painted walls she had a fussy floral wallpaper and the bold colours elsewhere had been picked to match the colours in the paper. Everyone who came to the nursery remarked that it was wonderfully colourful and great fun. Apart from the untiring way she championed the children, this has to be her greatest triumph. Out of the same budget, I was given the chance to choose the decoration for the baby room. With her encouragement, I went for a Sanderson patterned wallpaper and the matching material for the curtains. On the three walls which were plain, we matched the blue in the pattern and when I went back to the nursery about six years after I had left, to celebrate Miss Armstrong's retirement, the room looked as fresh and new as it had done when I'd been in charge.

During the time I worked in the nursery, the Sister left to get married. The council had thought they would fill her post quite quickly but by the time she had worked out her notice there was still no sign of a replacement. Miss Armstrong carried on for a couple of weeks without a full day off but by then it was becoming imperative that someone take her place. Although we all sent her away during the day to give her a few hours' break, she was becoming very tired. That was when the council approached me and asked me if I would like to apply for the job. I much preferred the 'hands-on' life with the children because a more senior post would simply drive me into the office with a load of paperwork. On top of that, there were endless meetings at County Hall or with the child care officers and I just wasn't prepared to do that. I did, however, agree to be 'acting-Sister-in-charge' so that Miss Armstrong could have her days off away from the nursery. The children's officer was delighted and promised that the council would swell my wage packet for the duration.

'It's so much better than employing an agency nurse who doesn't know the running of the nursery or the children,' she said shaking my hand vigorously. 'This way, we keep things as near to normal as possible.'

I had expected the arrangement to last a couple of weeks but in the event, I was acting-Sister for three months – less four days. Remember the four days: they are important.

My worst fears about the job were realised. It was endless office work, telephone calls and visits from authority figures. I did all right, and everyone was pleased with how it was going but mine was the loudest cheer when the new Sister arrived.

At the end of the three months (less four days), I was called into the office. The child officer thanked me for my help and shook my hand warmly but behind her back, I could see that Miss Armstrong was looking very pink and annoyed.

'The council have agreed to give you three pounds a week as an ex-gratia payment for taking the responsibility while Miss Armstrong had a day off,' she beamed.

I frowned. 'But I thought as acting-Sister, I would be paid as such,' I said. Judging by her furious nod, Miss Armstrong obviously thought the same.

'Had you done it for the full three months,' smiled the Child Officer, 'the council would have agreed to that. But as it is, you didn't complete the three months so I think this suits us well.'

'I did three months less four days,' I snapped.

'Quite so,' she agreed and that was that. I was furious, but what could I do? They had saved themselves an agency wage and got my services on the cheap. My only consolation was that Miss Armstrong had managed to have her allotted days off while I was covering for her.

After three happy years, I was saying my goodbyes again. The truth of the matter was that I became bored with doing the same thing for too long so I decided to do a one-year course in a premature baby unit in Birmingham to gain an accredited certificate. I left the nursery to take a temporary nanny's post in Worthing. It was only for a month during the school holidays but it was very well paid. My charge was a little girl called Fleur. She had been born to her parents late in life and she already had two much older siblings, Addison and Gabriella. I didn't see much of the two older girls so mostly it was Fleur and me. The family had a dog, Snoopy, which was rather overweight so whenever I took the baby out in the pram, I took the dog as well. We lived right along the seafront and I loved it. On my second day, I was walking along the path overlooking the sea when the pram

canopy fell from the screw mooring it to the pram and it frightened Fleur. I put it back and comforted her but when I looked
around for the dog, she was nowhere to be seen. Snoopy was a
Golden Labrador and looking up, I saw her way off in the
distance. Shouting her name, Fleur and I raced along the seafront to catch her up. The baby thought running with the pram
was great fun and laughed uproariously as we bounced along.
Eventually, I reached the dog, who was still taking no notice at
all of my frantic cries.

I grabbed her collar. 'You bad dog,' I scolded. 'What were you
doing?'

It was only then that I realised that 'she' had a brown collar
instead of the red one she'd set out with and that 'she' was a
boy! The owner looked rather startled. I apologised profusely
and set off again to look for Snoopy. By the time I got back
home for Fleur's feed, I was almost in tears. Only my second
day and I'd lost the family dog. I was bound to be asked to leave.
Ah well, it was fun while it lasted.

As I turned into the driveway, who should be sitting on the
doorstep but Snoopy. When I told my employer what had
happened, she teased the dog mercilessly.

'What did you do to Pamela?' she would ask the poor dog.
'What?'

As soon as she said it, Snoopy would go to the mat in the
kitchen and sit there with her top lip curled in embarrassment
and her head hung in shame.

They were a lovely family and I was tempted when they offered
me a more permanent job, but the hospital where I had enrolled
to do the course was reputed to be the best in its field and I was
lucky to secure the position. My greatest love had always been
looking after babies and I thought it would be a good idea to
gain more skills. I also had a restless spirit – I liked a place for
a while but I never wanted to become too comfortable. I was
never brave enough to travel far from home, but if I had been

228

young today, I probably would have gone abroad. As it turned out, I was going a little further up country because my next post was in a totally different area. In September 1971, I moved to Birmingham.

Chapter 19

Birmingham was a bit of a culture shock. It was big, busy and hot. The summer was glorious by the seaside but of course in a city, it feels close and humid. At that time, Birmingham, in the West Midlands, had the highest population in the country outside London. It had been a market town but it had swelled considerably during the eighteenth century as the Industrial Revolution gathered pace. The city suffered heavy bombing during World War Two but by the 1950s/60s it was already undergoing massive reconstruction. The most famous of these buildings was the Bullring and New Street Station. They were hailed as new and modern but quickly deteriorated and in later years they gained the reputation of being hideous concrete monstrosities. The city had also had a huge influx of people from the Commonwealth, which meant that its population was mixed and diverse. In the 1970s Birmingham was the most prosperous provincial city in Britain.

The hospital where I was to get my training had been a maternity unit since 1929. The only purpose-built buildings had been set up as an experimental premature baby unit in 1933 and the pioneering doctor who had started the work, Dr Mary Crosse, who lived from 1900 to the early Seventies, was awarded an OBE in 1948. She actually died of cancer in the hospital the year I was there. Although the place was a maternity hospital, the management committee gave Mary a room in one of the nurse's homes, where she could spend the last few days of her life in peace, out of respect for the woman who had begun the work. The rest of the hospital and the staff quarters were housed in several Victorian houses set along two streets. In its heyday, the hospital had up to two thousand five hundred births every year and its eighty beds were in constant use. The hospital was also known for its successful human milk bank, where nursing mothers could donate their breast milk for the use of others. When I was there, the hospital was in one of the most seriously overcrowded immigrant areas in the country so the vast majority of the babies we looked after came from totally different cultures.

My room was at the top of a house, one of several houses where the nurses lived. I shared with another girl who had the same surname as me, although we were not related. She was a Geordie and at first I found it hard to catch what she was saying with her strong accent. I think she may have had the same problem with my Southern accent but we got on well and we also got on well with the other girls in our 'set'. She and I would often host them in our room and give them a jacket potato and tea and cake in the evening. We would listen to music or sing songs together and generally while away a pleasant evening.

My enthusiasm for life was a little less happy when it came to being in the unit. To be perfectly frank, I hated the place from the moment I stepped over the threshold. I don't really understand why. Doing the course was everything I'd wanted, but perhaps I had been trying to recapture the atmosphere of my previous premature baby unit and it was nothing like that place. Perhaps it was because I had come from a situation where I had been in charge of responsibilities and now I had to go back to being a student and behaving like one. Coupled with that, I annoyed Sister Booker, a large Scottish woman who ruled the place with an iron rod, on my first day. She was pushing a trolley of water bottles through a swing door when one door swung back and bashed the trolley. A bottle fell to the floor and smashed and in my first day nerves, I giggled. I went to help her and cleared up the mess but I could tell by the sour expression on her face that she wasn't a happy bunny. Once again the old mantra, 'we do things this way because we've always done it this way' was prevalent. I quickly learned not to question anything but it frustrated me beyond words, especially if I could see a thing would work a lot better by adopting another method.

We ate our meals in the main hospital and the staff coffee room was there too, but we spent all our on duty times in the actual premature baby unit itself. There was a large open nursery downstairs on the other side of a set of double doors, and the milk kitchen, which was only used for the storage of the feeds, was next to it. The rest of the unit was made up of small rooms, where the stronger babies were cared for. There was an upstairs, which consisted of more small rooms and a couple of rooms kept for the mothers of babies who were almost ready to go home. We also had a larger area, which was used as a clinic for babies returning for check-ups and accessed from the outside via by a fire escape.

As a student, I had classes when I would take notes and be taught about the care of premature babies. We had a strict dress code: we wore white dresses and a nurse's cap with a red band on it and were supposed to have a clean dress on every day. Whenever we nursed the babies we had to wear a white gown over our clothes. They were usually hung on a coat hanger on the back of the door and changed every day. Our hair was supposed to be short or tied back, and our nails had to be short too. Nail varnish, lipstick and other make-up was strictly forbidden. Every time we handled a baby we had to wash our hands. The washing, nappies and baby gowns were put into a pedal bin so that we didn't have to touch the lids. We also had to adhere to a 'dirty side' and a 'clean side' when working beside the baby's incubator. This meant that you fed the baby from one side of the incubator and changed his nappy using the other side. The floors had to be cleaned every day with a damp mop, as did the window ledges, sinks and door handles. This was done by an in-house cleaner. The cots and baby scales were washed every day as well, which was our responsibility. We took special care when cleaning the incubators. It was no bad thing because there was little or no cross infection, probably because the regime was so strict.

Babies' bottles were sterilised with Milton solution (one part Milton to eighty parts water) and as in the previous nursery, everything had to be completely submerged for at least two hours before it could be used again. All the new mums had to attend a film given by the Milton people before they went home to make sure they fully understood how to use the product. Mrs Hyams could have done with seeing that!

The feeds were made up to order in a central milk kitchen and everything was autoclaved (a method of sterilisation by steam) and kept individually wrapped. It was sent to the wards to be kept in the clean milk kitchen until needed. Dirty milk bottles were washed in a separate area. They were thoroughly soaped using a bottle brush and then sent back to the central kitchen to be autoclaved before use.

We were taught how to properly wash the babies, taking care to clean the eyes, the armpits, the groin and buttocks, and the hands, which might be clenched, with water and a swab. This had to be done every day. The umbilicus was cleaned with a Hibitane and spirit mixture and then powdered with Ster-Zac powder each time the nappy was changed. It was important to keep it dry because moisture would encourage infection. Babies weren't given a bath until the cord had completely separated. The babies were bathed in Infacare solution, the only bar soap in the whole nursery being the one used by the nursing staff. These stringent and careful measures were maintained to give the babies a better chance of survival and put them at less risk of infection.

Sometimes the mothers did some things which seemed very odd to us. One baby had something Sellotaped to his forehead. My friend went into his room to check on him and was so alarmed, she got the Sister. It turned out to be the dried-up umbilical cord, which his mother had taped to his forehead to ward off evil spirits! With the utmost tact, Sister explained that in our nursery that wouldn't be needed and the mother duly took it off.

If we had a very sick baby, we were used to the vicar or minister coming to baptise the child or say prayers by the incubator but now I had to get used to people from other faiths in the nursery. The Muslim cleric would come to whisper words from the Koran in the baby's ear and we had to tread carefully for fear of offending them. As ever, it was important to lessen the risk of infection so we had to limit the number of people coming into the nursery. Also, we had to devise a way of allowing the cleric to get close enough to the baby to whisper those all-important words without them feeling that he had been singled out for special treatment. Some of them were offended by a woman, i.e. Sister Booker, telling them what to do. It was a delicate balancing act.

One of the first procedures I was taught was how to use the dextrostix, a small flat spill with one end impregnated with chemicals. I had to prick the baby's heel with a sterile prick and then smear some blood onto the dextrostix. After waiting a full minute I would wash the excess blood away with some sterile water and compare the changes in colour on the strip with the colours on the side of the jar. Matching the colours was only a rough guide but it told us if the baby had hypoglycaemia, which is low blood sugar. We also had to look for other symptoms like being slow to feed, or having cyanotic attacks (going blue) or if the baby made jittery movements. Even observing a 'concerned' look on the baby's face made us step up our observations on the child.

Although we never made them up unless we were on milk kitchen duties, I learned how to calculate what feeds to give a baby. For instance, if a baby weighed two thousand, seven hundred and fifty grams and was four days old, I calculated that he needed one hundred millilitres of milk for every one thousand grams of body weight, which meant the baby would have a total of two hundred and seventy-five millilitres a day. That would work out that each feed would be fifty-five millilitres if the baby was on five feeds a day. Considering I was rubbish at maths in school, it taxed my brain a bit but I got there in the end.

We not only looked after the babies but we had to know how to instruct the mothers so that they were competent when their babies went home. We all took great pains to help them feel happy and know that they were able to cope once they were 'on their own', although in actual fact they weren't really alone. There was always a back-up team ready to help them in the GP's surgery or the Baby Clinic and the mums knew that if they were desperate, they could always ring the hospital even after they'd gone home. Instructing the mums on the care of their babies and how to make up the feeds and change the Milton solution was built into our everyday routine. They took home written instructions in case they forgot something but increasingly we were getting mums who couldn't speak any English at all. This meant that the hospital had to employ interpreters to help us.

All our premature babies were given folic acid and Abidec drops at fourteen days old and Coliron from twenty-eight days. Abidec was a vitamin A, B and D mixture and folic acid was iron, as was Coliron. These prevented the baby from becoming anaemic. They were put into the baby's feeds and the mums would be given a prescription to take to the chemist. The mums would also be advised not to let the baby get too hot or too cold. Because their babies were so tiny, there was a temptation to overdress them, 'in case they got cold.' Keeping the room temperature at about 68°F (20°C) was best but clothing should be loose enough to allow free movement. Everybody advocated putting babies outside in the fresh air and in fact if we had a baby who was very small at birth and had been in the nursery for some time, provided that baby was progressing well, the hospital had a couple of coach-built prams and we would put the baby outside the unit in the warm sunshine. The babies in the other premature baby unit had been fed on Carnation milk to bulk up their weight very quickly but here, these babies were fed on Ostermilk 1.

Having given what must have seemed like a long and daunting list of dos and don'ts, the last thing Sister told the mums as they left was, 'Give your baby lots and lots of love.'

The duty roster was a lot like it had been in my previous premature baby unit. I spent a lot of my spare time with the other girls in my 'set' and we used to go out en masse for meals. We loved dressing up in our glad rags and finding some pub where the meals were wholesome and not too expensive. The hospital was in a tree-lined residential area so we had to travel into 'Brum' (as the locals called it) for the pictures or a dance. On days off, we would get together and go to Warwick Castle or Coventry for the day. Even a walk along the canal was lovely, and yet all I wanted was to leave. Far from enjoying my time on the ward, I felt trapped. The routine was much the same as it had previously been but the atmosphere wasn't nearly as nice. I wasn't very keen on city life either. Although there were some beautiful places around Birmingham, being somewhere else began to dominate my thoughts. It's hard to explain why. I suppose I was confused about what I wanted to do but one thing was for sure: I didn't want to stay in the unit.

I applied for several jobs and for the first time in my life, I didn't get them. I had been used to a prospective employer looking at my references and jumping at the chance to have me on board. Up until now, I had been spoilt for choice but this time it was different. One Matron actually told me off for not completing the course and told me to go back. I felt I really couldn't do it so I sought the advice of my church leaders and they encouraged me to stay as well! It wasn't the answer I wanted to hear but gradually I began to see that I was gaining something else by staying. Firstly, I had made an agreement and I should stick with it. Commitment is important to me. Secondly, I was gaining backbone and the ability to cope, no matter what the circumstance, became more important than my immediate happiness. I was also enjoying a totally different type of social life. I had the opportunity to go on mission with various groups and Saturday night at Hockley was fantastic. We gathered in a small rundown church hall, where the drip-fed oil heaters bounced on the floorboards as the meetings, always loud, crowded and eventful, went on until way past eleven o'clock. I loved it.

I had just made the decision to carry on and complete the course when, out of the blue, I had a phone call from Mrs Bancroft.

'Pamela, I am going abroad for the summer. We shall be there for six months. We're staying at a lovely place and I have rented a bungalow in the grounds. You can have your own car and plenty of free time. It's going to be wonderful! Do say you will come.'

As I stood in the phone booth, I had just come off night duty and I was dog tired. I watched the rain pouring down the window and I was cold and hungry. What a perfect solution. Sun, sand and sangria . . .

'Sorry,' I heard myself saying, 'but I'm staying here to complete my course. Have a lovely time, won't you.' I think I realised at that moment that it's not always having a bed of roses that makes us happy. I couldn't let this course beat me; I wanted to succeed more than I wanted a way out and a cushy life.

The hospital was famed for its human milk bank and part of my duties was to spend some time there making up the feeds. They ran it a bit like a space capsule. We had to scrub as if we were about to enter a theatre for surgery and we wore white gowns and masks. The feeds were measured out and put into bottles, which had been autoclaved and then sealed before getting them ready to send to the wards. Breast milk was a lifeline to some of the smallest babies. Their digestive system may not have been mature enough to cope with some of the milk substitutes and so without sounding too dramatic, having breast milk could have been a case of life or death. Any mum who had been on the unit was only too happy to supply the human milk bank with any spare milk she might have. Although she was paid a nominal sum of money, for most mums it was a way of paying back what had been done for her baby. For the mums who perhaps through no fault of their own didn't have enough milk for their babies, it must have seemed like the most generous of gifts.

Once we had taken the feeds to the unit, I put on my nurse's cloak and went with the district midwife to collect the milk from the mothers. We travelled all over Birmingham, collecting containers of expressed breast milk and each ounce donated was charted in a book. We took miniscule amounts from some mothers and large quantities from others. The hospital provided each mum with a hand pump and she was told to keep any expressed breast milk in the fridge. As soon as the milk was brought back to the milk bank, it was strained through muslin to remove any hairs or fluff from the mother's clothing. All the milk was put into special vats to be pasteurised in just the same way as the Milk Marketing Board pasteurised cow's milk from the farms. It all went in together but as we opened some of the bottles, the strong smell of spices filled the air.

'This comes from an Indian mother,' the Sister told me with a smile. 'Their babies get a subtle taste of curry in the breast milk, as that's what their mothers are eating.'

The pasteurisation took away the smell altogether and the milk was fine to use. Pasteurisation didn't take that long. The milk was heated to 133°F (56°C) for thirty minutes and then cooled rapidly to 50°F (10°C).

At the end of the month, the amounts contributed to the milk bank were all calculated and each mother was paid accordingly.

'One of my mums paid the deposit on her house with what she got for her breast milk,' Sister told me proudly, and when my eyebrows shot up, she added, 'she's had seven babies and is pregnant with her eighth.'

All the mothers donating breast milk had to be screened. Any mother who had Hepatitis B or antibodies to syphilis was not accepted and if their baby was ill at any time, or for that matter, the mum herself was unwell with a cold or something, she was told not to donate breast milk. Care was also taken to screen out anyone who smoked more than ten cigarettes a day or was taking regular drugs.

The midwives often told us stories about what happened out on the district. My friend Judy was called to a farm to deliver a baby. The labour was going along nicely and she and the mother were enjoying the experience. Every now and then, the farmer would crash into the kitchen and shout up the stairs. ''Ow's it going then?'

'Fine,' Judy called down the stairs. 'Mother and baby are doing very well.'

'Bairn ain't there then?' yelled the father.

'Not yet,' said Judy with a smile for the mother.

After about two hours, the farmer was getting exasperated. ''Ow much longer is thee goin' to be?'

Judy tut-tutted and frowned. 'We can't hurry these things,' she called downstairs. 'It shouldn't be long now.'

'Tell 'er to get a move on,' shouted the farmer irritably. 'I needs 'elp wi' milking!'

* * *

Another friend, Sally, was called to an Asian family. When she arrived there were three little girls huddled together in the kitchen and the father was pacing the floor. Upstairs, the mother was in tears.

'Please,' she said in her broken English, 'you make it a boy.'

'I'm afraid I can do nothing about that now,' Sally laughed. 'The die is already cast.'

The woman began to cry again. 'If the baby is another girl,' she sobbed, 'he will send me back to India.'

Sally felt terrible, but what could she do? She comforted the mother as best she could and prayed that everything would be all right. The baby was delivered just before midnight, a healthy child with a lusty cry and best of all, a boy! The mother immediately kissed Sally's hands. 'Thank you, thank you,' she gasped.

'No, really,' Sally protested, 'it was nothing to do with me.'

A little later the father came upstairs. Seeing his wife's tears, he expected the worst. His lips were set in an angry line as he walked to the crib and pulled back the covers. When he saw the baby was a boy he was elated. He kissed his wife and called his other children upstairs. They came in cautiously, but when their father's joy was obvious, they rushed to the crib to see their new baby brother. While Sally cleaned the mother up and washed the baby, the father went out into the neighbourhood. By the time Sally came downstairs, half the Asian men in Birmingham were crushed into the small sitting room. As she left, the father pushed something into her hand.

'You be sure to come next time,' he beamed. 'You are very good midwife.'

Outside in the street, Sally looked down at her hand. He'd given her fifteen pounds.

Mrs Dominic had a 'small for dates' baby. That was the term given to a baby who had gone to full time but when he had been born, he was obviously a lot smaller than he should have been.

The birth was normal but within hours, Mrs Dominic was as large as ever. The doctors discovered she had a cyst in the womb. The cyst had restricted the baby's growth and now that the baby and the placenta were gone, it had swelled to fill the whole space left behind. When she came to see her baby, one nurse who didn't realise who she was sent her away with, 'This is the ward for mothers who have already had their babies.'

With tears in her eyes, Mrs Dominic kissed her baby goodbye and went for surgery. Happily, she made a good recovery and her cyst was caused by an imbalance in her hormones.

Mrs Behari had been safely delivered of a baby girl but she couldn't bond with her. Nurse Evelyn Ross, a tall willowy Jamaican girl, and I were tidying the baby's room. We looked into the baby's cot and we both cooed. 'Isn't she lovely?' I said.

'Look at all that beautiful hair,' Evelyn smiled. 'She's gorgeous.'

Mrs Behari looked up sharply. 'You like?' she said to Evelyn. 'You take!'

We made a hasty retreat. I knew enough about her circumstances to know that she and her husband already had two girls and they had desperately wanted a boy. Mrs Behari hadn't had a single visitor since she'd come in and it was highly likely that she would be beaten when she got home with the baby. Her husband would blame her for having a girl and say she was not a good wife. As Evelyn and I walked past the window on our way to the nurses' home, Mrs Behari banged on the glass.

'You come back for baby!'

Baby Davies was born by caesarean section. He was perfect from the eyes down but the top of his head had not been formed properly. He had a lusty cry and was a hungry baby; he weighed nearly eight pounds. The mother was still in recovery when Baby Davies was brought to the nursery. He was put into isolation and his father came to see him shortly afterwards. The doctors told him Baby Davies could not possibly survive. There was nothing they could do to help him and the father should prepare himself for the worst. Sister had put a towel over the top of the baby's head to spare his father's feelings but the poor man wept when he saw his son.

Things have changed a lot since the 1970s. Back then people made decisions which in this day and age would be unthinkable. 'If you want your wife to have more children,' the doctor advised, 'don't let her see this one. It will put her off totally and she will never want another baby.'

'How long will my son survive?' a distraught Mr Davies asked.

'It's not an exact science,' said the doctor shaking his head, 'but I would say a few hours at the most.'

Baby Davies' mother would be 'out of it' for the rest of the day anyway, so Mr Davies agreed to do what the doctor advised. The truly awful thing was, Baby Davies lived for another three weeks. His father came to see him regularly but when she finally woke up from the operation, the nursing staff told his wife the baby didn't survive the birth. The poor man was on the horns of a dilemma.

'I have never lied to my wife in my life,' he wept, 'but how can I tell her now? She will hate me if I do, and she will hate me even more if she ever finds out what I've done.'

My heart went out to him. It never should have happened. Baby Davies died peacefully but whether or not his mother ever knew that he had lived for three whole weeks, I couldn't say.

On a much happier note, it was always a bit of an occasion when a baby went home for the first time. Sometimes other members of the family turned up on the ward. I remember one occasion when a family came with Mum to take the baby home. Everyone was looking at the baby as she was being dressed and telling the mum how beautiful she was. Fearing her older sister might be feeling left out, her grandfather gave her a side hug and said, 'And *you're* absolutely gorgeous.'

'No, I am not,' said the big sister indignantly. 'I'm Susan Victoria Sewell!'

When I was in the children's nursery doing my training, I'd had to do child observations. Here in the premature baby unit, I had to do the same thing, but this time to observe a baby. I was given Baby Nye. Admitted to the unit following a normal delivery, she was a first baby and the labour was quite quick, lasting only four hours and eighteen minutes.

I took Baby Nye's temperature and it was 95°F (35°C). She felt cold and was cyanosed (blue) all over. When the Sister in charge saw the baby she told me to apply oxygen via a face mask. Three minutes was all it took to have a good effect. She was nursed naked apart from a nappy in an incubator, with the oxygen flowing at five litres. Once I had weighed her and cleaned her up, I put a heat shield over her to help raise her temperature. She weighed four pounds, eleven ounces and her heartbeat was one hundred and forty beats per minute. Her dextrostix was forty-five milligrams per cent. I was supervised as I put a feeding tube in her stomach and then Sister gave her a stomach wash out. She obtained three millilitres of thick mucus; she left ten millilitres of dextrose, ten per cent, down the baby's stomach.

The doctor examined the baby and concluded that Baby Nye was about thirty-four weeks' gestation and she was to be fed by her weight so I worked out what she was to have. The next day, her dextrostix remained steady but Baby Nye was 'jittery'. That meant that her arms and legs shook involuntarily with short, jerky movements. She took her feeds half by bottle but the rest down the nasogastric tube.

That night, the night staff reported that Baby Nye appeared to have a slight fissure (hole) in the anal margin but the doctor ordered no special treatment. She had a lumber puncture and a blood test but there were no abnormalities except that her calcium levels were a bit low. She was prescribed calcium chloride, one hundred milligrams every six hours, to be mixed in with her feeds. Her overall improvement was already showing less than twenty-four hours later. When she was weighed the next day, Baby Nye had lost eight ounces since birth, which didn't give any cause for concern because all babies lose weight to begin with. They usually start to gain weight by the sixth day and any weight loss after that would be worrying. She was moved from the unit into the small, hot nursery, where the temperature was kept at 80°F (27°C) and she continued to be both bottle and tube fed, but by her seventh day, Baby Nye had lost even more weight. She was now only four pounds but everyone was confident that she would thrive because she was feeding well. Her parents came and asked a lot of questions. I observed that they loved their baby very much and this was plainly a very difficult time for them.

However, five days later the baby was ill and the doctor was called. He prescribed ephedrine nasal drops for her nose because she was snuffly, although her chest was clear. He gave the baby a thorough examination and ordered an abdominal X-ray because her abdomen was distended. Her condition was giving rise to some concern and so she was put on penicillin and kanamycin. Her mother came with the grandmother because the husband was abroad, visiting a sick relative. The priest accompanied them and because there was some concern about her condition, Baby Nye was christened Anita.

Now back in the incubator, happily Anita's condition slowly improved overnight. She was kept on three hourly observations and once she had passed a good stool, her abdomen was not nearly as distended. The staff were asked to collect her urine for twenty-four hours, (not that easy for a female!) and now she was passing loose stools.

By the beginning of May, Anita was taken off the antibiotics after she had had a full dose of seven days. I went off duty for four days and when I got back, she was upstairs in the nursery where we put the more healthy babies. She was crying lustily for her feeds and I noticed straight away that she had at last put on weight. She weighed five pounds, two ounces and both her parents came to see her. Six days later, Mrs Nye came to stay in the unit to get used to handling her baby. She stayed in the unit for two nights. When she went home, Anita Nye looked very pretty in her pink and white outfit. Her clothes had been lovingly handmade. Her discharge weight was five pounds, twelve ounces and her mother was asked to bring her back to the baby clinic in a month's time for a check-up.

The story of Anita Nye was one of the many happy endings, or should I say beginnings, we gave to the babies in the nursery. It wasn't hard to let them go when they were healthy and obviously much loved. And even if you weren't too sure about a baby's home conditions, you knew there were other agencies around to keep an eye on them. Besides, there was always the next baby to care for or giving cause for concern. The turnover was so quick there was no time to form any lasting bonds.

Chapter 20

I had fallen into the pattern of spending some of my days off with my old friend Evie Perryer. She was now married and had children of her own. They were delightful children and I loved them to bits. Working with small babies meant that I missed the funny little quips children come out with. Staying with Evie's children reminded me of them and they gave me some wonderful memories. We were in the kitchen one day when her little girl came in, carrying the plate with an apple her mother had just given her. She was about three or four at the time and her little face was screwed up in disgust. 'Mummy,' she announced, 'This apple is really shark!'

We'd already been chuckling over something Evie's little boy had said. He had been to Sunday School and was singing a chorus as he was playing with his farm animals. The actual words were, 'Let's all get together in communion sweet, walk, walk in the light . . .' When children don't understand something, they transpose words that they do understand, and so we heard him belting out, 'Let's all get together in a chewing-gum sweet . . .'

One time when I was staying with Evie, she introduced me to an RAF officer, who sometimes came to spend his off duty in their home. Evie and her husband had an open house and people like me (and Ben too) enjoyed their company and a small share in family life. Ben invited me, just as a friend, to go with him to a meeting in London, which was organised by a Soldiers,

Sailors and Airmen's Christian Fellowship. We were to have a meal in a London hotel, followed by a talk in one of the large meeting rooms given by Colonel Dobbie, who had been the Governor of Malta during the siege of 1940–42. Under his leadership, the whole island had been awarded the George Cross for their bravery in resisting the enemy. I thought he'd be a very interesting person to listen to because not only had he been a part of something remarkable in Malta during the Second World War but as a young staff officer on 11 November 1918, it was he who signed the order at Advanced GHQ to the effect that all troops on the Western Front should cease hostilities at 11 a.m. That marked the official end of the First World War and in doing so, he was always quoted as saying, 'I stopped the beastly thing!'

In the hotel, we mingled with some of the elite of the British Armed Forces and Ben renewed acquaintances with old friends, including one who was dressed in army uniform. We were still eating our meal, but his friend was on the way out of the dining room.

'I say, Tommy,' said Ben. 'What suite are we in this year?'

The army chap looked a little confused and then he said, 'I don't know, old boy. Had apple pie and ice-cream myself.'

I nearly choked but neither of them seemed to see how funny it was. When we got back to Evie's and I told them everything that had happened, including the 'apple pie' incident, she and her husband fell about laughing while Ben took a deep breath. 'Well, of course,' he said stiffly, and clearly not seeing the joke at all, 'he's Army.' And we all fell apart again.

Poor Ben, we teased him mercilessly and yet he was always a really good friend. He once showed Evie the menu he had in the officers' dining room on his base. She gasped at the high-class cuisine, each course complete with its own wine. We were more used to eating mince and mash with peas. The next time we all sat down for a meal, Evie's husband reprimanded her for not putting the napkins on the table. She gave him a withering look which said, 'you know we don't have any napkins', but he rushed off to the bathroom and came back with the toilet roll. The three of us tore off a piece each and lay it on our laps as if this was what we always did. This time Ben joined in the joke and we laughed our way through the meal.

Our old friend Ros had gone to work in a nursery in Bermuda and a couple of times, Ben hitched a lift with one of his RAF mates, going all that way to see her and take her out for a meal. Wow, how cool was that?

If I had thought Christmas 1963 had been miserable, when Matron Dickenson had been difficult and two members of staff had walked out, Christmas 1971 came a close second. I was on night duty, which I never enjoyed, so I missed out on a lot of the socialising that went on around that time. The night sister must have been a pupil in the same Queen of Mean charm-school Matron Dickenson went to. When the day staff gave us the report they said, 'We've put all the Christmas stuff upstairs in Room Six. There are mince pies and Christmas cake and someone has given us wine and there's a big tin of sweets. Help yourselves to whatever you want.' We all licked our lips and looked forward to our meal breaks but Sister had other ideas. As soon as the day staff left, she locked the room and put the key in her pocket. 'I don't want you girls sloping off all the time,' she announced. 'We'll open up once we've done all the feeds.'

The canteen was closed for the holiday and she made sure we had plenty to do all night so nobody had a break at all. We were starving hungry and we'd resorted to cupping water in our hands to drink because we were so thirsty. When the day staff came back and we waited for the report to finish, she feigned surprise as she put her hand in her pocket. 'Oh dearie me! We never went in for any Christmas fare, did we girls? What a shame!'

Of course by that time we were too tired to want to eat mince pies. All we could think about was getting our weary bodies to bed. It's not very nice of me but I think if I had had a magic wand, I would have turned her into the Christmas turkey.

I began having difficulties on the ward with Sister Booker, the sister in charge. She was a hard taskmaster but I grew to respect her, and she me. The greatest compliment I ever had in that place was one I overheard accidentally. We had just had a very sick premature baby admitted to the ward. He weighed less than a bag of sugar and had little chance of survival. The doctor had just finished doing a thorough examination when I walked into the ward to put some clean nappies in the cupboard. The cupboard was round a corner and the two of them hadn't seen me come in. As I knelt to pack the nappies away, I heard the doctor say, 'I want this baby on fifteen-minute observations. I want someone who will do it for the next two hours without fail.'

'I'll get Nurse Cox,' said Sister Booker, 'She's one of my most trusted nurses.'

Wow! I felt a mile high and somehow all the angst and frustration of the past year had been worth it for that one moment.

I never did like it in that place but at last the date of my leaving was moving slowly closer. I had almost completed the course and the final exam was looming large. With about a week to go, I was in the ward with a baby, giving her a cuddle when someone came in to leave her some clean gowns. She hesitated by the door. 'You'll be really sad to leave here, won't you?' she said sympathetically.

I stared in disbelief. 'Why do you say that?'

'Because you're always singing,' she said, closing the door.

I thought a lot about that. I wasn't even aware that I was singing all the time but I guess it helped me to think about something else rather than my feelings. I still wanted to go early, but by staying the course, I had learned more than I bargained for. I had learned to rise above my circumstances and get on with it, but it was more than that. I had come to a place where I was at peace with myself and so long as I had that, I could survive anything.

When I left Birmingham, I left behind some good friends, with whom I still keep in touch, and I left a much stronger person. I had my qualification and I had gained the respect of my tutors and Sister Booker, but now I wanted a change. I took a complete break from looking after children for eighteen months, first going to a Bible college and then to a Christian holiday conference centre, where I took up housekeeping duties and was a general dogsbody. Everything changed when a young man called David Weaver came for a holiday. He was handsome and he had a ready smile. We liked each other straight away and went out together on my day off. In the evening, he spent a good deal of his holiday 'hanging around' the coffee bar where I was working. When he went back home, we wrote to each other several times a week and spent hours on the telephone. I had fallen hopelessly in love! Eventually I moved to Worthing so that we could be together and that was a cue to apply for another post working with children. When I came back to child care, it was in a totally different set up.

My new post was in a private day nursery. The owner euphemistically called it a nursery school but we had no nursery teacher and no teaching area. There were three rooms with a total of thirty children in each room. They weren't always there all the time: some did mornings only, some did afternoons only and a few were there all day. The nursery had been the lifelong dream of the owner. It had been purpose-built and was open from 8.30 a.m. until 6 p.m. I was in charge of the middle room. I started in November 1973 and by January 1974, David and I had just got engaged and were looking for somewhere to live. The pay was terrible. I only earned fourteen pounds, fifty pence a week and with stoppages, I took home eleven pounds, eighty pence. That sort of money wouldn't even cover the rent on a flat. We found a furnished flat for thirteen pounds a week but I still had to find the train fare to get to the nursery. David's wage was only twenty-nine pounds a week; he was a delivery driver, so things were going to be tough. The trouble was, despite the money, I loved it in the nursery.

The fees were low in comparison to today's childcare costs. Full time was eleven pounds, fifty pence per week, a morning and lunch was five pounds, twenty pence and an afternoon and tea was also five pounds, twenty pence. Sometimes the children would have something for lunch that they weren't used to at home.

'What did you have for dinner?' I heard one child's mother ask when she came to collect her.

'Dicky spot,' came the reply.

Her mother shot me a concerned look. 'Spotted Dick,' I replied with a grin.

Then there was the other time when I saw Gregory poking his piece of lettuce with a fork.

'Come on, Gregory,' I said. 'Eat up your salad.'

'I don't like salad,' he said dourly. 'I only like beef burglars.'

Lunch wasn't the only meal when the children encountered something they weren't used to. 'What did you have for tea today?' one mum asked as she put her child's coat on.

'Black sandwiches,' said the child.

Once more I grinned. 'They were Marmite,' I said.

The owner cut a few corners as far as the meals went because a standard catering tin of luncheon meat was cut up so small, it fed the whole nursery AND the staff. Potato came in a large container. There was one ice-cream scoop for each child and two for the staff and each of us had a dessertspoonful of peas. Yes, I was hungry, but I got deliciously thin in preparation for my wedding!

The mid-morning break was always taken with the children,

as was the afternoon tea break. We had one biscuit each. The staff had a lunch hour but we weren't paid for that.

My housing problem was solved about three weeks before I got married. My employer's husband was a local builder and she told me to go to his offices. I was offered a one-bedroom unfurnished flat within walking distance of the nursery at the princely sum of five pounds a week. The offer was amazingly generous . . . or was it? I worked for another three years in the nursery at the same fourteen pounds a week. When I came back from my honeymoon, I was told that because I had only worked in the nursery for six months, I wasn't entitled to the two weeks I had just had as paid holiday. That meant I had to take it as unpaid leave. Things were very tight that month! When I pointed out that if this was the case, I should be able to have two weeks' holiday in November, I was told I could do that but it would be classed as my holiday for the following year. When I finally took two weeks' holiday in the summer of 1975, it was the first paid leave I had had since I joined the nursery in 1973!

I wasn't the only one to feel the pinch. The girl in room three, Helen, used to buy things out of her own pocket for the nursery. She bought some toys and puppets to go with the books we read with the children at the end of the day. After a good few months, the bookcase looked very impressive. One day the owner came in and saw them.

'These are lovely,' she said. 'Who bought them?'

'I did,' said Helen.

'Umm,' said the owner thoughtfully. 'I'm obviously paying you too much.'

We more or less did what we wanted in the room in which we had responsibility, and that was the beauty of it. I split the day up into sections and began with free play in the room. After drinks time, we went outside and the children enjoyed playing on the bigger toys in the nursery garden. We used to meet up with the children from the other two rooms so they had plenty to do and lots of other children to play with. We came back just before lunch and after we'd taken everybody to the toilet, we ate a lunch with the children. We took an hour break after lunch and made the children sleep on stretchers for an hour, with one girl looking after them. One day when I was helping to get the children up again after their rest, Robert put his hand over his trousers. 'Oh,' he said blushing a deep red, 'my botty just burped.'

During the afternoon, we would have another play session with different toys so that the children didn't get bored with playing with the same things. People donated us toys so we had a great many lovely things. One man from my church used to work for the GPO (General Post Office, which was the name of the Royal Mail back then). During some restructuring he got hold of some obsolete telephones. The nursery had two Bakelite phones in each room. The children loved playing with them and I wish I still had them – they'd be worth a small fortune now! After tea time, someone took the children into the staff room for that story just mentioned while we cleared up the rooms. By the time the last of the children had gone, we had cleaned the classrooms and put everything away. It was hard work but we were a good group of girls and we enjoyed ourselves.

My room had a book corner. There were a couple of easy chairs so that the children could sit comfortably as they read a book of their choice. There was also a Wendy house, which was well furnished with toys. The nursery guinea-pig, oddly named Quackers, lived in my room while room one had the fish and room three looked after a rabbit. At Christmas time, we would create a nativity tableau and invite all the mums to come. The children always rehearsed very well and knew their parts. They didn't have to learn any lines but the children could recognise when it was their turn to 'go on stage'. The owner always wanted her little bit of glory and every year she would turn up just before it started and stuff a sweet in everybody's mouth as they walked into the room. The *Worthing Herald* sent their photographer and he would get them to wave at the end but somehow Joseph complaining that the toffee in his mouth was stuck on his teeth didn't do it for me. Never mind, we all enjoyed the experience.

It's funny how the average nativity play sticks in the memory not for its brilliance but the faux pas that usually accompanies it. There was that tender moment when Mary laid baby Jesus in the manger and a loud clatter rattled along the wooden floor. It was followed by an even louder wail, 'Jesus' arm has fallen off!'

Then there was the time when the innkeeper, having been given instructions to shake his head and put his hand up to refuse entry, was so moved to hear that Mary needed help that he took her arm and said, 'Don't cry, you can have my bed if you like.'

Another year, the Angel Gabriel decided to settle an old score with one of the Wise Men on stage. Give him his due, the wise man gave as good as he got, but until we managed to break it up, a wailing angel and a screaming Wise Man had rather spoiled the heavenly image we were trying to recreate.

Then there was the time another angel who was part of the 'heavenly host' arrived with her dress tucked in her knickers. And there was the angel who, obviously feeling tired after a long rehearsal, lay down in the crib, put her thumb in her mouth and closed her eyes. Deaf to my frantic off-stage whispers, she slept throughout the whole performance. There were no video cameras to catch the scene but they will be indelibly marked in my memory until the day I die.

In the final run-up to Christmas, the children had a Christmas party. We had jelly and cakes and played party games. Their present from the nursery was small (usually a few sweets) but gratefully received. Whenever a birthday came along, we would celebrate it by giving the child a birthday card and letting them stand in the middle of a circle while we all sang 'Happy Birthday'.

I had a wind-up cake decoration which had been in my family for years (and still is). I used to bring it in and the birthday boy or girl was allowed to wind it up. It played 'Happy Birthday' as it revolved and each child was so excited when it was their turn to turn the key. We also had a pretend birthday cake made out of a sweet tin and covered in paper to look like icing. I would put the appropriate number of candles in the holders on the cake and the child was allowed to blow it out after we'd all sung. Such simple pleasures but the children thought it was wonderful.

We all put so much extra into everything we did. The girl in charge of room three wasn't the only one to use her hard-earned money for the children. We would buy craft materials and we spent time painting the windows with cartoon characters and lining the walls with coloured paper to put the children's pictures on. We often did a 'show' and then invited the children from the other two rooms to come and watch, and they would do the same for us.

Once a year, a professional photographer would come to the nursery and we'd spend the morning or afternoon having their pictures taken. They were expensive but most of the mums bought their child's first 'official' photograph. We would also arrange for younger siblings to come in as well to have their pictures taken with big brother or sister. The older siblings would have been at school. The only time I remember a mum refusing to buy a photograph was when Thomas had his picture taken. The day the photographer arrived it was his first day at school and he was missing his mum. I still have the picture she refused. Poor Thomas is staring down the lens of the camera with two huge pools of unshed tears in his eyes and an obviously quivering chin.

The children came from ordinary homes and most of them were happy and well looked after. Their mums either worked full or part time and the nursery met their requirements for childcare.

Having said that, we did have a few children who were not so well looked after. Joshua's parents were getting an acrimonious separation. One evening just as we were locking up, they both came to the nursery in separate cars and argued over who should take him home. I was in the office with the woman in overall charge of the nursery, Mrs Lucas, when I saw the pair of them, one holding Joshua's feet and the other his body, begin a tussle in the car park. I was partially hidden behind a curtain, but Mrs Lucas ducked down on the floor and pulled the telephone with her. While I was giving a running commentary, she was phoning the police. They arrived very quickly and persuaded the warring parents to put Joshua in one of the cars. They didn't intervene in the fight but stood beside them as they argued about who was taking their son home. Fortunately, Joshua seemed to think the tussle was a bit of a game. He certainly wasn't afraid and eventually the matter was settled and everyone went away.

Jenny and Nigel had a really beautiful mother. She had a lovely personality and was glamorous as well, with a perfect figure, blonde hair, blue eyes and immaculate make-up. The family were quite well off because she was always beautifully dressed and she drove a flashy red sports car. Sometimes her sister would turn up to collect the children from the nursery. The sister could have been a twin. She was certainly as blonde and glamorous as Jenny and Nigel's mother. One Monday morning, the sister came in to tell us that Jenny and Nigel might be a bit upset.

'My sister was killed in a car crash on Saturday,' she told us, her voice thick with emotion. 'We're not sure what's going to happen yet, but until we do, we want Jenny and Nigel to have as normal a life as possible.'

We were deeply shocked. It didn't mean much to the children, probably because they didn't really understand. They would say, 'Mummy's gone to be with Jesus,' in a voice that sounded like she'd gone to the shops, but we did our best to keep things as low key as possible, even though we spent most of the day fighting back the tears. Soon after, the children left the nursery to go and live with their auntie.

When Princess Anne married her husband, Captain Mark Phillips, in 1973, there was a lot of talk about weddings in the nursery. David and I married in 1974 and that had the children making me wedding pictures and buying me wedding presents, so it came as no surprise when in the following year, we had a 'wedding of the year' in the nursery. All the children were 'guests' when little Ellie and Bradley got 'married'. We had a trendy vicar with long hair (a wig) and a dog collar, and two of the children held a bower aloft as the bride and groom kissed. At first we just did it 'in house' but the children didn't stop talking about it so we did it again for the mums. There wasn't a dry eye in the place. I took the camera to work and used up the whole film taking photographs. We pinned them on the noticeboard and several mums ordered copies. One of the girls was teasing the nursery bridegroom. 'Oooh, you looked so handsome,' she said. 'When you're all grown up, perhaps you would marry me?'

'When I'm all grown up,' said four-year-old Bradley sagely, 'you'll be dead.'

The nursery was quite well stocked with toys. We were sometimes donated 'old' toys but we had a small budget and every year we were allowed to buy something new for each room. By careful planning we were able to keep up-to-date and to have plenty of variation. Each room had its own painting easels, and we had an old baby bath on its own stand, which was filled with silver sand. Sometimes the children would play with the sand when it was dry and at other times we would make it quite wet. The toys in the sand tray when it was dry were entirely different to those when it was wet. The children would stand at the easels to paint, using large brushes and pots with individual colours. The pots had lids on them and the brush fitted into a hole in the lid. That prevented us from ending up with mud-brown paint. A popular variation for painting was doing bubble pictures. We would colour some water with food colouring in a shallow tray and give the children a straw. Once they had mastered blowing rather than sucking the straw, bubbles would form and if we put a sheet of paper lightly on the top, you got a pretty picture. We also cut up potatoes and did potato cuts. We made hand prints and on a few days when we didn't mind all the hard work, we would do foot prints with the children. How they loved the mess!

Less messy play would have been using playdough. We made our own, which was much cheaper than the shop-bought variety and could be kept in the fridge. The recipe was two cups of flour, two cups of warm water, one cup of salt, two tablespoons of vegetable oil and one tablespoon of cream of tartar. We mixed all the ingredients together over a low heat. When it was ready, we would divide it and use food colouring to colour it. The cream of tartar was a preservative and we kept it fresh by keeping it in an airtight tin. Pastry dough made a good alternative but even though we put plenty of salt in it, that didn't last so long because after a while it began to smell horrible.

If the cook was feeling generous, she would make up a little water icing and we would decorate rich tea biscuits. The children generally had one at their break time and took another home. If we were doing this sort of thing, we generally had to supply our own ingredients. One afternoon, I bought a loaf of bread and the children in my room made sandwiches. There was one little girl called Sally, who was very small and rather thin. When we had finished making the sandwiches, we had enough for everyone to eat one at break time. I noticed that Sally couldn't get her sandwich in her mouth quick enough. She never stayed for lunch but she did seem to be extremely hungry. I gave her my sandwich as well and then discussed the matter with Mrs Lucas and we alerted Social Services. It turned out that Sally's mother was suffering from a serious illness and was unable to care for her properly. Sally and her older sister were put in the care of foster parents until her mother was better able to cope.

We had no piano but singing was very much a part of our routine. We taught the children finger play and nursery rhymes. Sometimes we would get the percussion instruments out as well and have a good old sing-song. I loved these times together and so did the children. They were far more confident than the residential nursery children and enjoyed being in nursery.

One child who came to be in my room had bright ginger curls. As he and his mother walked into the room, she told me his name was See-Ann. Mrs Lucas frowned and looked at the name on the admission paper. The child's name was indeed Sean but of course it's pronounced 'Shaun'.

'What a nice name,' Mrs Lucas remarked.

'Yeah,' said the mum, 'I read it in the paper.'

I stayed in the day nursery until I was pregnant with my first child. The week before I left, dear old Quackers the guinea pig died. When I buried him in the grounds, well away from where the children played, I was crying so much I could hardly see what I was doing. It wasn't just the size of my bump getting in the way, but that little creature had meant a lot to me. The girls teased me a bit, saying he must have known I was going. He was old and in truth, although I didn't wish him dead, I hated the thought that the next girl might not love him as I had done or look after him so well. He had come home with me every Christmas and Easter since I'd been there. Time moves on, and I was entering uncharted waters. I had been looking after other people's children all my life and now it was time to have one of my own. I may have said goodbye to nursery life but I still haven't said goodbye to working with children. As I brought up my girls, I was a child minder and then a playgroup leader and now I look after my grandchildren. Children never fail to make me laugh, and we have such fun together. I can only hope that I have given some of them half the pleasure they have given me.

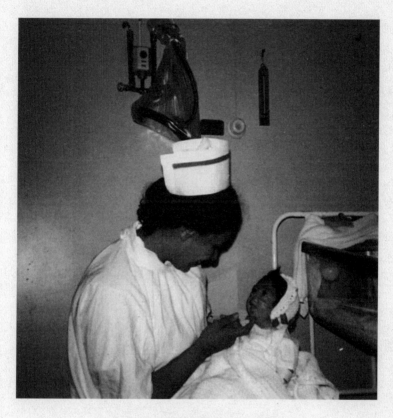

A photo of Pam during her time
working with premature babies.

Read on for an exclusive short story from Pam Weaver and the first chapter of her bestselling novel, *Better Days Will Come.*

Son of Pale Face

There is a nail-biting moment when we check the height restriction but everybody passes with flying colours. While I grab their backpacks and coats, Christopher, Thomas and Liam, their faces bright with excitement, join the end of the queue waiting to go on The Corkscrew.

'Are you sure about this?' I ask Rob.

Avoiding my eye, he gives me a brief nod. 'You go. We'll be fine.'

Oh joy . . . that means I can do what I'm desperate to do. I stagger to the nearby café and plonk myself down at a table. In my condition, even though it's only a matter of weeks, taking a ride on The Corkscrew doesn't seem like a good idea. I'm so glad of the chance to sit down.

Things are turning out really well today and yet just a few short months ago we were in crisis. It had come to a head one Saturday after the boys came back from their various club activities. We'd found a brand new toy car on the hall table. Rob and I had never seen it before and whoever had been playing with it had also scratched the top of the table, doing some very expensive damage.

Christopher and Thomas looked a bit blank. 'It's nothing to do with me!' Liam shrieked.

Rob's expression said it all. We all knew Liam was lying. I looked at him helplessly.

'Honest, Mum,' he said, digging himself in deeper. 'It's the first time I've ever seen that car.' He picked it up. 'It's very nice, isn't it?' he went on in a silly voice. 'I like the colour too. I wonder who could have put it there. Where have you come from, little car?'

Rob put his hands on his own two sons' shoulders and led them towards the patio doors. 'Come on, boys,' he said quietly, 'Let's leave them to it.'

'But it wasn't me,' Liam cried after them. 'Why do I always get the blame for everything?'

'Oh, Liam . . .' I began.

'And I don't need you here, Mum.' He stared at me, his eyes bulging, his cheeks aflame.

I was at a complete loss as to what to say. He certainly looked guilty, but he was so adamant.

'Darling,' I began again, but he just turned on his heel and ran up the stairs.

This wasn't the first time something like that had happened. A couple of weeks before, someone had 'borrowed' Christopher's bike without asking. When it reappeared, the mudguard was buckled and it had a flat tyre. All three of the boys had a terrible fight, so bad that Rob had to separate them. When the inquest began, I could vouch for the fact that Thomas had been upstairs all afternoon. But even though he had the same telltale coloured mud on his trousers, Liam was adamant that he was not responsible for taking the bike.

Later, as I began to add up the other 'little incidents' my stomach churned. The shoe mark on the side of Rob's car where a small foot had kicked the bodywork; the pieces Thomas couldn't find when he was making his latest model aeroplane . . . Liam's behaviour was turning our peaceful home into a war zone.

Of course we'd always known it wasn't going to be easy to stitch people from two single families into one, but Rob's two boys had adjusted to the change a lot more easily than my son.

From my seat in the café, I can watch them unobserved. The boys are dancing with excitement but Rob has the air of a lamb being led to the slaughter. I smile to myself. My big tough guy is looking a bit unsure. They've been waiting about twenty minutes but the queue is still quite long. Well, there's still time to duck out. I chew my lip thoughtfully and wonder if I should say something, but then the waitress comes and I order a coffee.

When we'd first got together, Rob and I came to an agreement. We decided to work together as a family but we would leave the serious discipline of our own children to each other. He would do anything for his boys, a loving father but strict, a lot more strict than I am with Liam. I was glad of the lines of demarcation and the system had worked well . . . until that Saturday afternoon. After the incident with the toy car, it didn't take a rocket scientist to know that my son was struggling.

Liam calls over the great divide and I look up. Some people near the front of the queue have dropped out. It looks as if one child needs the toilet and the rest of the family, although pretty annoyed, are going with him. Now my family are six people closer to the front. Liam gives me the thumbs up and I wave back.

I had hoped my sister might tell me what to do. After Paul died, we got into the habit of getting together once a month for lunch. We met a couple of days after that Saturday and Lindsay must have seen from my expression that I had something on my mind.

'So you're absolutely sure it was Liam who took the toy car?' she said when I told her what had happened.

I nodded sadly. 'Afraid so. When we tackled Christopher and Thomas, they seemed totally surprised.'

'They could have been lying.'

I shook my head. 'I'm getting to know how they look when they're guilty, Lindsay,' I said. 'Christopher always goes bright red and Thomas can't look you in the eye when he's up to something. Liam denied it but he put on that silly cartoon voice, the one he always uses when he knows he's done something wrong. I'm afraid as far as I'm concerned, that gave the game away right away.'

Lindsay stabbed her jacket potato and the prawn mayonnaise oozed all over the plate. 'So, what happened when you tackled Liam about it?'

'He just shouted at me.'

I couldn't bring myself to tell her the details, how he'd lashed out at me, even hitting me in his anger. 'Go away Mum. I don't want you here. I hate you . . .' Then bursting into tears, he'd slammed the door to his room leaving me feeling like a whipped dog.

Lindsay shrugged sympathetically. 'I don't know what to say.'

I'm still miles away as the waitress brings my coffee to the table but then I hear Liam shout again and a car comes sliding towards the platform. The boys are next. I watch them all climbing in, Christopher and Thomas in front, Rob and Liam behind. We all grin at each other and wave as the ride begins. They look so good together. Happy families? To a degree, but one part of this body feels out of joint.

When Liam's father was killed, I genuinely wished my life could end. It was only my curly-haired two-year-old who kept me sane. He didn't understand why his daddy wasn't there anymore. He'd cling to me, needing me, frantic if I was away from him for too long. His need for me was what kept me going all through those first awful months. That, and the need to fight my own corner.

Before his car accident, Paul had only just set up the business, buying and selling antiques. The family had urged me to sell it after he died, saying the money would set me up nicely, but somehow or other I couldn't do it. It felt too much like being disloyal.

Lindsay's husband had been very insistent. 'But you don't know anything about antiques,' he'd said crossly. 'With all due respect, you only have to make one disaster and everything will go down the tubes.'

I was furious at the time, but it gave me great pleasure to see the expression on his face when I thanked him for saying it a couple of years later.

'Your comment was just the spur I needed,' I'd said sweetly.

Absolute Antiques didn't exactly keep us in clover but it did give us a decent living. It gave me an unexpected bonus too. I'd honestly never thought I'd find love again. Rob worked for one of the local auctioneers. We met through work but we soon discovered that we had an awful lot more in common than a love of antiques. He'd been left to bring up his two sons alone after his wife had died. The previous two years had been a terrible time for him but he'd nursed her until it was no longer possible for him to cope alone. Poor Rob. Life is so unfair at times and cancer is such a filthy disease. One thing I do know, he'd go through hell or high water for his kids.

In the beginning we just used to pour out our troubles to each other but after a while we discovered that before we had married our respective partners, we had both enjoyed amateur dramatics. We joined the local club and began the long haul back into life after bereavement. It was great that our boys got on so well too. Christopher was two years older than Thomas and Liam but it didn't seem to matter. So six years after Paul died and three after Sarah had gone, Rob and I married. Despite my family's dire predictions, everything was working out very well. Apart from the problem with Liam, that is.

'You've got to be a lot more firm with him,' my mother had said, after he'd kicked down the flowers in her border.

'Liam is having a hard time right now,' I said, anxious to give him the benefit of the doubt.

'For heaven's sake!' my mother said crossly. 'We're all having a hard time. He's got to learn he can't go about pinching other people's stuff and messing up gardens just because he's feeling miserable.'

As I sip my coffee, I reflect that she's probably right. Perhaps I should be tougher with him.

The Corkscrew is gathering momentum. Can you believe the speed of that thing? It clatters along at what seems like 150 miles per hour. Everybody's screaming and although I know where they are, I can't make out their faces. Just as well, perhaps. If any of them hate it, there's no way I can get them to stop the ride anyway. I put my cup down and go back to my thoughts.

Saturdays were always something of a juggling act and that particular Saturday was even more frenetic than most. Christopher was captain of the school cricket team and had an all-day match. Thomas' model aircraft club had a show in the morning. At the same time, Liam had yet another swimming lesson but despite his best efforts, he still hadn't made a lot of progress.

Before we went to the cricket match to meet up with Rob and the boys, I took Liam to Badger's Antiquarian Books. I wanted to chat with the owner about an assignment of books I'd just bought. As we came out of the shop, Liam showed me a book on marine wildlife he'd bought with his pocket money. 'One day,' he said proudly, 'I'm going to see the Great Barrier Reef first hand.'

I laughed. 'You'll have to master your swimming first,' I blurted out in classic 'foot in mouth' mode.

'OK, Mum. Then I'll just look at the pictures.'

When I saw his angry glare that's when it hit me, so while the boys were altogether in the pavilion enjoying a spot of lunch, I pulled Rob to one side.

'I think perhaps Liam is feeling left out because your boys are so good at everything.'

He looked at me thoughtfully. 'You could be right, I suppose, but what can we do about it?'

I sighed helplessly. He put his arms around me and drew me close. 'Things will settle down soon, darling. It'll be alright.'

'I hope so,' I said with little conviction that it would.

By late Saturday afternoon, his boys were on top form. Christopher's team had beaten the county champions by eleven runs and Thomas was telling us how fantastic it was to get his prototype model aircraft airborne. Liam was very quiet.

On the way home, we stopped for a pizza but when we got back indoors, I couldn't find the pizza cutter anywhere. Everybody helped me to turn the drawers upside down but it was hopeless.

'Perhaps,' said Christopher looking straight at Liam, 'somebody has pinched it.'

'Yeah,' Thomas agreed.

There was an embarrassing silence and Liam went beetroot.

'That's enough,' Rob said shortly.

I reached out to touch my son but he dodged my hand and thundered up the stairs. I was going to follow him but Rob said quietly, 'Leave him, darling. Give him a bit of time to lick his wounds.'

The rest of us sat at the table and Christopher surprised me by saying, 'I didn't mean anything by it, Mum. I was just messing about.'

'He didn't mean anything,' Thomas echoed.

The boys, subdued, waited while Rob hacked the pizza with the bread knife but nobody felt much like eating. After twenty minutes of chewing what felt like cardboard I left the table and made my way upstairs.

Liam wasn't in his bedroom but the pizza cutter was. He'd been using it to make patterns on the cover of a book. My heart sank. *Oh, Liam. What am I going to do with you?*

So, where was he? I tried the bathroom. That was empty too. My heart skipped a beat. Surely he wasn't in Christopher's room? My imagination was working overtime. What damage was he doing in there? But Christopher's room was empty, as was his brother's. That only left our room. All the boys knew it was private, unless we said they could come in. I pushed open the door slowly.

He was under the duvet . . . on Rob's side of the bed.

I sat on the edge of the bed, my mind in a whirl. What on earth was I going to say to him? Dear Lord, why doesn't child rearing come with a tailor-made manual?

I pulled back the cover and exposed him a little. He was bathed in perspiration and he had obviously been crying. I had no words so I pulled him gently towards me and he came willingly into my arms.

'Listen, Liam,' I told him. 'Before we talk, I want you to know that no matter what you do, I will never, ever stop loving you.' I held him as he cried. 'You don't have to be like Christopher or Thomas.'

He pulled away and looked up at me earnestly. 'But why not, Mum?'

'We're all made differently,' I said, going down the usual trite pathway. 'It doesn't matter if you can't play cricket or work on a model aircraft. It doesn't even matter about the swimming . . .'

'I know all that, Mum,' he said with an expression on his face way beyond his years.

Now I was puzzled. 'Then what . . .?'

'Why doesn't he tell me off?' Liam demanded. 'Why can't Rob be my dad too?'

The Corkscrew is on the last part of the run now. I can't bear to watch this bit and yet I am compelled to. Upside down, spinning at a fair rate of knots . . . it's making my stomach turn. I down the last of my cold coffee and stand up with the bags.

Rob didn't tell Liam off but the following Saturday he took him back to the shop from where he'd pinched the toy car. Of course we didn't tell him that Rob had already been to see the shopkeeper to make sure Liam would be treated fairly. Liam was embarrassed but with Rob holding his hand, he apologised and the shopkeeper agreed that, even though it would take several weeks, Liam should pay for the car out of his own pocket money. After that, no more was said and the bad behaviour stopped.

The ride is over. The Corkscrew is unloading its passengers and there's a mêlée of bodies coming away from the entrance. When they get out of the car, Rob looks a bit unsteady on his feet but the boys are still hyper-excited.

'That was well cool,' Christopher shouts across to me.

'Yeah,' says Thomas. 'You should've come too, Mum.'

'Can we go again?' Liam asks and I see a flicker of panic in Rob's eye.

'You had to wait three quarters of an hour to get on last time,' I say quickly. 'The queue is even longer now.'

Thankfully, Liam concedes it's too long to wait. 'Come on,' he urges the others, 'Let's have a go on the Grand Rapids.'

The Grand Rapids looks thrilling, but it's a lot less scary than the Corkscrew.

The Grand Rapids involves lots of dark tunnels and water. I can't wait. It's my turn to make up the even number. Rob can look after the coats this time. The boys race off, their energy levels unbelievably high as they horseplay their way to the entrance.

'I was hoping I'd be too tall for The Corkscrew,' Rob whispers as we walk past a disappointed child crying beside the height restriction gate. 'I never was much good at fairground rides. They make me so giddy and sick.'

I gasp. 'You never said.'

Suddenly Liam breaks free from the others and comes racing back. He flings himself at Rob, wrapping his arms around his waist and giving him a big hug.

'Thanks for taking me on The Corkscrew, Dad,' he beams, and then he races back to his brothers.

273

I slip my hand in Rob's and our fingers entwine. All at once, I am unbelievably happy even though my pale-faced husband can only look down at me with a slightly green smile.

Better Days Will Come

Prologue

He was fingering the chain, letting it run through his fingers. Was it time to let the locket go? Would he ever need it? After all, nobody suspected a thing. Why should they in a sleepy backwater like Worthing? He might not have the heady power of previous years but that was no bad thing. When you reached the top, there were any number of people wanting to take you out. It had been a stroke of genius living here. The best place to hide was where everyone could see you. Which brought him back to the locket and the little secret inside. Keep it, or ditch it? He held it up to the light and realised that he wasn't ready to burn all his bridges just yet. All he needed was somewhere safe.

One

'Looks like they're going to make a start on repairing the pier at last,' Grace Rogers called out as she entered the house but there was no reply. She pulled her wet headscarf from her head and shook it. Water droplets splattered the back of the chair. She ran her fingers through her honey-blonde hair which curled neatly at the nape of her neck and then unbuttoned her coat and hung it on a peg behind the front door.

She was a small woman, with a neat figure, pale eyes and long artistic fingers. She'd missed the bus and had to wait for another, so she was soaked. Someone had said that the Littlehampton Road was flooded between Titnore Lane and Limbrick Lane. She wasn't surprised. The rain hadn't let up all week. She kicked off her boots. Her feet were wet too but that was hardly surprising either. There was a hole in the bottom of her left shoe. Grace pulled out a soggy piece of cardboard, the only thing between her foot and the pavement, and threw it into the coalscuttle.

The two reception rooms downstairs had been knocked into one and the kitchen range struggled to heat such a large area. The fire was low. Using an oven glove, Grace opened the door and put the poker in. The fire resettled and flared a little. She added some coal, not a lot, tossed in the soggy cardboard, and closed the door. Coal was still rationed and it was only November 12th. Winter had hardly started yet.

'Bonnie?'

No response. Perhaps she was upstairs in her room. Grace opened the stair door and called up but there was no answer. She glanced up at the clock on the mantelpiece. Almost three-thirty. It would be getting dark soon. Where was the girl? It was early closing in Worthing and Bonnie had the afternoon off, but she never went anywhere, not this time of year anyway, and certainly not in this weather. Rita, her youngest, would be coming back from school in less than an hour.

Grace dried her hair with a towel while the kettle boiled. Her bones ached with weariness. She'd jumped at the chance to do an extra shift because even with Bonnie's wages, the money didn't go far. When Michael died in the D-Day Landings, she'd never imagined bringing up two girls on her own would be so difficult. Still, she shouldn't grumble. She was a lot better off than some. Even if the rent did keep going up, at least she had a roof over her head, and the knitwear factory, Finley International, where she worked, was doing well. They were producing more than ever, mostly for America and Canada. The war had been over for eighteen months and the country needed all the exports it could get. A year ago they had all hoped that the good times were just around the corner but if anything, things were worse than ever. Even bread was rationed now, and potatoes. Three pounds per person per week, that was all, and that hadn't happened all through the dark days of the war.

Her hair towelled dry, Grace glanced up at the clock again. Where was Bonnie? She said she'd be home to help with the tea. She screwed up some newspaper and stuffed it into the toes of her boots before putting them on the floor by the range. With a bit of luck they'd be dry in the morning.

Grace brushed her hair vigorously. She was lucky that it was naturally curly and she didn't have any grey. The only time she went to the hairdresser was to have it cut.

The kettle boiled and Grace rinsed out the brown teapot before reaching for the caddy. Two scoops of Brooke Bond and she'd be as right as ninepence. She was looking forward to its reviving qualities. She sat at the table and reached for the knitted tea cosy.

The letter was underneath. It must have been propped against the salt and pepper and fallen over when she'd opened the door and created a draught. Grace picked it up. The envelope was unsealed. Was it meant for her or Bonnie? And who had put it there? She took out a single sheet of paper.

A glance at the bottom of the page told her it was from Bonnie. Grace sighed. That meant her daughter was either staying over with her friend from work, or she'd decided to go to the pictures with that new boy she was always going on about. Grace didn't know his name but it was obvious Bonnie was smitten. They'd had words about it last night when Grace had seen her with a neatly wrapped present in striped paper and a red ribbon on the top. Bonnie had sat at the table and pulled out a dark green jewellery box. Grace knew at once that it had come from Whibley's, a quality jeweller at the end of Warwick Street. Although she had never personally had anything from the shop, they advertised in every newspaper in the town and the box was instantly recognisable.

Before Bonnie had even lifted the lid, Grace had stopped her. 'Don't even be tempted,' she cautioned. 'Whatever it is, you can't possibly keep it.'

Bonnie looked up, appalled. 'Why ever not?'

'You're too young to be getting expensive presents from men,' said Grace.

'Oh, Mum,' said Bonnie turning slightly to lift the lid. 'I already know what's inside. I just wanted to show you, that's all.'

Grace caught a glimpse of some kind of locket on a chain before closing the box herself. 'I mean it,' she'd said firmly. 'You hardly know this man and I've never met him. How do you know his intentions are honourable?'

Bonnie smiled mysteriously. 'I know, Mum, and I love him.'

'Don't talk such rot,' Grace had retorted angrily. 'You're far too young . . .'

Bonnie's eyes blazed. 'I'm the same age as you were when you met Daddy.'

'That's different,' Grace had told her.

They had wrestled over the box with Bonnie eventually gaining the upper hand, and thinking about it now made Grace feel uncomfortable.

She got a cup and saucer down from the dresser and sat down. As she poured her tea Grace began to read:

Dear Mum,

   I am sorry but I am going away. By the time you read this, I shall be on the London train. You are not to worry. I shall be fine. I just need to leave Worthing. I am sorry to let you down but this is for the best. I shall never forget you and Rita and I want you to know I love you both with all my heart. Please don't think too badly of me.

   All my love,
   Bonnie.

As she reached the end of the page, Grace became aware that she was still pouring tea. Dark brown liquid trickled towards the page because it had filled her cup and saucer and overflowed onto her tablecloth. Her hand trembled as she put the teapot back onto the stand. Her mind struggled to focus. *On the London train.* It had only been a silly tiff. Why go all the way to London? She glanced up at the clock. That train would be leaving the station in less than five minutes. She leapt to her feet and grabbed her boots. It took an age to get all the newspaper out before she could stuff her feet back inside the wet leather. *I just need to leave Worthing.* Why? What did that mean? Surely she wasn't going for good. Her mind struggled to make sense of it. You're only eighteen, Bonnie. You always seemed happy enough. Grace stumbled out into the hall for her coat. The back of her left boot stubbornly refused to come back up. She had to stop and use her finger to get the heel in properly but there was no time to lace them. As she dashed out of the door she paused only to look at the grandmother clock. Four minutes before the train was due to leave. Without stopping to lock up, she ran blindly down the street, her unbuttoned coat flapping behind her like a cloak and her boots slopping on her feet. Water oozed between the stitches, forming little bubbles as she ran.

There were lights on in the little shop on the corner of Cross Street and Clifton Road and the new owner looked up from whatever he was doing to stare at her as she ran down the middle of the road towards him. The gates were already cranking across the road as she burst into Station Approach. She could feel a painful stitch coming in her side but she refused to ease up. The rain was coming down steadily and by now her hair was plastered to her face. As she raced up the steps of the entrance, the train thundered to a halt on platform 2.

Manny Hart, neat and tidy in his uniform and with his mouth organ tucked into his top pocket, stood at the entrance to the station platform with his hand out. 'Tickets please.' If he was surprised by the state of her, he said nothing.

'I've got to get to the other side before the train leaves,' Grace blurted out.

He glanced over his shoulder towards a group of men, all in smart suits, walking along the platform. 'Then you'll need a platform ticket.' Manny seemed uncomfortable.

Grace's heart sank. Her purse was sitting on the dresser in the kitchen. 'I'll pay you next time I see you.'

But Manny was in no mood to be placated. 'You need a ticket,' he said stubbornly. The men hovered by the entrance, while on the other side of the track the train shuddered and the steam hissed.

'You don't understand,' Grace cried. 'I've simply got to . . .' Her hands were searching her empty pockets and she was beginning to panic. She was so angry and frustrated she could have hit him. She looked around wildly and saw a woman who lived just up the road from her. 'Excuse me, Peggy. Could you lend me a penny for a platform ticket, only I must catch someone on the train before it goes.'

'Of course, dear. Hang on a minute, I'm sure I've got a penny in here somewhere.' Peggy Jones opened her bag, found her purse and handed Grace a penny. As it appeared in her hand, Grace almost snatched it and ran to the platform ticket machine, calling, 'Thank you, thank you' over her shoulder. To add to her frustration, the machine was reluctant to yield and she had to thump it a couple of times before the ticket appeared.

The passengers who were getting off at Worthing were already starting to head towards the barrier as she thrust the ticket at Manny Hart. He clipped it and went to hand it back but Grace was already at the top of the stairs leading to the underpass which came up on the other side and platform 2. Now she was hampered by the steady flow of people coming in the opposite direction.

'Close all the doors.'

The porter's cry echoed down the stairs and into the underpass. The train shuddered again and just as she reached the stairwell leading up she heard the powerful shunt of steam and smoke which heralded its departure. She was only halfway up the stairs leading to platform 2 when the guard blew his whistle and the lumbering giant was on the move. How she got to the top of the stairs, she never knew but as soon as she emerged onto the platform she knew it was hopeless. Through the smoke and steam, the last two carriages were all that was left. The train was gone.

Someone was walking jauntily towards her, a familiar figure, well dressed, confident and whistling as he came. He flicked his

282

hat with his finger and pushed it back on his head and his coat, open despite the rain, flapped behind him as he walked. Norris Finley, her boss, was a lot heavier and far less attractive than when they were younger but he still behaved like cock of the walk. What was he doing here? Usually, Grace would turn the other way if she saw him coming but her mind was on other things. Throwing aside her usual reserve, she roared out Bonnie's name. As the train gathered speed, she burst into helpless heart-rending tears, and putting her hands on the top of her head, she fell to her knees.

'Are you all right, love?' She heard a woman's voice, kind and concerned. The woman bent over her and touched her arm.

'Grace?' said Norris. 'You seem a bit upset. Anything I can do?'

Grace heard him but didn't respond. She was still staring at the disappearing train, and finally the empty track. She couldn't speak but she felt two arms, one on either side, helping her to her feet. Where was Bonnie going? Who on earth did she know in London?

'Do you know her, dear?' the woman's voice filtered through Grace's befuddled brain.

'Yes.' The man was raising his hat. 'Norris Finley of Finley's International,' he said.

The woman nodded. 'I'll leave you to it then, sir,' and patting Grace's arm she said, 'I'm sure it's not as bad as you think, dear.'

Norris tucked his hand under Grace's elbow and led her back down the stairs into the gloomy underpass.

'She's gone,' Grace said dully when they were alone. 'My Bonnie has left home.'

'Left home?'

She was crying again so they walked on in silence with Grace leaning heavily on his arm. Norris winked as he handed his ticket to Manny Hart and steered Grace onto the concourse.

'Is she all right?' said Manny, suddenly concerned. He took off his hat and scratched his slightly balding head.

'Mrs Rogers has had a bit of an upset, that's all,' said Norris pleasantly.

'If you had let me go,' Grace said, suddenly rounding on Manny, 'I might have been able to stop my daughter making the biggest mistake of her life.'

Manny looked uncomfortable. 'I cannot help that,' he said defensively. 'You know I would do anything for you, Grace. The men on the platform were government inspectors for when the railway goes national next year. Rules are rules and I have to obey.'

'Mrs Rogers . . . Grace,' said Norris. 'You're soaked to the skin. Let me take you home. My car is just outside.'

'Your paper, sir,' said Manny.

'Eh?' Norris seemed a little confused.

'You dropped your paper.' He handed him a rolled-up newspaper.

'Oh, right,' grinned Norris, taking it from him.

Manny watched them go.

'Nice man, that Mr Finley,' the woman remarked as she handed Manny her ticket and he nodded.

Outside it was still tipping with rain. 'I'll walk,' said Grace stiffly. 'It's not far and I'm wet through anyway.'

There were still people waiting for taxis or buses. 'Absolutely not, my dear Mrs Rogers,' Finley insisted. 'Hop in.'

As he climbed into the car, he handed her his folded handkerchief before they set off. He drove away like a madman but her mind was so full of Bonnie, Grace hardly noticed. She wiped her eyes and blew her nose. Outside her house, Grace turned to him. 'She left me a note,' she said hopelessly. 'I found it when I got in from work.'

'Where's she gone?'

Grace looked up at him. 'That's just it,' she said. 'I don't know. All she said was she had to leave Worthing.'

'*Had* to leave?' He raised his eyebrows and let out a short sigh. 'Ah well, you can't keep her tied to your apron strings all her life. She's a sensible girl, isn't she? She'll be fine.'

Grace's eyes grew wide. 'Promise me you didn't have anything to do with this?'

'Of course I didn't! Why should I?'

'Why were you there then? What were you doing on the platform?'

'I've been in Southampton on business,' he said irritably.

'Did you see her get on the train?'

'No, but then I'm hardly likely to, am I?' he said. 'I travel first class. Does Bonnie travel first class? No, I didn't think so, so why would I have seen her? Don't be so melodramatic, Grace.'

Grace fumbled for the door handle but couldn't open the door. 'I didn't expect any sympathy from you but Bonnie leaving like this . . . it's breaking my heart.'

'For God's sake, Grace. Nobody died, did they?' Norris said coldly. 'She'll be fine.' He got out of the car and came round to the passenger side. Just as he opened the door Grace's neighbour walked by under a large umbrella.

'There you are, Mrs Rogers,' Norris said loudly and cheerfully as he stepped back. 'Back home safe and sound. Can I help you with your door key?'

Grace shook her head. The door was open anyway. She hadn't stopped to lock it. She turned and he waved cheerfully as he got back into his car. He drove off at speed, leaving Grace standing like a dumb thing on the pavement.

'You'll catch your death of cold,' said a voice. 'You look soaked to the skin.' Their eyes met and she hesitated. 'You all right, Grace?' Her neighbour who lived next-door-but-one, Elsie Dawson, was on her step putting her key into her own door. Dougie, her son, stood behind his mother waiting for her to open it. Elsie, her middle son Dougie and daughter Mo were good friends with Rita and Bonnie, and they had all enjoyed sharing times like Christmas and Easter together. Bob, Elsie's oldest boy, was in the army now and Mo was in the same class as Rita at school but Dougie was what the powers that be called 'retarded', a term which made Grace cross. He might struggle with understanding, but he wasn't stupid. Once he knew what you wanted, Dougie would put his hand to anything.

'I'm fine, thank you,' Grace said with as much dignity as she could muster. But once inside the house, she sat alone on the cold stairs and gave way to her tears once again.

As the train sped towards London, Bonnie stared out of the window. She should have done this earlier in the day while she still had the opportunity. The light was going and by the time she reached Victoria station it would be dark. Never mind, George would be there to meet her. If for some reason they missed each other, he'd told her to wait by the entrance of platform 12.

She had finished work a lot earlier than she'd thought she would. The people in the wages department had worked out that she was owed a half day's holiday so rather than give her the extra in her wage packet, she had been told she could go by ten o'clock. Seeing as how she had arranged to meet George in time for the train, it meant she had a couple of hours to kill. Her case was already in the left luggage department at Worthing and she couldn't go back home, so she went to his digs.

Mrs Kerr, his landlady, was her usual unwelcoming self. 'He's not here,' she'd said curtly, 'and I have no time to entertain his guests.' She had obviously taken her apron off to answer the door and now she was putting it back on again.

'Do you know where he might be?' Bonnie had asked.

'He's going to London.'

'I know that,' Bonnie had said. 'I just wondered if he was still here.'

Mrs Kerr shrugged. 'As far as I know, he's gone to the old factory.'

Bonnie had frowned. 'But why? It's all shut up, isn't it?'

'All I know is he said he'd found something. Now I'm very busy.'

'Do you know what he'd found?' Bonnie persisted.

'Am I my brother's keeper?' Mrs Kerr snapped as she shut the door.

Bonnie had stood on the pavement wondering what to do.

There was still plenty of time before the train so she'd decided to walk to the factory. She didn't have to go right into West Worthing. There was a Jacob's ladder in Pavilion Road which was between the stations and came out at the bottom of Heene Road. Although she was wearing her best shoes, which were quite unsuitable for walking, it hadn't taken her long to get to Finley's Knitwear.

She had met George Matthews at a dance in the Assembly Hall. He was a friend of a friend and they'd hit it off straight away. He was so debonair, so handsome and so unlike any of her other friends that it wasn't long before she was hopelessly in love with him. He worked at the knitwear factory in Tarring Road, the same as her mother. He was a machine operator, while her mum worked in the packing room. George was getting good money but he was ambitious so when it was announced that the factory would be moving to new premises, he felt it was time to move on.

'I don't think the boss is a very nice person,' he'd told her. 'Don't let him get too close to you.'

'Whatever do you mean?' she'd asked, thoroughly alarmed.

He'd hesitated for a second then changed the subject. 'There are real opportunities in places like South Africa, and Rhodesia and Australia, the sort of opportunities the likes of you and me will never get in this country. We can get away from all the corruption in high places. It'll be a whole new start, far away from the war and everything to do with it.'

'If Mr Finley is up to something,' she'd asked, 'should I say something to my mother?'

He'd shaken his head. 'Your mother and all the other girls are safe enough if you keep your distance, but he's deep, that one.'

Out of loyalty, he stayed long enough to help clear up the old place, but just lately he'd seemed even more troubled about something. 'I'm glad we're going,' he said one day. 'I really don't want to work for Finley any more.'

Once again she'd asked why but he told her not to worry her pretty little head.

'How will we get to South Africa?' she'd asked.

'Leave all that to me,' he'd said mysteriously, and then he'd filled her imagination with sun-drenched beaches and cocktails before dinner and making their fortune. They'd made love in his digs at Pavilion Road. They had to be very careful for fear of his landlady, who was a deeply religious woman, but while she was wrestling with the Devil at the prayer meeting every Tuesday night, Bonnie and George were wrestling between the sheets. And while Mrs Kerr studied the Bible every Thursday, they filled themselves with more carnal delights. Bonnie smiled cosily as she remembered those wonderful nights together.

'Tickets please.' The conductor on the train brought her back to the present day and Bonnie handed him her ticket.

When she'd told him about the baby, George had been wonderful about it. That's when he had bought her the locket. It was so beautiful she'd vowed to wear it all the time. He'd said she should get a job until it was time for the baby to be born and then they would set sail. Having a baby in South Africa wasn't as safe as here in England. He'd promised to get her passport all sorted and she'd saved up the £2 2s 6d she needed. The last thing she'd done as she'd left the house was to remember to take her birth certificate. Bonnie couldn't wait. It was so exciting.

'I shall need references,' she'd told George.

'I'm sure you can get someone to vouch for you,' George said, nibbling her ear in that delicious way of his. 'I think you're a very nice girl.'

She'd giggled. He had a way of making her feel that it would all work out. Right now everything was such a mess but once they were married, it would be all right. She was sure of it.

She had decided to ask her old Sunday school teacher to give her a reference. She didn't really know why, but she trusted Miss Reeves absolutely. She didn't tell her everything, of course, but then how could she? It was easier to be economical with the truth although it did make her feel a bit guilty. Still, it wasn't as if she was lying to the vicar or something. All she did was tell her just enough for Miss Reeves to write a glowing reference addressed '*To whom it may concern*'.

'I know the woman you'll be working for quite well,' George assured her when he gave her the slip of paper. 'Mrs Palmer is a nice woman. You'll like her.'

Bonnie frowned. 'How do you know her?'

He'd pulled her close. 'Don't I know just about everyone who's anyone, silly?'

When she had surprised him at his digs after the row with her mother last night, he had taken her to his room. 'You'll get me thrown out onto the street,' he'd said and she'd laughed. 'Who cares? We're going to live in South Africa,' she'd said, her cornflower-blue eyes dancing with excitement.

George had drawn her down onto the bed with a kiss. Bonnie closed her eyes as she relived the moment. He was so good-looking, so strong, so manly . . . She sighed. She hated doing this to her mother but she had to. If she'd told her mother what she and George were planning, she would have talked her out of it. Grace was a good mother but she still thought of Bonnie as 'her little girl'. Bonnie smiled to herself. If only she knew. She certainly wasn't her little girl any more. Since she'd met George, she had become a fully-grown woman.

When her father had been killed in the D-Day Landings, Grace Rogers had been totally lost without him. The day the telegram came, she'd sat on the stairs, hardly even aware that she had two daughters to look after. Rita was the only one able to pacify her and they sat crying together. Without their father, life had become so difficult. They never had much money even though her mother worked all the hours God gave. Bonnie knew her mother would be upset to lose her wage, but it was all swings and roundabouts. There would be one less mouth to feed and Bonnie was determined she'd send a bit of money as soon as she and George were settled in South Africa. Of course, she would write to her mother long before they got there and once they were there, Grace could hardly refuse her consent to their marriage.

Bonnie stared at the name and address on the piece of paper she had been given. Mrs Palmer, 105 Honeypot Lane, Stanmore. Telephone: Stanmore 256. She couldn't wait to see George at the station. Everything was going to be absolutely fine, she just knew it. With a smile of contentment, Bonnie leaned her head against the carriage window and closed her eyes.

Rita was puzzled. When she'd arrived home from school after choir practice, she found her mother sitting in the darkness on the stairs. Rita could tell at once that she had been crying but she didn't seem to be aware that she was wet through and shivering with the cold.

Rita sat down beside her. 'Mum?'

Grace stood up. 'I'm going to get changed.' She knew Rita was wondering what was wrong but she didn't look back as she wearily climbed the steep stairs.

There was little warm water in the tap and the bathroom was very cold, but Grace washed herself slowly. How was she going to tell Rita? She and Bonnie were very close, so close they might almost be twins rather than two years apart. Bonnie had left no note for Rita. The girl would be heartbroken.

As she crossed the landing, a thought struck her. What if Rita already knew Bonnie was going? Maybe they'd planned it this way together. Grace felt a frisson of irritation. How dare they!

By now, she was frozen to the marrow. Pulling out some warmer clothes, Grace dressed quickly; a dry bra, her once pink petticoat, and a blue cable knit jumper over a grey skirt. She sat on the edge of the bed to roll her nylon stockings right down to the toe before putting them on her feet and easing over the heel. Her clothes were shabby, the jumper had darns on one elbow and at the side, her petticoat had odd straps because she'd used one petticoat to repair another, and her skirt, which came from a jumble sale, had been altered to fit. The one luxury she allowed herself was a decent pair of stockings. She rolled them slowly up her leg, careful not to snag them on a jagged nail, and checked her seams for straightness. Fastening the stockings to her suspenders, Grace towel-dried her hair and pulled on her wrap-around apron before heading back downstairs to confront Rita.

'Something's happened,' said Rita as she walked back into the kitchen. 'What's wrong, Mum?'

'Your sister has left home,' Grace said, her lips in a tight line, 'but of course you already knew that, didn't you?'

Rita's jaw dropped.

'Left home?' Rita looked so shocked, Grace was thrown. 'Where's she gone?'

'I don't know.'

'What do you mean, you don't know?'

'Precisely what I said, I don't know,' cried her mother, her voice full of anguish. 'I was so sure you'd know all about it.'

Rita seemed bewildered. Grace threw an enamel bowl into the stone sink with a great clatter. All the while that she had believed Rita knew about Bonnie, there was the hope that she could bully her whereabouts out of the girl. 'Mum?'

For a few seconds, Grace stood with her back to her daughter, her hands clenching the sides of the stone sink, as if supporting the weight of her body, then she turned round. Rita was alarmed to see the tears in her eyes. Grace reached out for her but when Rita stood up, scraping her chair on the wooden floor behind her, she ran upstairs. Grace could hear her opening drawers, looking in the wardrobe and searching for the battered suitcase that they kept under the bed. As she listened, she relived every moment of her own fruitless search not half an hour ago. She opened the stair door and sat down. A moment or two later, Rita joined her and laid her head on Grace's shoulder.

Rita chewed her bottom lip. Left home . . . Bonnie didn't confide in her much these days, but Rita was sure she would have said something if she'd known she was going away. Was she ill or something?

'Has she done something wrong, Mum?'

No answer.

'When is she coming back?'

'Darling, I've told you,' Grace sighed. 'I don't know.'

Rita's stomach fell away. She couldn't bear it if Bonnie was gone. Sometimes Bonnie and her mother had words but neither of them held grudges. It just wasn't their way. A sudden thought struck her. She lifted her head. 'Shall I go and see if she's at Sandra's place?'

'She's not at Sandra's. She's gone to London.'

'London?'

'She told me in a note.'

'What note?'

Grace stood up and they both went back into the kitchen. She showed Rita the single sheet of paper.

'*I shall never forget you and Rita* . . . it all sounds so final,' said Rita.

Her mother couldn't look her in the eye. She got the saucepan out of the cupboard, put it onto the range and reached for a couple of potatoes. 'Let's clear the table please.'

Rita gathered her schoolbooks into a pile. Tears were already brimming over her eyes. Why go to London? It was fifty miles away. Bonnie didn't know anyone in London, did she? Rita opened her mouth to say something but thought better of it when she saw her mother's expression.

'There's nothing we can do, love,' Grace said firmly but in a more conciliatory tone. 'Your sister has left home. I don't know why she's gone but it's her choice and we'll just have to get on with it.'

The potatoes Grace had cut up went clattering into the pan. She covered them with water before putting them on the range. Their eyes met and a second or two later, unable to contain her grief any more, Rita burst into tears and ran upstairs.

* * *

Victoria station was alive with people. Bonnie had arrived in the rush hour. She went straight to platform 12 as agreed with George, but after waiting a long two hours, she was so desperate for the toilet, she had to leave. She wasn't gone for more than ten minutes but he must have come and gone during that time and she'd missed him. Why didn't he wait? Where could he have gone? She didn't know what to do, but she was afraid to move from their agreed meeting place in case she'd got it wrong and he was simply late. As time wore on, it grew colder. The station was getting quieter. She began to feel more conspicuous now that the evening rush hour was drawing to a close, and a lot more anxious. Oh, George, where are you? She scoured the heads of the male passengers, willing George's trilby hat to come bobbing towards her, but it was hopeless. A few passengers who had obviously been to the theatre or some other posh frock do milled around, talking in loud plummy voices. Bonnie bit back her tears and shivered. She wished she and George could have travelled together but she hadn't expected Miss Bridewell to let her go early. She'd worked her notice so that she could get the week's pay owing to her and some of her holiday money. The extra money would come in handy if the job in Stanmore didn't work out for some reason.

'I've got on to a mate who can put us up,' he'd told her. 'Save a bit of money that way. He's not on the telephone so I'll go up and make the arrangements beforehand. I'll meet you at platform 12.'

She saw a party of cleaners emerge from a small storeroom and begin to sweep the concourse and then she noticed a man approaching. Bonnie looked around anxiously. Why was he coming her way? She didn't know him.

'Excuse me, Miss,' he said raising his hat. 'I couldn't help noticing you standing there. Has your friend been delayed?'

Bonnie didn't answer but she felt her face heating up and her heart beat a little faster. Oh, George, she thought, where are you? Please come now . . .

'If you're looking for a place to stay,' he continued, 'I know where a respectable girl like you can get a room at a cheap price.'

Bonnie looked at him for the first time. He was smartly dressed in a suit and tie. He looked clean and presentable. He looked like the sort of man she could take home to her mother but she didn't know him from Adam and she had read of the terrible things that could happen to young girls on their own in London in Uncle Charlie Hanson's *News of the World*. She turned her head, pretending not to have heard him.

'Forgive me,' he smiled pleasantly. 'I only ask because I can see you look concerned. I don't normally approach young women like this.'

Bonnie began to tremble. *Oh, where are you, George . . .*

'Could I perhaps offer you a cup of tea in the tea bar?' He was very persistent but that was what the *News of the World* said they were like. Men like him duped girls into going with them and corrupted them into a life of prostitution.

She shook her head. Even though she was tired and sorely tempted, Bonnie didn't go with him. She had seen the man watching her from behind a pillar for some time and she didn't like it. She picked up her suitcase and walked towards the newspaper vendor to buy a paper.

Eventually she stopped a passing policeman and after explaining that she had missed her friend, he at first directed her, then, having heard her story about the man who kept pestering her, decided to walk with her to a small hotel just around the corner. Bonnie booked a room for the night. It wasn't until she got undressed that she realised that the locket George had given her was no longer around her neck. Her stomach fell away. Where had she lost it? Had it come off when she was in that horrible factory? What a ghastly day it had been. Everything was going wrong. Bonnie climbed into bed and cried herself to sleep.